# Elixir and Phoenix
# for
# Beginners

*Build real-world Elixir and Phoenix
apps the practical, TDD way*

### Karthikeyan Paramasivan

**bpb**

www.bpbonline.com

First Edition 2026

Copyright © BPB Publications, India

ISBN: 978-93-65897-562

## LIMITS OF LIABILITY AND DISCLAIMER OF WARRANTY

# Dedicated to

*My lord and savior, Jesus Christ*

*and*

*My family members*

# About the Author

**Karthikeyan Paramasivan** is a seasoned backend developer with over a decade of experience in building web applications across diverse domains. He has worked extensively with Elixir, Phoenix, Node.js, PHP, and AWS, and is passionate about designing secure, scalable, production-ready systems and distributed systems.

He began his career in 2009 as a PHP programmer, earning the Zend PHP5 certification early on. Over time, he expanded his expertise to modern technologies, contributing to projects in logistics, finance, insurance, and large-scale real-time applications. His journey into Elixir started with building a ridesharing application similar to Uber, and since then, he has been deeply involved in creating Elixir- and Phoenix-based solutions for complex business needs.

David's development philosophy centers around writing clean code, applying best practices, and following robust security standards. Beyond his professional work, he is an advocate for continuous learning and knowledge sharing. With this book, he brings his practical insights and experience to beginners, helping them understand Elixir step by step through examples, exercises, and a real-world project.

# About the Reviewer

**Yatender Singh** is a highly experienced senior software engineer with over 12 years of professional software development experience, specializing in sophisticated server-side applications. Since 2016, he has dedicated over 10,000 hours to Elixir, Phoenix, LiveView, and Absinthe GraphQL, designing, building, and optimizing scalable systems. Yatender has a proven track record across diverse domains, including travel, blockchain, betting and gambling, and social networking. He is currently applying his extensive knowledge at Priceline.com in Berlin, Germany.

# Acknowledgement

First and foremost, I thank my lord and savior, Jesus Christ, who has been my constant source of wisdom, strength, and guidance throughout this journey. Without his grace, this book would not have been possible. I am also deeply grateful to my family members for their unwavering support, encouragement, and patience, which carried me through the long hours of writing and revisions.

I would also like to express my heartfelt gratitude to BPB Publications for their invaluable support in bringing this book to life. Their editorial guidance, encouragement, and professional expertise have been instrumental in shaping the final manuscript. From the very beginning, they believed in the vision of this book and provided me with the time and resources to complete it. The BPB team has done truly wonderful work, and I am sincerely thankful for their dedication to making this project a reality.

Lastly, I extend my gratitude to the readers of this book. By choosing to learn Elixir through these pages, you have entrusted me to be part of your learning journey. I hope this book serves you well, strengthens your programming skills, and inspires you to build impactful, real-world applications.

# Preface

This book is designed to provide a hands-on and beginner-friendly journey into Elixir. Elixir has rapidly grown in popularity for building scalable, maintainable, and concurrent applications. This book aims to simplify complex concepts and present them in a way that is accessible to aspiring developers.

The content begins with foundational knowledge of Elixir and functional programming, gradually progressing toward advanced topics like concurrency, OTP, and distributed systems. Along the way, readers will engage in practical exercises and work on real-world examples, ensuring a balance between theory and practice.

This book is structured into twelve chapters:

Chapter 1: Introduction to Elixir and Functional Programming- This chapter lays the groundwork for your journey into Elixir. You will learn about the history, purpose, and strengths of Elixir, including its roots in Erlang and the BEAM virtual machine. The discussion introduces functional programming concepts such as immutability, higher-order functions, and declarative coding. It also highlights why Elixir is well-suited for today's distributed and scalable systems. By the end, you will have installed and set up your Elixir environment and gained a clear understanding of the paradigm shift from traditional programming.

Chapter 2: Elixir Syntax and Data Types- With your environment ready, this chapter introduces you to Elixir's syntax and the various data types the language provides. We will cover integers, floats, strings, atoms, lists, tuples, maps, and structs, along with the role of modules and functions in organizing code. Control flow structures such as if, case, and cond will also be explained. Practical examples ensure you understand how each element works in real applications, helping you develop a strong foundation before moving on to more complex concepts.

Chapter 3: Elixir Collections and Pattern Matching- Collections and pattern matching are at the heart of Elixir programming. In this chapter, you will learn how lists, maps, and other collections are used to structure data. We explore how pattern matching enables concise and expressive ways to deconstruct values and bind variables. Recursion, a core concept in functional programming, is explained with examples that show how Elixir handles loops without traditional constructs. Practical exercises will strengthen your understanding and give you the confidence to use these techniques in everyday coding tasks.

**Chapter 4: Concurrent Programming in Elixir-** Concurrency is central to Elixir's strengths, and this chapter provides a comprehensive guide to writing concurrent and fault-tolerant applications. We begin with lightweight processes, exploring their creation, management, and communication through message passing. Building on this, you will be introduced to OTP, including GenServers, Supervisors, Dynamic Supervisors, Tasks, and Agents, which form the backbone of resilient systems. Fault tolerance and crash-handling mechanisms are also emphasized, showing how Elixir applications can recover seamlessly. Practical exercises ensure that you finish with confidence in applying these principles to real-world projects.

**Chapter 5: Understanding Distributed Systems-** This chapter explores Elixir's ability to power distributed systems, one of the language's defining capabilities. Starting with the fundamentals of distributed computing, you will learn how Elixir, built on the Erlang VM, simplifies the complexities of building fault-tolerant, scalable applications across multiple nodes. We explore distributed OTP applications, strategies for handling failures and network partitions, and Elixir's role in enabling high availability. Practical examples and case studies bring these concepts to life, ensuring you not only understand the theory but also gain the skills to implement distributed systems effectively.

**Chapter 6: Mix Tooling, Testing, and Debugging in Elixir-** Robust applications require strong tooling and reliable testing, and this chapter equips you with both. You will gain hands-on experience with Mix, Elixir's build tool, learning how to manage dependencies, compile projects, and generate documentation. ExUnit, Elixir's built-in testing framework, is introduced to help you write effective test suites that ensure correctness and stability. Debugging strategies and tools are also discussed to help you diagnose and resolve issues quickly. Whether you are a beginner or an experienced developer, this chapter enhances your workflow and strengthens your ability to deliver high-quality applications.

**Chapter 7: Elixir's Metaprogramming-** Metaprogramming sets Elixir apart by enabling developers to write code that generates code. This chapter explores macros, compile-time execution, and how quoting and unquoting work in Elixir. We discuss the difference between compile-time and run-time, providing practical use cases where metaprogramming simplifies otherwise repetitive or complex tasks. With carefully designed examples, you will learn how to harness the power of macros responsibly. This chapter empowers you to extend the language itself and adapt Elixir to suit the specific needs of your projects.

**Chapter 8: Working with Phoenix and Ecto-** Phoenix is the web framework that makes Elixir a real-world contender in modern web development. This chapter walks you through building your first Phoenix application and understanding its request/response lifecycle. We then move on to Ecto, Elixir's database wrapper, which simplifies database interactions while promoting safe and maintainable code. You will learn to create schemas, migrations, and queries. The chapter concludes with a practical exercise that integrates Phoenix and Ecto, helping you build full-stack web applications with confidence and clarity.

**Chapter 9: Creating Deployable Releases-** Deployment is an essential part of any application's lifecycle. This chapter introduces release management in Elixir and explains how to package your applications for production. You will learn how Mix can be used to create self-contained releases that bundle the runtime, dependencies, and code together. We also cover deployment strategies, versioning, and best practices for running Elixir applications in different environments. By the end, you will understand how to deliver production-ready applications and maintain them effectively after deployment.

**Chapter 10: Build Phoenix Components for Real-world Apps-** Phoenix Components bring reusability, modularity, and clarity to application development, and this chapter is your guide to mastering them. You will learn the foundational concepts of creating and organizing components, passing data, handling state, and managing dynamic rendering. Advanced techniques such as using slots for flexible layouts and testing for reliability are also covered. By the end, you will be prepared to adopt a component-driven architecture that simplifies development and enhances maintainability.

**Chapter 11: Project on Building Real-world Application-** This chapter brings together everything you have learned by guiding you through the development of a Task Management CRUD application using Phoenix 1.7. Beginning with project setup, you will implement features such as listing, creating, editing, and deleting tasks, all using a strict TDD workflow. You will also work with Ecto schemas, contexts, controllers, HEEx templates, and Phoenix Components to ensure reusable design patterns. The chapter concludes with refinement, debugging, and deployment, giving you practical confidence to build and deliver production-ready applications.

**Chapter 12: Future Directions-** In the final chapter, we revisit the core ideas learned throughout the book, including functional programming, concurrency, OTP, and Phoenix. Best practices for code organization and project structuring are emphasized to help you write maintainable applications. We also explore Elixir's ecosystem, communities, and resources for further learning. Finally, we discuss where Elixir is heading and how you can continue your journey as a developer. This chapter ensures that you finish the book with both confidence and a clear path forward.

By the end of this book, readers will have not only learned Elixir concepts but also gained the confidence to apply them in real-world scenarios. I hope this book inspires you to embrace functional programming and leverage Elixir's power to build scalable, reliable, and modern applications.

# Code Bundle and Coloured Images

Please follow the link to download the
*Code Bundle* and the *Coloured Images* of the book:

# https://rebrand.ly/f6d84a

The code bundle for the book is also hosted on GitHub at
**https://github.com/bpbpublications/Elixir-and-Phoenix-for-Beginners**.
In case there's an update to the code, it will be updated on the existing GitHub repository.

We have code bundles from our rich catalogue of books and videos available at
https://github.com/bpbpublications. Check them out!

# Errata

We take immense pride in our work at BPB Publications and follow best practices to ensure the accuracy of our content to provide with an indulging reading experience to our subscribers. Our readers are our mirrors, and we use their inputs to reflect and improve upon human errors, if any, that may have occurred during the publishing processes involved. To let us maintain the quality and help us reach out to any readers who might be having difficulties due to any unforeseen errors, please write to us at: errata@bpbonline.com

Your support, suggestions and feedbacks are highly appreciated by the BPB Publications' Family.

## Piracy

If you come across any illegal copies of our works in any form on the internet, we would be grateful if you would provide us with the location address or website name. Please contact us at business@bpbonline.com with a link to the material.

## If you are interested in becoming an author

If there is a topic that you have expertise in, and you are interested in either writing or contributing to a book, please visit www.bpbonline.com. We have worked with thousands of developers and tech professionals, just like you, to help them share their insights with the global tech community. You can make a general application, apply for a specific hot topic that we are recruiting an author for, or submit your own idea.

## Reviews

Please leave a review. Once you have read and used this book, why not leave a review on the site that you purchased it from? Potential readers can then see and use your unbiased opinion to make purchase decisions. We at BPB can understand what you think about our products, and our authors can see your feedback on their book. Thank you!

For more information about BPB, please visit www.bpbonline.com.

# Join our Discord space

Join our Discord workspace for latest updates, offers, tech happenings around the world, new releases, and sessions with the authors:

https://discord.bpbonline.com

# Table of Contents

# CHAPTER 1

# Introduction to Elixir and Functional Programming

## Introduction

If you are new to Elixir, you might wonder why another language is worth your time. Think of the internet services you use every day: chat apps, video calls, live scoreboards. They serve millions of people at once and must stay online even when something goes wrong behind the scenes. Elixir was created to make that kind of reliability and speed easy rather than painful. In this chapter, we will give you an exploration of how Elixir, and the virtual machine it runs on, called the BEAM, helps beginners build rock-solid applications without getting lost in low-level details.

## Structure

This chapter will cover the following topics:

- Background and its benefits
- Overview of Erlang and BEAM
- Basics of functional programming in Elixir
- Elixir installation and setup

# Objectives

This chapter serves as a comprehensive introduction to Elixir and functional programming, aiming to arm readers with a solid foundation in these subjects. By the end of this chapter, you will have gained an understanding of the background and benefits of Elixir, grasped the basics of functional programming within its context, and acquired the knowledge to set up Elixir on your own machine. You will learn about Erlang, a robust language upon which Elixir is built, and the BEAM virtual machine, which provides the high concurrency and fault tolerance that Elixir applications enjoy. This foundational knowledge will prepare you for not just understanding how Elixir works, but also why it is an advantageous tool for certain types of applications, particularly those requiring high reliability and concurrency management.

# Background and its benefits

The background of Elixir is as follows:

- **BEAM meaning**: The BEAM is the engine that runs Elixir code. It was built in the 1980s for telephone switches that could never drop a call. Its key idea is to run tiny, isolated processes that talk by sending messages. Each process is so light that a single laptop can start hundreds of thousands of them without breaking a sweat. Elixir inherits this superpower but wraps it in a clean, modern syntax.

- **Concurrency vs. waiting for your turn**: If you have written JavaScript with Node.js, you may know the term asynchronous, doing something else while waiting for a file or network reply. Node manages this with one big event loop. It works, but heavy work can still block that single loop. The BEAM instead gives every task its own miniature thread (a process). They are preempted (paused and resumed) by the VM, so no single task hogs the CPU. You write code that looks synchronous, no deep callback chains, but it still runs side by side with thousands of others.

- **Builtin safety nets**: In many languages, that would bring your whole program down. On the BEAM, every process is watched by a supervisor, a parent who restarts children in milliseconds. This pattern, called a supervision tree, makes your app self-healing. Beginners can focus on happypath logic, knowing the runtime will tidy up many errors automatically.

- **Upgrading without downtime**: The BEAM supports hot code upgrades. You can load new versions of modules into a running system, and old processes will gently finish their work before switching. This feature is optional, but it shows how the platform was built for always-on services.

- **Easy clustering**: If you are running out of CPU on one machine. Then start with another CPU and connect it with a shared cookie. The nodes discover each other, and processes can send messages across the network almost as easily as within one computer. No special loadbalancer setup is required to get started.

# Benefits

Elixir bundles a set of advantages that feel advanced yet remain approachable for people writing their very first modules.

- **Lots of concurrent tasks**: If you need a separate task for every chat room, sensor reading, or HTTP request then spawning a BEAM process is cheaper than creating an operatingsystem thread, so you can start hundreds of thousands without worrying about locks or shared memory.

- **Automatic recovery**: Each process is supervised by a parent. If something crashes, only the faulty process restarts while the rest of your system keeps humming. You focus on the happypath logic; the runtime supplies the safety net.

- **Predictable response times**: The scheduler gives every process a tiny time slice, preempting long work so short requests are never starved. Your APIs stay snappy even under heavy load, no need to micromanage priorities.

- **Live upgrades**: Deploy bug fixes and new features while users stay connected. Hotcode swapping lets you patch production at lunchtime, confirm the change in your logs, and continue coding without a maintenance window.

- **Resource savings**: Because processes are lightweight and memory is shared efficiently, Elixir apps often serve more traffic on fewer machines. WhatsApp's legendary one server per million users story shows the upside.

- **Simple horizontal scaling**: When traffic grows, start another node, connect it to the cluster, and the BEAM routes messages across machines. No special loadbalancer gymnastics required.

# Overview of Erlang and BEAM

Erlang is a functional, concurrent programming language developed by *Ericsson* in the 1980s for building robust, fault-tolerant, distributed systems. Its primary use case was for telecom systems, which needed to have high availability, handle numerous simultaneous connections, and recover gracefully from failures.

## Key features of Erlang

The key features of Erlang are as follows:

- **Concurrency**: Erlang is known for its lightweight process creation and handling. Processes communicate using message passing, which ensures no shared state and reduces the risk of concurrent access issues.

- **Fault tolerance**: Erlang supports the *let it crash* philosophy, where processes can fail without crashing the whole system. Supervision trees can restart processes that fail, ensuring system resilience.

- **Hot code upgrades:** Erlang systems can be updated without being taken offline, a critical feature for systems requiring high availability.

- **Distributed**: Erlang supports native mechanisms to communicate between nodes, making it easier to build distributed systems.

- **BEAM**: BEAM is the Erlang virtual machine on which Erlang (and, by extension, Elixir) runs. It is designed to run Erlang's lightweight processes efficiently and provides built-in support for the features listed above.

Refer to the following figure:

*Figure 1.1*: Key features of a distributed system

Mix is Elixir's built-in project generator and task runner. With one concise commandline interface, you can create a new project, compile source code, manage dependencies, and run tests, everything needed to build and maintain Elixir applications.

# Elixir's relationship with Erlang and BEAM

Elixir is a modern language built on top of the BEAM VM, meaning it inherently benefits from all the robust, concurrent, and distributed features of Erlang. Here are some of the reasons why this is beneficial:

- **Modern syntax**: Elixir provides a more contemporary syntax and tooling compared to Erlang, making it more approachable to new developers.

- **Extensibility**: Elixir introduces metaprogramming capabilities, allowing developers to extend the language naturally.

- **Interoperability**: Elixir can interoperate with Erlang seamlessly. This means you can call Erlang libraries directly from Elixir and vice versa.

- **Frameworks**: Elixir has introduced popular frameworks like Phoenix (for web development) and Nerves (for embedded software), allowing developers to build various applications.

- **Interoperability with Erlang**: Elixir provides seamless interoperability with Erlang libraries. This is particularly beneficial as it allows Elixir developers to leverage the robust and mature ecosystem of Erlang, which has been developed over decades, particularly in areas like telecommunications, distributed databases, and networking.

In Elixir, you can invoke Erlang functions by prefixing them with a colon (:) followed by the name of the Erlang module and then the function. The Erlang standard library is vast and can be called directly in this manner.

Let us consider a simple example where we use Erlang's lists module to calculate the sum of a list:

```
1. iex(1)> sum = :lists.sum([1, 2, 3, 4, 5])
2. 15
```

Another common use case is working with dates and times using the Erlang :calendar module:

```
1. # Getting the current date and time in Elixir using Erlang's calendar
   module:
2. iex> {date, time} = :calendar.local_time()
3. {{2023, 10, 10}, {12, 54, 34}}
```

The ability to directly utilize Erlang functions and modules in Elixir code is a testament to the close relationship between the two languages. This not only saves time and effort for developers but also ensures that Elixir can leverage the stability, maturity, and efficiency of existing Erlang libraries.

# Basics of functional programming in Elixir

Let us focus on functional programming by breaking it down for better understanding:

- **Immutable data**: In Elixir, once a data structure is created, it cannot be changed. Instead, new data structures are derived from the original. Imagine if every time you wrote something on a piece of paper, you could not erase or change it. In Elixir, once you create a piece of data, it is like that written note; it stays the same forever. If you want something different, you have to use a new sheet of paper:

```
1.  # Let's define a list of fruits
2.  fruits = ["apple", "banana", "cherry"]
3.
4.  # Now, let's say we want to add "date" to our list of fruits
5.  new_fruits = ["date" | fruits]
6.
7.  # Check the contents of both lists
8.  IO.puts("Original fruits: #{inspect(fruits)}")
9.  IO.puts("New fruits: #{inspect(new_fruits)}")
```

We started with a list of **fruits: ["apple", "banana", "cherry"]**.

We wanted to add **"date"** to this list. Instead of altering the original list, Elixir created a new list for us, **new_fruits**.

When we printed the original fruits, they remained unchanged, showcasing that data in Elixir is immutable. The original list did not get altered or modified. Instead, we got a brand-new list with the changes.

This behavior ensures predictability in our code. When data cannot be changed unexpectedly, it reduces bugs and errors, especially in concurrent systems where multiple processes might be interacting with the same piece of data.

- **First-class functions**: Functions are first-class citizens, meaning they can be passed around like any other value.

- **Pure functions**: A pure function is one where the output value is determined only by its input values, without observable side effects. This means that for a given input, the function will always produce the same output.

In the following example, the add function is pure. Given the same numbers, **a** and **b**, it will always return the same result, and it does not have any side effects:

```
1.  defmodule MathOperations do
2.    # This is a pure function.
3.    def add(a, b) do
4.      a + b
5.    end
6.  end
```

- **Higher-order functions**: These functions take one or more functions as arguments or return a function as a result.

# Elixir installation and setup

Installing Elixir is usually straightforward, regardless of your operating system. Here is a brief guide on how to do it:

- **Installing on macOS:** If you use Homebrew, installation is a breeze:

  1. `$ brew update`

  2. `$ brew install erlang elixir`

- **Installing on Ubuntu:** Up-to-date instructions for installing Elixir using a variety of package managers are available at **https://elixir-lang.org/install.html#gnulinux**.

- **Installing on Windows:** For Windows users, an installer is available on the official Elixir website **https://elixir-lang.org/install.html#windows**.

- **Verifying installation:** After installation, you can verify whether Elixir has been installed successfully by running the following command:

  1. `elixir -v`

  This command will display the Elixir version installed on your system.

- **Additional setup:**

  o **Install Hex:** Hex is the package manager for the Erlang ecosystem. You can install it with:

  1. `mix local.hex`

  o **Install Phoenix (Optional):** If you are interested in building web applications, you can enhance your development experience by installing the Phoenix framework.

  To install Phoenix, you can run the following command:

  1. `mix archive.install hex phx_new`

Official installation page link: **https://hexdocs.pm/phoenix/installation.html**

- **Integrated development environment (IDE):** While you can use any text editor for Elixir development, some IDEs, such as Visual Studio Code or IntelliJ IDEA with the Elixir plugin, offer Elixir-specific syntax highlighting, code completion, and other useful features.

- **Interactive Elixir (IEx):** Once Elixir is installed, you can start an interactive session using the iex command. This interactive shell is beneficial for testing out small bits of Elixir code.

Elixir offers easy installation methods for most platforms. Once installed, you can explore the vast capabilities of the language, from building concurrent applications to web development with the Phoenix framework.

Note: **Refer to the official Elixir documentation for the most up-to-date installation instructions and best practices.**

# Conclusion

Erlang and BEAM are great for making strong, distributed, and multitasking systems. Elixir is a different language that uses Erlang's good points but adds easier ways to write and expand code. This means programmers can rely on Erlang's long history of being solid while enjoying Elixir's easier-to-use design and tools. As we wrap up this chapter, we understand how strong Erlang is and how Elixir makes it even better.

As we move on to the next chapter, we will look closer at how Elixir is written and the different kinds of data types you can use in it. We will learn about the simple parts of writing Elixir code and how to put code together in chunks. You will see how to make the code do what you want and work with different kinds of data types. At the end of the chapter, you will practice what you have learned to get a good grip on Elixir's writing style and features. This step-by-step learning is important to get really good at Elixir and use it to make strong and flexible apps.

# Multiple choice questions

1. **Which virtual machine does Elixir run on?**
    a. JVM
    b. Python VM
    c. BEAM
    d. Ruby VM

2. **What is the Elixir tool used for managing dependencies?**
    a. npm
    b. mix
    c. bundler
    d. pip

3. **Which of the following is NOT a feature of functional programming in Elixir?**
    a. Mutable data structures
    b. Pure functions

c.   First-class functions

d.   Higher-order functions

4.   **Elixir's fault tolerance is inherited from which language?**

a.   Python

b.   Ruby

c.   Erlang

d.   JavaScript

5.   **Which Elixir framework is intended for web development?**

a.   React

b.   Phoenix

c.   Laravel

d.   Rails

# Answer key

1.   c.

2.   b.

3.   a.

4.   c.

5.   b.

# Points to remember

- Elixir is a functional programming language designed for building scalable and maintainable applications, with Erlang's runtime giving it capabilities for high concurrency, fault tolerance, and distribution.

- The *let it crash* philosophy in Erlang, inherited by Elixir, promotes building self-healing systems through process supervision, allowing individual components to fail without affecting the entire system.

- The BEAM virtual machine is optimized for running Elixir's lightweight processes, enabling the creation of systems that can handle millions of concurrent operations.

- Hot code swapping is one of Erlang's standout features available in Elixir, allowing for updates to be made on a live system without downtime.

- Elixir's tooling includes Mix for project management, Hex for package management, and IEx for an interactive shell, which together provide a powerful and efficient development workflow.

- Seamless interoperability with Erlang means that all of Erlang's libraries and functionalities are available to Elixir developers without any performance penalties.

- The Elixir community has contributed a growing ecosystem of libraries and frameworks, such as Phoenix for web development and Nerves for embedded systems, further broadening the applications of the language.

- Understanding Elixir's underlying principles and its relationship with Erlang is essential for fully leveraging the language's potential in creating resilient, concurrent applications.

# Join our Discord space

Join our Discord workspace for latest updates, offers, tech happenings around the world, new releases, and sessions with the authors:

https://discord.bpbonline.com

# CHAPTER 2
# Elixir Syntax and Data Types

## Introduction

In this chapter, we will explore the fundamental concepts of Elixir data types, complemented by practical exercises to solidify your understanding. The significance of mastering Elixir data types lies in analogy to kitchen utensils, each meticulously crafted to serve a distinct purpose. Just as a fork is inappropriate for consuming soup and a spoon is not intended for slicing bread, so too do data types in programming languages fulfill specific roles. In this chapter, we will uncover the intricacies of each data type, equip ourselves with the tools to effectively utilize them, and enhance our proficiency in Elixir programming.

## Structure

This chapter will cover the following topics:

- Integers
- Floats
- Boolean
- Strings
- Atoms

- Maps

- Lists

- Tuples

- Keyword list

- Structs

- Modules and functions in Elixir

- Control flow structures

# Objectives

The aim of this chapter is to acquire a comprehensive understanding of the diverse data types in Elixir, emphasizing their distinct features and applications. The readers will hone the ability to judiciously select and implement appropriate data types within various programming contexts, thereby optimizing code efficiency and performance. Ultimately, the objective is to significantly elevate one's expertise in Elixir programming through a thorough mastery of data type utilization and comprehension.

# Integers

Like most languages, Elixir has integers. An integer can be any whole number, be it positive, negative, or zero. Notably, Elixir provides the functionality of using underscores to enhance the readability of large numbers. For instance, the notation **1_000_000_000** is perfectly valid and is interpreted identically to **1000000000**. This particular feature of Elixir is especially commendable for its contribution to code clarity. See how Elixir uses underscores in large numbers for clarity in these IEx examples:

```
1. iex> 1000000000
2. 1000000000
3. iex> 1000_000_000
4. 1000000000
```

You can do all mathematical operations in Elixir. Here are some examples of basic mathematical operations performed in Elixir:

```
1. iex(1)> 1 + 1
2. 2
3. iex(2)> 2 - 1
4. 1
```

```
5. iex(3)> 2 * 2
6. 4
7. iex(4)> 2 / 2
8. 1.0
```

For division, as you can see, you are getting the result in float. To get the result in integer, you can use the div function, which performs an integer division, as shown in the following code:

```
1. iex> div(2,2)
2. 1
3. iex> div(2,1)
4. 2
```

The Integer module has several built-in functions, such as finding whether the given number is even or odd. Here is how you can use the Integer module in Elixir to check if numbers are even or odd:

```
1. iex> require Integer
2. Integer
3. iex> Integer.is_even(10)
4. true
5. iex> Integer.is_odd(10)
6. false
```

For additional functions, please refer to the Elixir documentation for the **Integer** module, available on their official website.

# Floats

A step ahead of integers, we have floats. These are numbers with decimal points, such as 5.16. In Elixir, floats are in 64-bit double precision. You can round off a float to the nearest integer using the round function. Here is an example of using the **Float.round** function to round a float to three decimal places:

```
1. iex> Float.round(9.5575, 3)
2. 9.557
```

As you can see, one would have expected the output to be 9.558 instead. This is not a bug but a known issue. You must use a decimal library if you want exact rounding for decimals.

# Boolean

In Elixir, as in many other programming languages, Booleans are represented by two values: true and false. These serve as the fundamental building blocks for handling decision-making in code, enabling programmers to manage control flow and logic based on conditions. Booleans are especially critical in scenarios where a binary decision is necessary, simplifying complex evaluations into simple yes-or-no choices.

Elixir handles Booleans in a straightforward manner, allowing seamless integration with conditional statements like if, unless, and case. This simplicity is pivotal for writing clear and effective code.

# Strings

Elixir strings are UTF-8-encoded binaries. UTF-8 is a popular encoding that can represent any character in the Unicode standard, yet is backward-compatible with ASCII. This means that Elixir strings can comfortably handle a wide range of characters from various languages and scripts, not just English. Here is an example demonstrating how Elixir's UTF-8 encoded strings can seamlessly handle a mix of characters from different languages:

```
1. # A string with characters from different languages
2. iex> multi_lang_str = "Hello, 你好, Bonjour, Привет"
3.
4. iex> IO.puts(multi_lang_str)
5. Hello, 你好, Bonjour, Привет
6. :ok
```

Elixir strings are essentially sequences of Unicode characters. Unicode is a standard for encoding a vast range of characters and symbols from all writing systems, past and present. When you see an Elixir string enclosed in double quotes, you see a sequence of these Unicode characters. Here are a few examples that illustrate how Elixir handles strings as sequences of Unicode characters, ranging from simple ASCII to special characters with unique Unicode code points:

```
1. # A simple string in Elixir
2. simple_str = "hello"
3. IO.puts(simple_str)   # Outputs: hello
4.
5. # A string with special Unicode characters
6. unicode_str = "héllò"
```

```
7. IO.puts(unicode_str)   # Outputs: héllò

8.

9. # Each character has a unique Unicode code point. Let's get the code
   point of 'é':

10. IO.puts(?é)   # Outputs: 233
```

These characteristics of Elixir strings make the language powerful for processing text data from diverse sources without running into unexpected encoding issues. They reflect Elixir's foundation on the Erlang VM, which was designed with robustness and wide-reaching connectivity in mind.

In addition to handling characters from various languages, Elixir provides several mechanisms to manipulate and work with strings effectively. Let us explore these features in more detail:

- **Escaping double quotes within a string**: In many programming languages, strings are denoted by enclosing them within double quotes. If you want to include a double quote inside a string, it needs to be *escaped*, so you prepend it with a backslash (\). This tells Elixir that the following character is to be interpreted as a literal character and not as a control character. Here is how you can include double quotes within a string in Elixir by using the escape character \ to ensure they are treated as literal characters:

  ```
  1. iex> str = "this is a string with \"double quotes\""
  2. iex> IO.puts(str)
  3. this is a string with "double quotes"
  ```

- **Concatenation using the <>/2 operator**: In Elixir, strings can be concatenated using the <> operator. It is slightly different from some other languages where (+) might be used for string concatenation. The /2 in <>/2 denotes a binary function (it takes two arguments):

  ```
  1. iex> concatenated_str = "hello" <> " " <> "world"
  2. iex> IO.puts(concatenated_str)
  3. hello world
  ```

- **String interpolation**: It is a convenient way to insert variables or expressions directly into a string. You use the #{} syntax to achieve this in Elixir. Whatever is inside the curly braces {} is evaluated as an Elixir expression, and its result is inserted into the string at that position:

  ```
  1. iex> name = "John"
  2. iex> age = 30
  ```

```
3. iex> interpolated_str = "My name is #{name} and I am #{age} years
   old."

4. iex> IO.puts(interpolated_str)

5. My name is John and I am 30 years old.

6.

7. # It can even evaluate expressions within the interpolation

8. iex> IO.puts("Next year, I will be #{age + 1} years old.")

9. Next year, I will be 31 years old.
```

Elixir offers a rich set of functions for string manipulation through its **String** module. Here are some of the most commonly used and useful functions:

- **String.length/1**: Returns the number of graphemes (perceived characters) in a string.

  Here is how you can determine the number of graphemes in a string using the **String.length/1** function:

```
1. iex> String.length("héllo")

2. 5
```

- **String.split/2**: Splits a string into a list of strings based on a delimiter.

  See how we can divide a string into multiple parts based on a specified delimiter with the **String.split/2** function:

```
1. iex> String.split("hello, world", ", ")

2. ["hello", "world"]
```

- **String.replace/3**: Replaces a specific pattern in a string.

  The following example demonstrates replacing a specific substring with another string using the **String.replace/3** function:

```
1. iex> String.replace("hello world", "world", "Elixir")

2. "hello Elixir"
```

- **String.downcase/1 and String.upcase/1**: Convert string characters to lower or upper case, respectively.

  Here is how to convert a string to either lower case or upper case using the **String.downcase/1** and **String.upcase/1** functions:

```
1. iex> String.downcase("HELLO")

2. "hello"
```

```
3. iex> String.upcase("elixir")
4. "ELIXIR"
```

- **String.trim/1**: Removes leading and trailing whitespaces from a string.

  This example demonstrates how to remove leading and trailing whitespaces from a string with the **String.trim/1** function:

```
1. iex> String.trim("  hello  ")
2. "hello"
```

- **String.contains?/2**: Checks if a string contains a particular substring or pattern.

  See how to determine if a string contains a specific substring or pattern using the **String.contains?/2** function:

```
1. iex> String.contains?("hello world", "world")
2. true
```

- **String.at/2**: Returns the grapheme at a particular index.

  Here is how to retrieve a specific grapheme from a string by its index using the **String.at/2** function:

```
1. iex> String.at("hello", 1)  # Returns "e"
2. "e"
```

- **String.starts_with?/2 and String.ends_with?/2**: Check if a string starts or ends with a particular pattern.

  This example shows how to check if a string starts or ends with a particular pattern using **String.starts_with?/2** and **String.ends_with?/2** functions:

```
1. iex> String.starts_with?("elixir", "eli")
2. true
3. iex> String.ends_with?("elixir", "xir")
4. true
```

- **String.capitalize/1**: Capitalizes the first grapheme and turns all other graphemes in the string into lowercase.

  Learn how to capitalize the first grapheme and turn all other graphemes into lowercase with the **String.capitalize/1** function:

```
1. iex> String.capitalize("elixir")
2. "Elixir"
```

# Memory considerations inside the BEAM

Strings in Elixir are immutable binaries. The BEAM copies data only when necessary; once you know where those copies occur, you can choose the cheapest technique for each job:

- **Variable rebinding:** The following code shows how a variable can be reassigned without mutating the original binary:

```
1. name = "Alice"

2. name = "Bob"
```

  **"Bob"** is created as a new binary, and name now points to it; the earlier **"Alice"** remains in memory until no process refers to it.

  Best practice of rebinding small strings is fine, but avoid rebinding large binaries inside loops; each assignment keeps the previous value alive until garbage collection runs. Build the final value once or stream chunks instead.

- **Concatenation (<>):** The next snippet demonstrates that every use of <> allocates a fresh buffer:

```
1. greeting = "hello" <> " world"
```

  <> copies both operands. Inside a loop that joins many lines, this behaviour multiplies allocations.

  Best practice use <> for a few short joins; for thousands, switch to iodata so the VM performs a single copy at the end.

- **Building large text with iodata**: Here we gather many small binaries into an iodata list, then flatten it once:

```
1. iodata =
2.   [["name,email\n"]
3.   | Enum.map(rows, fn r -> [r.name, ",", r.email, ?\n] end)]
4.
5. csv = IO.iodata_to_binary(iodata)    # one allocation
```

  Iodata postpones copying until **IO.iodata_to_binary/1**, so only the final 2 MB buffer (for 50,000 rows) is allocated, not hundreds of megabytes of intermediates.

- **Slicing and pattern matching**: The following match pulls out a header byte without copying the underlying bytes:

```
1. <<sigil::binary-size(1), rest::binary>> = "Ωmega"
2.
3. sigil and rest become sub-binaries that share the original buffer.
```

Best practice is the use of sub-binaries for cheap parsing. If the source payload is very large and will be discarded immediately, copy just the slice you need with **binary_part/3** so the big buffer can be freed sooner.

- **Sending binaries between processes**: This code shows that large binaries cross process boundaries by reference, not by copy:

```
1. payload = String.duplicate("x", 4_096)   # 4 KB
2. send(other_pid, payload)        # zero-copy transfer
```

The BEAM copies binaries under 64 B; anything larger travels by pointer.

The best practice is to send large binaries as they are; reference counting prevents duplication. For floods of tiny messages, batch them into a larger frame to reduce copy overhead.

By following these guidelines, you minimize unnecessary allocations, keep the garbage collector calm, and ensure that your Elixir applications remain responsive even when processing large text or binary payloads.

# Atoms

Atoms in Elixir serve as constants, and their values are essentially their own names. This means that atoms with the same name are identical, making them useful for representing distinct values or states. For instance, **:cow** and **:milk** are atoms, with **:cow** being equal to itself but not to **:milk**. Atoms can also depict the outcome of operations, such as **:ok** and **:error**. Interestingly, the Boolean values **true** and **false** in Elixir are also atoms. There is a syntactic sugar in Elixir that lets you omit the leading colon for the atoms **false**, **true**, and **nil**.

To define an atom, you typically use a sequence of Unicode characters like letters, numbers, underscores, and @. However, if you need to use characters outside of these typical ones, such as spaces, you can enclose the atom's name in double quotes, like: *This is an atom with spaces*.

Elixir provides utility functions for atoms. For example, you can convert an atom to a charlist using **to_charlist(atom)** or a string using **to_string(atom)**. These functions are inlined by the compiler for performance reasons. Some examples include **Atom.to_charlist(:"An apple")** resulting in **'An apple'** and **Atom.to_string(:bob)** yielding **"bob"**.

# Limitations and cautions

Here are some important limitations and precautions to consider when working with atoms in Elixir:

- **Memory consumption**: Atoms are not garbage-collected. This means once an atom is created, it remains in memory for the duration of the system's process. If you dynamically create a large number of atoms (for example, by converting user input directly into atoms), you can exhaust the virtual machine's atom table and cause the system to run out of memory.

- **Fixed atom limit**: The BEAM VM, which runs Elixir, has a default limit of around 1,048,576 atoms. While this might sound like a lot, if atoms are generated dynamically, especially from untrusted input, you can hit this limit.

- **Avoid user-generated atoms**: You should be cautious about converting user input directly into atoms. If there is a need, always ensure a predefined list of acceptable values to prevent arbitrary atom creation.

- **String to atom conversion**: Functions like `String.to_atom/1` should be used with caution, especially if the input is not controlled. Instead, when dealing with dynamic data, you can use functions like `String.to_existing_atom/1`, which will raise an error if the atom does not already exist.

Therefore, atoms are powerful and useful constructs in Elixir, but like any tool, they need to be used appropriately. Being aware of their non-garbage-collected nature is crucial to avoiding potential system issues.

# Maps

Maps in Elixir serve as the main structure to hold key-value pairs for storing associated data. Maps are created using the `%{}` syntax, with key-value pairs represented as `key => value`. A distinctive feature of maps is that keys can be of any type, and they do not impose order on their key-value pairs.

Here are examples showing how to create and use maps in Elixir, demonstrating the flexibility of keys and the syntax for setting key-value pairs:

```
1. iex> my_map = %{"key" => "value", :symbol_key => 123}
2. %{:symbol_key => 123, "key" => "value"}
3. iex> map_with_various_keys = %{:a => 1, "b" => 2, [1,2,3] => 3}
4. %{:a => 1, [1, 2, 3] => 3, "b" => 2}
```

Duplicate keys are not allowed. If duplicate keys are present in a map definition, the last one is used.

The key lookups in maps are fast compared to lists. If you have key-value pairs stored in a list and you want to find a value based on its key, you would have to potentially look at every element in the list until you find it. However, with a map, due to its internal structure and the way it organizes data, you can find the key much more quickly, especially as the size of the dataset grows.

In simple terms, if you are frequently looking up values by their keys, it is much more efficient to use a map than a list in Elixir.

Maps implement the Enumerable protocol, so functions in the Enum module can operate on them. There are several built-in Kernel functions available for map operations; let us see some of them now:

- **New**: `Map.new()` creates a new empty map:

```
1. iex> Map.new()
2. %{}
```

You can also convert an enumerable into a map, as shown in the following code:

```
1. iex> list = [name: "John", age: 28]
2. [name: "John", age: 28]
3. iex> Map.new(list)
4. %{name: "John", age: 28}
```

**Caution: This is useful for converting keyword lists or other enumerables to maps. However, if the enumerable is not in a {key, value} format, you may encounter errors or unexpected results.**

- **Put**: `Map.put(map, key, value)` adds or updates the given key with the provided value:

```
1. iex> map = %{name: "Alice"}
2. %{name: "Alice"}
3. iex> Map.put(map, :name, "Bob")
4. %{name: "Bob"}
5. iex> Map.put(map, :age, 28)
6. %{name: "Alice", age: 28}
```

- **Get**: `Map.get(map, key, default \ nil)` fetches the value for a specific key or returns the default value if the key does not exist:

```
1. iex> map = %{name: "Alice", age: 28}
2. %{name: "Alice", age: 28}
3. iex> Map.get(map, :name, "Unknown")
4. "Alice"
5. iex> Map.get(map, :gender, "Unknown")
6. "Unknown"
```

The `Map.get` function provides a straightforward way to access values in a map, returning a specified default value if the key is not found. This function is useful when you want to avoid errors from accessing nonexistent keys and need a simple value retrieval without pattern matching.

Next, let us look at the `Map.fetch` function, which offers a more structured response. It returns a tuple with `:ok` and the value if the key exists, or `:error` if it does not. This is particularly useful for scenarios where you need to explicitly handle the presence or absence of a key:

```
1. iex> Map.fetch(map, :name)
2. {:ok, "Alice"}
3. iex> Map.fetch(map, :gender)
4. :error
```

On the other hand, `Map.fetch!` is more assertive. It returns the value directly if the key exists, but it will raise a `KeyError` if the key is not found in the map. This behavior is useful when you expect the key to always be present and prefer the program to fail loudly if it is not:

```
1. iex> Map.fetch!(map, :name)
2. "Alice"
3. iex> Map.fetch!(map, :gender)
4. ** (KeyError) key :gender not found in: %{name: "Alice", age: 28}
5.     (stdlib 5.0) :maps.get(:gender, %{name: "Alice", age: 28})
```

Caution: **Use Map.fetch!/2 judiciously. If there is any doubt about the key's presence, consider using Map.fetch/2 or check for the key's existence with Map.has_key?/2 first.**

- Merge: `Map.merge(map1, map2)` merges two maps into one. If there are conflicting keys, the values from **map2** will overwrite those from **map1**:

```
1. iex> map1 = %{name: "Alice", age: 28}
2. %{name: "Alice", age: 28}
3. iex> map2 = %{age: 29, city: "Phoenix"}
4. %{age: 29, city: "Phoenix"}
5. iex> Map.merge(map1, map2)
6. %{name: "Alice", age: 29, city: "Phoenix"}
```

Caution: **Be wary of key overlaps between the maps, as map2's values will prevail. If specific merge behavior is desired for collisions, consider using Map.merge/3.**

- **Delete**: `Map.delete(map, key)` deletes the entry in the map for a specific key:

```
1. iex> map = %{name: "Alice", age: 28, city: "Phoenix"}
2. %{name: "Alice", age: 28, city: "Phoenix"}
3. iex> Map.delete(map, :age)
4. %{name: "Alice", city: "Phoenix"}
```

**Caution: This function deletes the key-value pair silently, even if the key does not exist. Ensure you really want to delete the key or check its existence first if you want to be sure.**

Similar to `Map.delete/2`, this function will silently ignore keys that do not exist in the map. If your intent is to confirm removal, you may want to first check if all keys are present on the map:

```
1. iex> map = %{name: "Alice", age: 28, city: "Phoenix", country:
   "USA"}
2. %{name: "Alice", age: 28, city: "Phoenix", country: "USA"}
3. iex> Map.drop(map, [:age, :city])
4. %{name: "Alice", country: "USA"}
```

# Lists

Elixir lists are a form of linked lists that can hold any number of elements, including elements of different types. They are defined between square brackets:

```
1. iex> my_list = [1, 2, 3, "four", :five]
2. [1, 2, 3, "four", :five]
```

Concatenation is the process of joining two end-to-end lists to produce a new list:

```
1. iex> [1, 2, 3] ++ [4, 5]
2. [1, 2, 3, 4, 5]
```

Appending is the process of adding an element to the end of a list. Technically, this is a special case of concatenation where the second list contains only one element:

```
1. iex> [1, 2, 3] ++ [4]
2. [1, 2, 3, 4]
```

Subtraction involves removing the first occurrence of elements from the second list from the first list:

```
1. iex> [1, 2, 3, 2] -- [2, 3]
2. [1, 2]
```

Prepending is the process of adding an element to the start of a list.

```
1. iex> [6 | [1,2,3] ]
2. [6, 1, 2, 3]
```

**Caution: In Elixir, prepending is more efficient than appending due to the linked list structure of Elixir lists.**

Every list in Elixir can be thought of as being made up of a *head* and a *tail*.

Consider the following example:

- **Head**: The first element of the list.
- **Tail**: The remainder of the list after removing the head.

For instance, in the list [1, 2, 3, 4]:

- The head is 1
- The tail is [2, 3, 4]

Elixir provides a unique syntax to split a list into its head and tail:

```
1. [head | tail] = [1, 2, 3, 4]
```

After this line, head would be **1**, and tail would be **[2, 3, 4]**.

This decomposition is fundamental in Elixir (and Erlang) and often comes into play in recursive functions. When recursively processing a list, a common pattern is to handle the *head* of the list and then recursively process the *tail* until the list is empty.

Let us see some of the useful **List** functions:

```
 1. iex> List.first([1, 2, 3])
 2. 1
 3.
 4. iex> List.last([1, 2, 3])
 5. 3
 6.
 7. iex> List.flatten([1, [2, 3], 4])
 8. [1, 2, 3, 4]
 9.
10.    # (deletes the first occurrence of 2)
11. iex> List.delete([1, 2, 3, 2], 2)
12. [1, 3, 2]
13.
```

```
14. iex> List.duplicate(:ok, 3)
15. [:ok, :ok, :ok]
```

We will do some practical exercises on Elixir lists at the end of this chapter.

# Tuples

In Elixir, tuples are fixed-size collections containing elements of any type. They are denoted by curly braces and are designed primarily for read-heavy operations.

```
1. # Defining a tuple
2. tuple = {1, :two, "three"}
```

Tuples provide constant-time access for reading any element, making them efficient for tasks where the structure does not change frequently. However, if you have to modify a tuple, a new tuple gets created, which is a linear-time operation.

> Caution: **Tuples should not be used as flexible collections like lists. Instead, they are best suited for fixed-size containers. Enum functions do not work on tuples.**

While accessing elements in a tuple is constant time, modifying its results is a linear-time operation since it creates a shallow copy. Lists are more suited for traversals and modifications.

Here are some useful functions for working with tuples in Elixir, demonstrating how to access, modify, and convert tuples:

- **elem/2**: Access an element in the **tuple** by its index:

```
1. iex> tuple = {1, :two, "three"}
2. {1, :two, "three"}
3. iex> second_element = elem(tuple, 1)
4. :two
```

- **put_elem/3**: Insert or replace a value into the **tuple** at a specific index:

```
1. iex> tuple = {1, :two, "three"}
2. {1, :two, "three"}
3. iex> new_tuple = put_elem(tuple, 1, :changed)
4. {1, :changed, "three"}
```

- **tuple_size/1**: Retrieve the number of elements in the **tuple**:

```
1. iex> tuple = {1, :two, "three"}
2. {1, :two, "three"}
3. iex> size = tuple_size(tuple)
4. 3
```

- **to_list/1**: Convert a tuple to a list:

```
1. iex> tuple = {1, :two, "three"}
2. {1, :two, "three"}
3. iex> Tuple.to_list(tuple)
4. [1, :two, "three"]
```

# Keyword list

Elixir keyword list is composed of two-element tuples where the first element, the key, is an atom, and the second element, the value, can be any term. Elixir offers a concise syntax for keyword lists, making them more readable.

For example:

- **Traditional tuple format**:
  **[{:exit_on_close, true}, {:active, :once}]**

- **Concise keyword list syntax**:
  **[exit_on_close: true, active: :once]**

Let us look into a few of the functions offered by the **Keyword** module in Elixir:

- **get**: Fetches the value for a specific key:

```
1. iex> list = [a: 1, b: 2, c: 3]
2. [a: 1, b: 2, c: 3]
3. iex> Keyword.get(list, :a)
4. 1
```

- **put**: Inserts or updates the value for a specific key:

```
1. iex> list = [a: 1, b: 2]
2. [a: 1, b: 2]
3. iex> Keyword.put(list, :c, 3)
4. [c: 3, a: 1, b: 2]
```

- **delete**: Removes the entries for a specific key:

```
1. iex> list = [a: 1, b: 2, c: 3]
2. [a: 1, b: 2, c: 3]
3. iex> Keyword.delete(list, :b)
4. [a: 1, c: 3]
```

- **has_key?**: Checks if a given key exists:

  1. `iex> list = [a: 1, b: 2]`
  2. `[a: 1, b: 2]`
  3. `iex> Keyword.has_key?(list, :a)`
  4. `true`

- **merge**: Combines two keyword lists:

  1. `iex> list1 = [a: 1, b: 2]`
  2. `[a: 1, b: 2]`
  3. `iex> list2 = [b: 3, c: 4]`
  4. `[b: 3, c: 4]`
  5. `iex> Keyword.merge(list1, list2)`
  6. `[a: 1, b: 3, c: 4]`

- **keys and values**: Return all keys or values from the keyword list, respectively:

  1. `iex> list = [a: 1, b: 2, c: 3]`
  2. `[a: 1, b: 2, c: 3]`
  3. `iex> Keyword.keys(list)`
  4. `[:a, :b, :c]`
  5. `iex> Keyword.values(list)`
  6. `[1, 2, 3]`

These are just a few of the functions offered by the **Keyword** module in Elixir. The module provides a comprehensive set of utilities to manipulate and query keyword lists effectively.

The following are the cautions:

- Keyword lists can have duplicate keys.
- Functions in the **Keyword** module do not ensure a specific order for the keys, so pattern matching based on order is not reliable.
- Operations on keyword lists might be slower than their map counterparts due to the need to traverse the list.

# Structs

In Elixir, a struct is a special data type that allows the definition of a set of fields and their associated values. Essentially, it is an extension of Elixir's map data type but with a fixed set of keys.

Let us explore how structs are used in Elixir, focusing on naming conventions, creation, updates, and their behavior in pattern matching:

- **Naming**: Structs are named after the module they are defined in. For instance, if you define a struct inside the **User** module, the struct will be named **User**:

```
1. defmodule User do
2.   defstruct name: "John", age: 30
3. end
```

- **Create/define a struct**: To create a struct, use the defstruct construct inside a module. This will define a new struct with the specified fields and their default values:

```
1. defmodule User do
2.   defstruct name: nil, age: nil
3. end
4.
5. user = %User{name: "Alice", age: 30}
```

- **Update fields in a struct**: You cannot add new fields to a struct after it has been defined, but you can update the values of existing fields:

```
1. user = %User{name: "Alice", age: 30}
2.
3. updated_user = %User{user | name: "Bob"}
```

**Note: The above operations return a new struct with the updated values. They do not modify the original struct because Elixir data structures are immutable.**

The following are the cautions:

- **Fixed keys**: Structs have a fixed set of fields. Attempting to assign a value to a field that has not been defined in the struct will raise an error.

- **No inheritance**: Unlike some object-oriented languages, Elixir does not support inheritance for structs. You cannot create a struct that inherits fields from another struct:

```
1. defmodule Mammal do
2.   defstruct legs: 4
3. end
4. # In some OOP languages, you might be able to have Dog inherit
     properties from Mammal.
5. # But in Elixir, this concept doesn't exist for structs.
```

```
6. # You'll have to explicitly define the properties you need in each
     struct.
7. defmodule Dog do
8.   defstruct legs: 4, breed: nil
9. end
```

- **Strict matching**: Pattern matching with structs ensures a match against that specific struct type. A **map**, even with the same fields, will not match against a struct in a pattern:

```
1. defmodule Vehicle do
2.   defstruct wheels: 4
3. end
4. car = %Vehicle{wheels: 4}
5. # This works - matching a struct against a struct.
6. %Vehicle{wheels: wheel_count} = car
7. IO.puts wheel_count  # Outputs: 4
8. # This will raise a match error even though the map has the same
     fields.
9. %{wheels: wheel_count} = car
```

Unlike maps, you cannot add or remove fields from a struct once it is defined. Ensure that your operations align with the struct's defined shape.

# Modules and functions in Elixir

In Elixir, efficient code organization and clarity are achieved through the use of modules and functions. In the following sections, we will cover these constructs in detail.

## Modules

In Elixir, modules are the primary means to organize and group sets of related functions. They serve as namespaces, helping you avoid naming collisions, and can be thought of as containers for related functions. Let us see some of the module attributes now:

- **Module documentation with @moduledoc**: The **@moduledoc** attribute allows you to provide a description for your module, which can be useful for other developers and for generating documentation using tools like *ExDoc*:

```
1. defmodule Calculator do
2.   @moduledoc """
3.   This module provides basic arithmetic operations.
```

```
4.    """
5.
6.    def add(a, b), do: a + b
7. end
```

- **Function documentation with @doc**: You can document your functions and macros using the **@doc** attribute. This documentation can be accessed via IEx and is also used by ExDoc:

```
1. defmodule Calculator do
2.    @doc """
3.    Adds two numbers.
4.    """
5.    def add(a, b), do: a + b
6. End
```

- **Using @behaviour**: In Elixir, behaviours provide a way to define a set of functions that a module must implement. This allows for a polymorphic way of invoking certain functionalities across different modules while ensuring they adhere to the same interface, similar to interfaces in object-oriented languages:

  Behaviours are defined using the **@callback** directive.

# Defining the behavior

Behaviors specify what functions a module should implement. For instance, in the **Notifier** module, we define a behavior with one callback, **send_notification**. Here is how it is defined:

```
1. defmodule Notifier do
2.    @callback send_notification(to: String.t(), message: String.t()) ::
   {:ok, String.t()} | {:error, String.t()}
3. end
```

This declaration mandates that any module claiming to implement this behavior must provide its own implementation of the **send_notification** function.

# Implementing the behavior

To conform to the defined behavior, different modules can implement the specified functionalities according to their operational context. For example, the **SmsNotifier** and **EmailNotifier** modules implement the Notifier behavior, each tailoring the **send_notification** function to their specific medium:

```
01. defmodule SmsNotifier do
02.    @behaviour Notifier
03.
04.    def send_notification(to, message) do
05.      # Simulate sending an SMS...
06.      {:ok, "SMS sent to #{to} with message: #{message}"}
07.    end
08. end
09.
10. defmodule EmailNotifier do
11.    @behaviour Notifier
12.
13.    def send_notification(to, message) do
14.      # Simulate sending an email...
15.      {:ok, "Email sent to #{to} with message: #{message}"}
16.    end
17. end
```

These implementations demonstrate how different modules fulfill the requirements of the **Notifier** behavior, with each handling the task of notification in a distinct manner. If a module declares it implements a behavior using **@behaviour** but fails to provide the required function implementations, Elixir generates a compile-time warning. This feature is crucial when designing systems with interchangeable parts that need to adhere to the same interface or when developing libraries that require future modules to conform to a specific set of functions. This ensures reliability and consistency across the application or library ecosystem.

# Deprecating functions with @deprecated

Over time, as your application evolves, you might want to deprecate some old functions in favor of new ones. The **@deprecated** attribute allows you to specify that a function or macro is deprecated:

```
1. defmodule Calculator do
2.    @deprecated "Use `subtract/2` instead."
3.    def minus(a, b), do: a - b
4.
5.    def subtract(a, b), do: a - b
6. end
```

# Using @on_load for module initialization

If you need to run some initialization code whenever a module is loaded, the **@on_load** attribute can be handy:

```
1. defmodule Initializer do
2.   @on_load :init_module
3.
4.   def init_module do
5.     IO.puts("Module loaded!")
6.     :ok
7.   end
8. End
```

When you compile and load this module, it will print **"Module loaded!"**.

# Specifying external dependencies with @external_resource

If your module relies on an external file (like a configuration file or a database migration), you can use the **@external_resource** attribute. If the external resource changes, the module will be recompiled:

```
1. defmodule Config do
2.   @external_resource "config/prod.exs"
3.
4.   def get_config do
5.     # Load the configuration from "config/prod.exs"
6.   end
7. end
```

These examples provide an overview of some of the most commonly used module attributes in Elixir. When used appropriately, they can make your code more maintainable, understandable, and robust.

# Functions

Functions in Elixir are blocks of code meant to perform a specific task. They take in parameters, process them, and then return a result.

Let us explore some of the features that can be applied to functions:

- **Named vs. anonymous functions**: Elixir supports both named and anonymous functions:

```
1. double = fn x -> x * 2 end
2.
3. defmodule NamedFunction do
4.   def triple(x), do: x * 3
5. end
```

Here, double is an anonymous function (does not have a name) that takes an argument **x** and returns its **double**. We define it using the **fn** keyword. On the other hand, inside the **NamedFunction** module, **triple** is a named function defined using the **def** keyword.

- **Anonymous functions (basic usage)**: Anonymous functions are a versatile feature in Elixir, useful for defining functionality without naming them, allowing for inline usage and easy passing as arguments:

```
1. sum = fn (a, b) -> a + b end
2. IO.puts(sum.(1, 2))   # This will print "3"
```

We define an anonymous function sum that adds two numbers, stored in the variable sum. To call an anonymous function, use the dot notation as shown.

- **Multi-clause anonymous function**: Anonymous functions can also have multiple clauses, similar to named functions, as shown in the following code example:

```
1. greet = fn
2.   :english -> "Hello"
3.   :spanish -> "Hola"
4.   _ -> "Hi"
5. end
6.
7. IO.puts(greet.(:spanish))   # This will print "Hola"
```

This anonymous function matches against the given input to return a greeting in the specified language. If the language is not recognized, it defaults to **"Hi"**.

- **Anonymous function (using capture notation)**: Elixir provides a shorthand for defining anonymous functions called **capture notation**:

```
1. multiply = &(&1 * &2)
2. IO.puts(multiply.(2, 3))   # This will print "6"
```

The capture notation is a compact way to define anonymous functions. &1 and &2 are placeholders for the first and second arguments, respectively.

- **First-class citizens**: Functions are first-class citizens that can be passed around like any other value, such as integers or strings:

```
01. defmodule MathOperations do
02.   def add(a, b), do: a + b
03.   def subtract(a, b), do: a - b
04.
05.   def operate(func, a, b) do
06.     func.(a, b)
07.   end
08. end
09.
10. # Usage:
11.
12. # Define two anonymous functions for addition and subtraction
13. add_func = fn a, b -> MathOperations.add(a, b) end
14. subtract_func = fn a, b -> MathOperations.subtract(a, b) end
15.
16. # Use the operate function with the defined anonymous functions
17. IO.puts(MathOperations.operate(add_func, 5, 3))      # This will
    print "8"
18. IO.puts(MathOperations.operate(subtract_func, 5, 3))  # This will
    print "2"
```

In the module **MathOperations**, we have an **operate** function that takes another function, **func**, as an argument. We can then use that passed-in function within the operation. This demonstrates how functions can be treated as values and passed to other functions as arguments.

# Control flow structures

Elixir is a functional programming language that provides various control flow structures and allows developers to direct the execution of code based on conditions or to repeat actions. These structures are crucial in building logic into applications. In this section, we will explore the primary control flow structures in Elixir: if, unless, case, cond, and with, along with practical examples:

- **if and unless**: **if** is used to execute code based on a condition. Elixir also offers unless, which is the equivalent of if not.

For example:

```
1. defmodule Example do
2.    def check_number(n) do
3.       if n > 0 do
4.          "#{n} is positive"
5.       else
6.          "#{n} is not positive"
7.       end
8.    end
9. end
```

- **case**: **case** allows for pattern matching against multiple values. It is particularly powerful in Elixir due to its deep integration with the language's pattern-matching capabilities.

For example:

```
1. defmodule Example do
2.    def classify(number) do
3.       case number do
4.          1 -> 'One'
5.          2 -> 'Two'
6.          _ -> 'Other'
7.       end
8.    end
9. End
```

- **cond**: **cond** is used when you need to check multiple conditions. It is similar to **else if** or **elsif** in other languages.

For example:

```
1. defmodule Example do
2.    def size(n) do
3.       cond do
4.          n > 0 and n <= 10 -> 'small'
5.          n > 10 and n <= 100 -> 'medium'
6.          n > 100 -> 'large'
7.          true -> 'invalid'
```

```
8.        end
9.      end
10. end
```

- **with**: The **with** statement in Elixir is a control flow structure used for sequential pattern matching. It is particularly useful when you have multiple operations that could potentially fail, and you want to execute them in a sequence where each step depends on the success of the previous one. This feature streamlines error handling and improves code readability, especially when dealing with a sequence of operations.

For example, consider a simple task of opening and reading a file:

```
1. defmodule FileReader do
2.   def read_file(file_path) do
3.     with {:ok, file} <- File.open(file_path),
4.          contents <- File.read(file) do
5.       File.close(file)
6.       {:ok, contents}
7.     else
8.       {:error, reason} -> {:error, reason}
9.     end
10.  end
11. end
```

In this example, **File.open** might fail if the file does not exist. The **with** statement ensures that **File.read** is only called if **File.open** succeeds, thus handling potential errors gracefully.

Let us say we have a data processing pipeline involving multiple steps:

```
1. defmodule DataProcessor do
2.   def process(data) do
3.     with {:ok, step1_result} <- step1(data),
4.          {:ok, step2_result} <- step2(step1_result),
5.          {:ok, final_result} <- step3(step2_result) do
6.       {:ok, final_result}
7.     else
8.       {:error, reason} -> handle_error(reason)
9.     end
10.  end
```

```
11.
12.   defp handle_error(reason), do: IO.puts("Error occurred: #{rea-
      son}")
13. end
14.
```

Each function **step1**, **step2**, and **step3** represents a stage in the pipeline and can potentially return an error. The with block cleanly handles this sequence, passing the result from one step to the next and dealing with any errors that occur.

You can also handle different errors by specifying patterns in the else block of the **with** statement. This allows you to catch and handle specific errors differently.

You can define custom error handling for different failure cases:

```
1. with {:ok, result} <- some_operation(),
2.      {:ok, another_result} <- another_operation(result) do
3.    # Success path
4. else
5.   {:error, :not_found} -> handle_not_found()
6.   {:error, reason} -> handle_generic_error(reason)
7. End
```

Here, we handle a **:not_found** error differently from other errors.

# Conclusion

Mastering the fundamental data types in Elixir is essential for writing clear, efficient, and maintainable code. By understanding and effectively utilizing integers, floats, Booleans, strings, atoms, maps, lists, tuples, keyword lists, and structs, you will be well-equipped to handle a wide range of programming challenges. The exercises provided below will help reinforce these concepts and prepare you for more advanced topics.

In the next chapter, we will understand Elixir's elegant handling of collections, the power of the Enum module, and the sophistication of pattern matching. As a functional language, Elixir stands out for its efficient and expressive ways of managing collections, such as lists, tuples, and maps, through a set of powerful enumerable functions. This chapter explores seamless integration of these functions with pattern matching, an essential feature that distinguishes Elixir from many other programming languages. Whether you are new to Elixir or looking to deepen your understanding, this chapter provides a comprehensive guide to harnessing the full potential of collections, Enum, and pattern matching in writing clean, efficient, and maintainable code.

# Practical exercises

This chapter covered a lot, and now it is time for some hands-on work. We are going to use a tool called **Mix**, which comes with Elixir. It helps us organize and test our code.

The benefits of using Mix are:

- **Organized**: With mix, our code has its special place, and our tests have another. It is like having separate drawers for socks and shirts.

- **Testing is easy**: We can quickly check if our answers to exercises are right.

**Create a project:**

Open your terminal and create a new project:

```
mix new chapter2
```

It is like setting up a new play area for our exercises.

If you look at the folder structure, you will see two main spots, which are shown as follows:

- **lib**: Put your exercise answers here.

- **test**: This is where you check if your answers are right.

**Testing**:

For each exercise, there is a way to test if you are on the mark. You will put these tests in the test spot.

To see if you got an exercise right, type:

```
1. mix test
```

If things light up green, you are good. If not, try again:

```
1. mix test
2. Compiling 1 file (.ex)
3. Generated chapter2 app
4. ..
5. Finished in 0.01 seconds (0.00s async, 0.01s sync)
6. 1 doctest, 1 test, 0 failures
```

You can keep trying until you get it. Every time you think you have got the right answer, run the test to check.

We are set up and ready. These exercises are a good way to see what you have learned.

# Exercise 1: Find the sum of the first n positive integers

You are given a number n. Your task is to find the sum of the first n positive integers. In simpler terms, you are to compute the sum: 1+2+3+···+n

We will solve this problem using two different approaches: formula-based and iterative.

The formula to solve this problem is n(n+1)/2. So, let us solve it first using the formula-based approach.

Create a test file under the test folder: **test/sum_integers_test.exs** and write your test cases.

```
01. defmodule SumIntegersTest do
02.   use ExUnit.Case
03.   alias SumIntegers
04.
05.   describe "formula_based/1" do
06.     test "calculate sum of n integers correctly" do
07.       assert SumIntegers.formula_based(0) == 0
08.       assert SumIntegers.formula_based(1) == 1
09.       assert SumIntegers.formula_based(5) == 15
10.       assert SumIntegers.formula_based(10) == 55
11.     end
12.   end
13. end
```

If you run **mix test,** you will see a failed test case since we have not yet created the **SumIntegers** module or the **formula_based** function.

Now, let us create a file inside the **lib** folder to implement our solution for the failed test cases:

```
1. # lib/sum_integers.ex
2.
3. defmodule SumIntegers do
4.   def formula_based(n) when n >= 0 do
5.     div(n*(n + 1), 2)
6.   end
7. end
```

Run the mix test again, and you will see your test cases passing. For some of our practical exercises, we will adopt the following method:

1.  Write test cases first.

2.  Implement the code next. This method is called the **test-driven development** (TDD) approach.

Now, we will attempt the iterative approach:

```
01. # test/sum_integers_test.exs
02.
03. defmodule SumIntegersTest do
04.   use ExUnit.Case
05.   alias SumIntegers
06.
07.   describe "formula_based/1" do
08.     test "calculate sum of n integers correctly" do
09.       assert SumIntegers.formula_based(0) == 0
10.       assert SumIntegers.formula_based(1) == 1
11.       assert SumIntegers.formula_based(5) == 15
12.       assert SumIntegers.formula_based(10) == 55
13.     end
14.   end
15.
16.   describe "iterative/1" do
17.     test "calculates sum of first n integers correctly" do
18.       assert SumIntegers.iterative(0) == 0
19.       assert SumIntegers.iterative(1) == 1
20.       assert SumIntegers.iterative(5) == 15
21.       assert SumIntegers.iterative(10) == 55
22.     end
23.   end
24. end
```

Next, create a file named **lib/sum_integers.ex** with the following content to implement the solution:

```
01. # lib/sum_integers.ex
```

```
02.
03. defmodule SumIntegers do
04.   def formula_based(n) when n >= 0 do
05.     div(n*(n + 1),2)
06.   end
07.
08.   def iterative(n) when n >= 0, do: iterative(n, 0)
09.
10.   defp iterative(0, acc), do: acc
11.
12.   defp iterative(n, acc) when n > 0 do
13.     iterative(n - 1, acc + n)
14.   end
15. end
```

In the iterative approach, we use a helper function with an accumulator to hold the current sum. The function recursively calls itself, reducing the value of **n** each time and adding it to the accumulator until **n** is zero:

```
1.  iterative(n - 1, acc + n)
2.
3.  (5 - 1, 0 + 5)   # acc = 5
4.  (4 - 1, 5 + 4)   # acc = 9
5.  (3 - 1, 9 + 3)   # acc = 12
6.  (2 - 1, 12 + 2)  #acc = 14
7.  (1 - 1, 14 + 1)  #acc = 15
```

# Exercise 2: Palindrome checker

Write a function to check if a given string is a palindrome, ignoring spaces, punctuation, and capitalization.

First, let us create test cases for the palindrome checker. These test cases will include positive (strings that are palindromes) and negative (strings that are not palindromes) cases.

Here is what the test module could look like:

```
01. defmodule PalindromeCheckerTest do
02.   use ExUnit.Case
03.   alias PalindromeChecker
```

```
04.
05.   describe "is_palindrome?/1" do
06.     test "checks if a string is a palindrome, ignoring spaces,
        punctuation, and capitalization" do
07.         assert PalindromeChecker.is_palindrome?("A man, a plan, a canal,
        Panama")
08.         assert PalindromeChecker.is_palindrome?("Madam")
09.         assert PalindromeChecker.is_palindrome?("Racecar")
10.         assert not PalindromeChecker.is_palindrome?("Hello")
11.         assert not PalindromeChecker.is_palindrome?("Elixir")
12.     end
13.
14.     test "returns true for empty string and single-letter strings" do
15.         assert PalindromeChecker.is_palindrome?("")
16.         assert PalindromeChecker.is_palindrome?("a")
17.         assert PalindromeChecker.is_palindrome?("A")
18.     end
19.   end
20. end
```

The **PalindromeCheckerTest** module is defined to hold the test cases for the **PalindromeChecker** module.

Within the first test block, we are checking common positive and negative cases for palindromes. We ensure that strings that are palindromes return true, and those that are not return **false**.

The second test block checks edge cases like empty strings and single-letter strings. Since a single letter is always equal to its reverse, and an empty string has no characters to compare, they are technically considered palindromes.

Now, we will build the **PalindromeChecker** module that does the following things:

1. Converts the string to lowercase.

2. Removes all non-alphanumeric characters from the string.

3. Compares the processed string to its reverse.

```
01. # lib/palindrome_checker.ex
02.
03. defmodule PalindromeChecker do
```

```
04.    def is_palindrome?(str) do
05.      cleaned_str = clean_string(str)
06.      cleaned_str == String.reverse(cleaned_str)
07.    end
08.
09.    defp clean_string(str) do
10.      str
11.      |> String.downcase()
12.      |> String.replace(~r/[^a-z0-9]/, "")
13.    end
14. end
```

Let us explore how the **PalindromeChecker** module implements its functionality, ensuring that strings are accurately evaluated as palindromes or not:

- **is_palindrome?/1**: This function is the **main public** function of the module. Its purpose is to determine if a given string (**str**) is a palindrome:

  o **Cleaning the string**: The first step inside this function is to clean the string by calling the **private** function **clean_string/1**. This step removes any characters from the string that are not alphanumeric (letters and numbers), converts the entire string to lowercase, and returns the cleaned version of the string.

  o **Palindrome check**: The cleaned string is then compared with its reverse using **String.reverse(cleaned_str)**. If the cleaned string and its reverse are identical, then the original string is a palindrome, and the function returns true. Otherwise, it returns false.

- **clean_string/1**: This is a **private** helper function (denoted by the **defp** keyword) that takes a string and performs two primary operations to clean it:

  o **Lowercasing**: The string is converted to lowercase using **String.downcase()**. This ensures that the function treats capitalized and non-capitalized versions of the same letter as identical, so **"A"** and **"a"** are considered the same.

  o **Removing non-alphanumeric characters**: The string is then processed to remove any characters that are not lowercase letters or numbers. This is done using the **String.replace/2** function with a regular expression (**~r/[^a-z0-9]/**). The regular expression matches any character that is **NOT (^)** a lowercase letter (a-z) or a number (0-9). Any matched characters are replaced with an empty string, effectively removing them from the original string.

In essence, the **PalindromeChecker** module works by first cleaning the input string to remove any potential discrepancies caused by capitalization or punctuation. Once cleaned, it simply checks if the string reads the same forwards and backward, determining if it is a palindrome or not.

# Points to remember

- Basic data types in Elixir include integers, floats, Booleans, atoms, strings, lists, and tuples.

- Integers are whole numbers; floats are numbers with decimal points.

- Booleans represent true and false values. In Elixir, true and false are actually atoms :true and :false.

- Atoms are constants where their name is their value, useful for identifiers.

- Strings are UTF-8 encoded text, enclosed in double quotes.

- Lists are collections of items, not necessarily of the same type, and can be easily concatenated.

- Tuples are similar to lists but are stored contiguously in memory, making them efficient for fixed-size collections.

- Maps are key-value stores used for storing associated data. Keys can be of any type. Maps are the go-to data structure for storing and accessing key-value pairs in Elixir.

- Functions are grouped into modules. Modules are the primary way to organize code in Elixir.

# Multiple choice questions

1. **What data type is used to represent whole numbers in Elixir?**
   a. Float
   b. Integer
   c. Boolean
   d. Atom

2. **Which of the following is not a valid Elixir data type?**
   a. Tuple
   b. Keyword List
   c. Float
   d. Hash

3.  **How do you represent a string in Elixir?**

    a.  Single quotes

    b.  Double quotes

    c.  Backticks

    d.  Curly braces

4.  **Which module in Elixir provides functions for working with integers?**

    a.  Enum

    b.  Kernel

    c.  Integer

    d.  Float

5.  **What is the result of the expression String.length("hello") in Elixir?**

    a.  4

    b.  5

    c.  6

    d.  0

# Answer key

1.  b

2.  d

3.  b

4.  c

5.  b

# Join our Discord space

Join our Discord workspace for latest updates, offers, tech happenings around the world, new releases, and sessions with the authors:

https://discord.bpbonline.com

# CHAPTER 3
# Elixir Collections and Pattern Matching

## Introduction

In this chapter, we will explore Elixir's elegant handling of collections, Enum modules, and pattern matching. As a functional language, Elixir stands out for its efficient and expressive ways of managing collections of lists, tuples, and maps through a set of powerful enumerable functions. This chapter seamlessly integrates these functions with pattern matching, an essential feature that distinguishes Elixir from many other programming languages. Whether you are new to Elixir or looking to deepen your understanding, this chapter provides a comprehensive guide to understanding the full potential of collections, Enum, and pattern matching in writing clean, efficient, and maintainable code.

## Structure

This chapter will cover the following topics:

- Elixir collections and processing
- Understanding recursion in Elixir
- Pattern matching and guards
- Practica examples

# Objectives

By the end of this chapter, readers should have a comprehensive understanding of Elixir's capabilities in handling collections, the fundamentals of recursion, and practical experience with pattern matching and guards. This knowledge is essential for anyone looking to master Elixir and leverage its full potential for efficient and effective software development.

# Elixir collections and processing

One of the standout features of Elixir is its handling of collections and the ease with which they can be processed. In this section, we will explore Elixir collections and demonstrate how to process them efficiently, complete with practical examples.

# Collections

Collections in Elixir are versatile data structures that allow you to group and manage multiple elements in a cohesive manner. These collections are fundamental to how data is handled in Elixir, providing the foundation for many operations and transformations. The most commonly used collections in Elixir are lists, tuples, and maps, each serving distinct purposes:

- Lists are ordered collections where elements are stored sequentially. They are highly versatile, often used when you need to maintain an ordered sequence of elements or frequently add/remove elements.

- Tuples are also ordered but are typically used for fixed-size collections where the position of each element has a specific meaning. Tuples are immutable, making them ideal for grouping related but different types of data.

- Maps are key-value pairs, allowing you to associate values with keys for fast lookups. Maps are particularly useful when you need to represent structured data or when the order of elements is not important.

Understanding these collections is crucial for effective data manipulation in Elixir, as they form the backbone of most Elixir applications. Each type has its strengths and is chosen based on the specific requirements of the task at hand.

# Processing collections in Elixir

Processing collections in Elixir is an essential skill that involves iterating, transforming, and aggregating data efficiently. The Elixir language provides a rich set of tools and functions that make these tasks both straightforward and powerful. Whether you need to process a small list of items or perform complex operations on large datasets, Elixir's collection processing capabilities are designed to be both expressive and efficient.

In Elixir, you can process collections using various approaches, from simple loops and pattern matching to more advanced techniques like comprehensions and higher-order functions. The language's functional nature encourages a declarative style of processing, which leads to clearer and more maintainable code.

For instance, common tasks such as filtering a list, mapping a function over a collection, or reducing a collection to a single value can all be accomplished using Elixir's built-in tools. This ability to work seamlessly with collections is a cornerstone of Elixir's efficiency in handling large-scale data processing tasks.

# Enum module

The Enum module is one of Elixir's most powerful tools for collection processing. It offers a wide range of functions to iterate, transform, and aggregate data in collections.

The Enum module in Elixir is part of its standard library and provides a plethora of functions for working with enumerable data types that can be enumerated over, such as lists, maps, and ranges.

Enum matters for the following reasons:

- **Simplicity and expressiveness**: Enum functions allow you to perform complex operations on collections in a concise and readable manner.
- **Functional approach**: It promotes a functional programming style, enabling you to write declarative code that is easy to understand and maintain.
- **Versatility**: From simple iteration to transformation, filtering, and sorting, the Enum module can handle a wide array of tasks.

The key functions of the Enum module are:

- **Map (Enum.map/2)**: Transforms a collection by applying a given function to each element. To better understand how Enum.map/2 works, let us look at its flow, starting from the collection, applying a function to each element, and producing a transformed list. Refer to the following figure:

Start $\longrightarrow$ Apply Function $\longrightarrow$ New List $\longrightarrow$ End

*Figure 3.1: Flow of Enum.map/2*

- **Filter (Enum.filter/2)**: Selects elements from a collection based on a specified condition. To see how Enum.filter/2 operates, the following figure illustrates how elements are checked against a condition, and only the matching ones are included in the result:

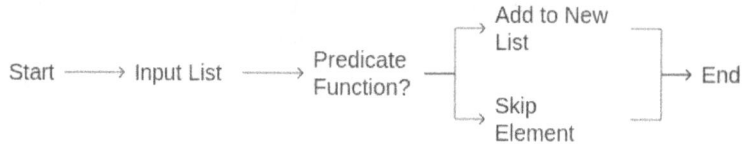

*Figure 3.2: Flow of Enum.filter/2*

- **Reduce (Enum.reduce/2 and Enum.reduce/3)**: Aggregates a collection into a single value using an accumulator. The following figure illustrates how Enum.reduce/2 and Enum.reduce/3 work by combining elements of a collection step by step, carrying forward an accumulator until a single result is produced:

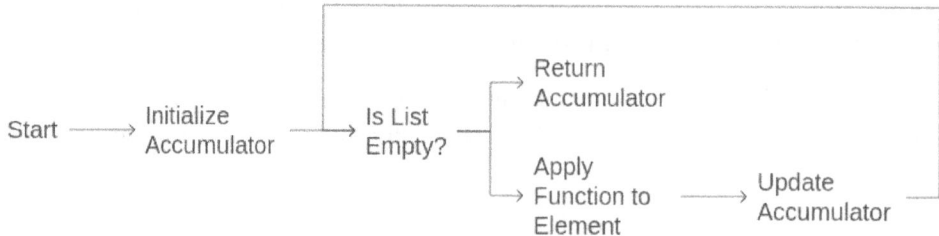

*Figure 3.3: Flow of Enum.reduce/2 and Enum.reduce/3*

- **Sort (Enum.sort/2)**: Sorts a collection based on a given comparison function. The following figure demonstrates how Enum.sort/2 organizes elements of a collection by repeatedly applying a comparison function to determine their correct order:

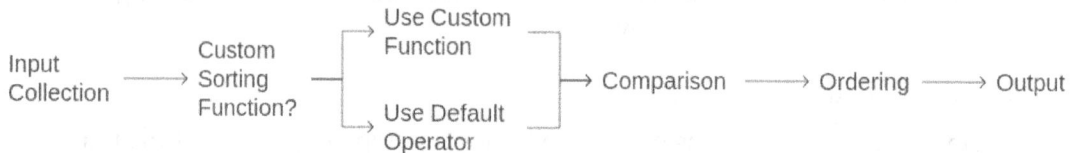

*Figure 3.4: Flow of Enum.sort/2*

- **Each (Enum.each/2)**: Iterates over a collection, applying a function to each element without transforming the collection. The following figure shows how Enum.each/2 works by applying a function to every element in the collection without producing a new transformed list:

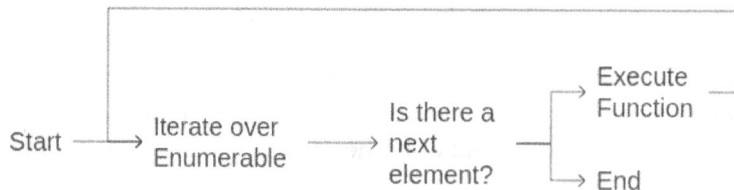

*Figure 3.5: Flow of Enum.each/2*

# Enum basic syntax

The syntax for using Enum functions is straightforward. Most functions take an enumerable as the first argument and a function (often an anonymous function) as the second argument. Here is a basic structure:

```
1. Enum.function_name(enumerable, fn element ->
2.   # process element
3. end)
```

# Stream module

The **Stream** module in Elixir is a powerful tool designed for working with large collections or when you need to process data lazily. Unlike the **Enum** module, which operates eagerly and processes entire collections at once, Stream allows you to create composable enumerations that are lazily evaluated. This means that elements are only processed as needed, which can lead to significant performance improvements when dealing with large datasets.

Streams are particularly useful in scenarios where you want to handle potentially infinite data, such as reading from a file or a live data feed, without loading everything into memory. By using streams, you can compose complex data processing pipelines that are both memory-efficient and easy to read.

For example, you can chain multiple stream transformations together, filtering, mapping, and reducing elements on the fly without ever generating intermediate collections. This makes streams an essential tool in any Elixir developer's toolkit, especially when working with performance-critical or memory-constrained applications.

# Data transformation approach

In order to illustrate how different Enum functions work for transforming data, we will create an employees list. Let us use the following list of employees and walk through various transformation functions with this dataset. For added complexity, we will also consider a scenario where each employee has a list of projects they have worked on:

```
employees = [
  %{name: "Alice", department: "Engineering", salary: 60000, projects:
["Project X", "Project Y"]},
  %{name: "Bob", department: "Marketing", salary: 45000, projects: ["Project Z"]},
  %{name: "Carol", department: "Engineering", salary: 75000, projects:
["Project X", "Project A", "Project B"]},
  %{name: "Dave", department: "Sales", salary: 50000, projects: []}
]
```

In the following examples, we will explore different data transformation techniques using Elixir's **Enum** module. Each example demonstrates how to modify or reformat data within a collection, such as increasing salaries, creating a formatted list of employee names, or extracting and flattening project lists. These examples will help you understand how to leverage the versatility of **Enum.map/2**, **Enum.map_join/3**, **Enum.flat_map/2**, and **Enum.flat_map_reduce/3** to perform complex transformations on your data:

- Transforming data with **Enum.map/2**

  **Objective**: Increase the employee's salary by 10%:

```
01. defmodule EmployeeProcessor do
02.   def raise_salaries(employees) do
03.     Enum.map(employees, fn employee ->
04.       Map.update!(employee, :salary, &(&1 * 1.1))
05.     end)
06.   end
07. end
08.
09. # Usage
10. EmployeeProcessor.raise_salaries(employees)
11. # Each employee's salary is increased by 10%
```

- Using **Enum.map_join/3**

  **Objective**: Create a string that lists all employees' names, separated by a comma:

```
1. def get_employee_names(employees) do
2.   Enum.map_join(employees, ", ", fn %{name: name} -> name end)
3. end
4.
5. # Usage
6. get_employee_names(employees)
7. # Returns "Alice, Bob, Carol, Dave"
```

- Applying **Enum.flat_map/2**

  **Objective**: Get a flattened list of all projects the employees are working on:

```
1. def names_and_total_salary(employees) do
2.   Enum.map_reduce(employees, 0, fn employee, acc ->
3.     {employee.name, employee.salary + acc}
```

```
4.        end)
5.  end
6.
7.  # Usage
8.  names_and_total_salary(employees)
9.  # Returns {["Alice", "Bob", "Carol", "Dave"], 230000}
```

- Using **Enum.flat_map_reduce/3**

**Objective**: Extract all unique projects from the employees' list and count the total number of projects:

```
1.  def unique_projects_count(employees) do
2.    Enum.flat_map_reduce(employees, [], fn %{projects: projects},
      acc ->
3.        {projects, acc ++ projects}
4.    end)
5.    |> then(fn {projects, _all_projects} -> {Enum.uniq(projects),
      length(projects)} end)
6.  end
7.
8.  # Usage
9.  unique_projects_count(employees)
10. # Returns {["Project X", "Project Y", "Project Z", "Project A",
      "Project B"], 5}
```

The complete code is given as follows:

```
01. defmodule EmployeeProcessor do
02.
03.   def raise_salaries(employees) do
04.     Enum.map(employees, fn employee ->
05.       Map.update!(employee, :salary, &(&1 * 1.1))
06.     end)
07.   end
08.
09.   def get_employee_names(employees) do
10.     Enum.map_join(employees, ", ", fn %{name: name} -> name end)
11.   end
```

```
12.
13.    def get_all_projects(employees) do
14.      Enum.flat_map(employees, fn %{projects: projects} -> projects
       end)
15.    end
16.
17.    def names_and_total_salary(employees) do
18.      Enum.map_reduce(employees, 0, fn employee, acc ->
19.        {employee.name, employee.salary + acc}
20.      end)
21.    end
22.
23.    def unique_projects_count(employees) do
24.      Enum.flat_map_reduce(employees, [], fn %{projects: projects},
       acc ->
25.        {projects, acc ++ projects}
26.      end)
27.      |> then(fn {projects, _all_projects} -> {Enum.uniq(projects),
       length(projects)} end)
28.    end
29. end
```

# Data aggregation

Aggregation is the process of combining data from a collection to produce a summary result, such as a sum or an average.

Data aggregation is a key concept in programming, particularly in functional languages like Elixir. It involves combining data from a collection, such as a list or a map, to produce a summarized result. This process is essential in scenarios where you need to extract meaningful insights or calculate summary statistics from a dataset.

In Elixir, data aggregation is often achieved through functions that process each element of a collection and accumulate a result. These functions can range from simple summing of values to more complex operations like calculating averages or grouping data based on specific criteria.

The beauty of Elixir lies in its functional approach and the availability of powerful enumerable functions in the **Enum** module. These functions provide a straightforward and expressive syntax for performing these aggregation tasks.

Let us explore some practical examples using a list of employees to illustrate how data aggregation can be effectively implemented in Elixir:

```
employees = [
  %{name: "Alice", department: "Engineering", salary: 60000, projects:
["Project X", "Project Y"], years_of_experience: 5},
  %{name: "Bob", department: "Marketing", salary: 45000, projects: ["Project
Z"], years_of_experience: 3},
  %{name: "Carol", department: "Engineering", salary: 75000, projects:
["Project X", "Project A", "Project B"], years_of_experience: 8},
  %{name: "Dave", department: "Sales", salary: 50000, projects: [], years_of_
experience: 9}
]
```

In the following examples, we will explore different approaches to data aggregation using Elixir's **Enum** module. Each example demonstrates a specific method for summarizing data, such as calculating total salaries, finding average values, or determining the total years of experience in a department. These examples will show you how to effectively aggregate data from a collection, leveraging Elixir's powerful enumerable functions to produce meaningful and concise summary results.

In **Enum.reduce/3**, the second argument 0 in our example is called the initial accumulator or seed. Think of it as the starting point for the running total. This is because we are summing salaries; we choose 0, the identity value for addition (adding zero never changes a number). During the first loop, the anonymous function receives the first employee map and the seed 0, adds the employee's salary to that seed, and returns the new total. That updated total becomes the accumulator for the next employee, and the process repeats until every record has been processed, at which point the accumulator holds the final sum of all salaries:

- Total salary calculation.

  **Objective**: Calculate the total salary of all employees:

  ```
  1. defmodule EmployeeAnalytics do
  2.   def total_salary(employees) do
  3.     Enum.reduce(employees, 0, fn %{salary: salary}, acc -> acc +
        salary end)
  4.   end
  5. end
  6.
  7. # Usage
  8. EmployeeAnalytics.total_salary(employees)
  ```

```
9.  # Returns the sum of salaries
10. 230000
```

- Average salary calculation.

  **Objective**: Calculate the average salary of all employees:

```
1.  def average_salary(employees) do
2.    total_salary = EmployeeAnalytics.total_salary(employees)
3.    Enum.count(employees) |> then(fn count -> total_salary / count
    end)
4.  end
5.
6.  # Usage
7.  average_salary(employees)
8.  # Returns the average of the salaries
9.  57500.0
```

- Total years of experience in a department.

  **Objective**: Find the total years of experience in a specific department:

```
1.  def total_experience_in_department(employees, department) do
2.    employees
3.    |> Enum.filter(fn %{department: d} -> d == department end)
4.    |> Enum.reduce(0, fn %{years_of_experience: exp}, acc -> acc +
    exp end)
5.  end
6.
7.  # Usage
8.  total_experience_in_department(employees, "Engineering")
9.  # Returns the total years of experience in the Engineering
    department
10. 13
```

- Average experience per department.

  **Objective**: Calculate the average years of experience per department:

```
1.  def average_experience_per_department(employees) do
2.    employees
```

```
3.      |> Enum.group_by(fn %{department: dept} -> dept end)
4.      |> Enum.map(fn {dept, emps} ->
5.          total_exp = Enum.reduce(emps, 0, fn %{years_of_experience:
   exp}, acc -> acc + exp end)
6.             {dept, total_exp / length(emps)}
7.         end)
8. end
9.
10. # Usage
11. average_experience_per_department(employees)
12. # Returns a list of departments with their average experience
13. [{"Engineering", 6.5}, {"Marketing", 3.0}, {"Sales", 9.0}]
```

In each of these examples, we have utilized various Enum functions to aggregate data in different ways. From calculating totals and averages to more complex grouping and filtering, these examples demonstrate the versatility and power of Elixir's enumerable functions in data aggregation tasks.

The complete code is given as follows:

```
01. defmodule EmployeeAnalytics do
02.    def total_salary(employees) do
03.       Enum.reduce(employees, 0, fn %{salary: salary}, acc -> acc + salary
   end)
04.    end
05.
06.    def average_salary(employees) do
07.       total_salary = EmployeeAnalytics.total_salary(employees)
08.       Enum.count(employees) |> then(fn count -> total_salary / count end)
09.    end
10.
11.    def total_experience_in_department(employees, department) do
12.       employees
13.       |> Enum.filter(fn %{department: d} -> d == department end)
14.       |> Enum.reduce(0, fn %{years_of_experience: exp}, acc -> acc + exp
   end)
15.    end
16.
```

```
17.    def average_experience_per_department(employees) do
18.      employees
19.      |> Enum.group_by(fn %{department: dept} -> dept end)
20.      |> Enum.map(fn {dept, emps} ->
21.        total_exp =
22.          Enum.reduce(emps, 0, fn %{years_of_experience: exp}, acc -> acc
       + exp end)
23.
24.        {dept, total_exp / length(emps)}
25.      end)
26.    end
27.  end
28.
```

# Data finding

Data finding is a crucial operation in programming. The goal is to locate elements within a collection that satisfy certain conditions or criteria. In Elixir, this operation typically involves searching through lists, maps, or any enumerable collection to find specific items based on attributes or conditions.

Elixir's **Enum** module provides a suite of functions designed for this purpose, offering both flexibility and power in searching through collections. These functions allow developers to write concise, clear, and efficient code for locating items within a collection, which is particularly useful in scenarios where data needs to be queried or filtered based on specific criteria.

Let us explore some practical examples using the employees list to illustrate how data finding can be effectively implemented in Elixir:

```
employees = [
  %{name: "Alice", department: "Engineering", salary: 60000, projects:
["Project X", "Project Y"], years_of_experience: 5},
  %{name: "Bob", department: "Marketing", salary: 45000, projects: ["Project
Z"], years_of_experience: 3},
  %{name: "Carol", department: "Engineering", salary: 75000, projects:
["Project X", "Project A", "Project B"], years_of_experience: 8},
  %{name: "Dave", department: "Sales", salary: 50000, projects: [], years_of_
experience: 9}
]
```

In the following examples, we will explore various techniques for finding specific data within a collection using Elixir's **Enum** module. Each example demonstrates a particular use case, such as finding an employee by name, locating all employees in a specific department, identifying the highest paid employee, or searching for employees with experience on a particular project. These examples will help you understand how to leverage functions like **Enum.find/2**, **Enum.filter/2**, and **Enum.max_by/2** to efficiently locate and retrieve specific elements from a collection based on defined criteria:

- Finding an employee by name.

  **Objective**: Find an employee's record by their name:

```
1. defmodule EmployeeFinder do
2.   def find_by_name(employees, target_name) do
3.     Enum.find(employees, fn %{name: name} -> name == target_name
   end)
4.   end
5. end
6.
7. # Usage
8. EmployeeFinder.find_by_name(employees, "Alice")
9. # Returns the record for Alice, if present
```

- Finding all employees in a department.

  **Objective**: Find all employees who belong to a specific department:

```
1. def find_in_department(employees, target_department) do
2.   Enum.filter(employees, fn %{department: dept} -> dept == target_
   department end)
3. end
4.
5. # Usage
6. find_in_department(employees, "Engineering")
7. # Returns a list of all employees in the Engineering department
```

- Finding the highest-paid employee.

  **Objective**: Locate the employee with the highest salary:

```
1. def highest_paid_employee(employees) do
2.   Enum.max_by(employees, fn %{salary: salary} -> salary end)
```

```
3.  end
4.
5.  # Usage
6.  highest_paid_employee(employees)
7.  # Returns the record of the employee with the highest salary
```

- Finding employees with specific project experience.

   **Objective**: Find employees who have worked on a specific project:

```
1.  def find_with_project_experience(employees, project_name) do
2.    Enum.filter(employees, fn %{projects: projects} -> project_name
      in projects end)
3.  end
4.
5.  # Usage
6.  find_with_project_experience(employees, "Project X")
7.  # Returns a list of employees who have worked on "Project X"
```

In these examples, we used functions such as **Enum.find/2**, **Enum.filter/2**, and **Enum.max_by/2** to find data within the collection. Each function serves a specific purpose: from locating a single item that meets a condition to filtering out multiple items based on a criterion. This demonstrates Elixir's robust capabilities in efficiently searching and finding data within collections.

The complete code is given as follows:

```
01. defmodule EmployeeFinder do
02.   def find_by_name(employees, target_name) do
03.     Enum.find(employees, fn %{name: name} -> name == target_name end)
04.   end
05.
06.   def find_in_department(employees, target_department) do
07.     Enum.filter(employees, fn %{department: dept} -> dept == target_
    department end)
08.   end
09.
10.   def highest_paid_employee(employees) do
11.     Enum.max_by(employees, fn %{salary: salary} -> salary end)
12.   end
```

```
13.
14.    def find_with_project_experience(employees, project_name) do
15.      Enum.filter(employees, fn %{projects: projects} -> project_name in
    projects end)
16.    end
17. end
```

# Data filtering

Data filtering is a fundamental operation in many programming tasks, where the goal is to sift through a collection and select elements that meet certain criteria. In Elixir, the **Enum** module offers powerful and versatile functions to perform this operation on various types of collections, such as lists or maps. Filtering allows developers to efficiently narrow down a dataset to the relevant subset.

Let us discuss practical examples of data filtering using the **employees** list. In the following examples, we will explore different methods of filtering data from a collection using Elixir's **Enum.filter/2** function. Each example demonstrates a specific scenario where filtering is used to extract a subset of data that meets certain criteria, such as filtering based on salary, identifying employees without projects, or extracting names from a specific department. These examples will help you understand how to effectively apply filtering to narrow down your dataset and retrieve meaningful information:

- Filtering based on salary range.

  **Objective**: Find **employees** whose salary falls within a specified range:

  ```
  1. def within_salary_range(employees, min_salary, max_salary) do
  2.    Enum.filter(employees, fn %{salary: salary} -> salary >= min_
       salary and salary <= max_salary end)
  3. end
  4.
  5. # Usage
  6. EmployeeFilter.within_salary_range(employees, 45000, 60000)
  7. # Returns employees with salaries between 45000 and 60000
  ```

- Filtering **employees** without projects.

  **Objective**: Identify employees who are not assigned to any projects:

  ```
  1. def without_projects(employees) do
  2.    Enum.filter(employees, fn %{projects: projects} -> projects ==
       [] end)
  ```

```
3. end
4.
5. # Usage
6. EmployeeFilter.without_projects(employees)
7. # Returns employees who are not assigned to any projects
```

- Filtering and transforming data.

  **Objective**: Extract names of employees from a specific department:

```
1. def names_from_department(employees, target_department) do
2.    employees
3.    |> Enum.filter(fn %{department: dept} -> dept == target_
      department end)
4.    |> Enum.map(fn %{name: name} -> name end)
5. end
6.
7. # Usage
8. EmployeeFilter.names_from_department(employees, "Marketing")
9. # Returns the names of employees in the Marketing department
```

In these examples, **Enum.filter/2** is used extensively to perform data filtering. The function iterates over the collection and applies the provided condition to each element, returning a new collection that contains only those elements for which the condition is true. This showcases Elixir's capability to handle data filtering in a concise and efficient manner, enabling clear and readable code for processing collections.

The complete code is given as follows:

```
01. defmodule EmployeeFilter do
02.   def within_salary_range(employees, min_salary, max_salary) do
03.     Enum.filter(employees, fn %{salary: salary} ->
04.       salary >= min_salary and salary <= max_salary
05.     end)
06.   end
07.
08.   def without_projects(employees) do
09.     Enum.filter(employees, fn %{projects: projects} -> projects == [] end)
10.   end
11.
```

```
12.    def names_from_department(employees, target_department) do
13.        employees
14.        |> Enum.filter(fn %{department: dept} -> dept == target_department
       end)
15.        |> Enum.map(fn %{name: name} -> name end)
16.    end
17. end
18.
```

# Data reducing

In programming, data reduction refers to the process of transforming a collection into a single value by iteratively applying a function to the elements of the collection. In Elixir, this is commonly achieved using the **Enum.reduce/3** function from the **Enum** module. Let us explore how data reduction can be effectively applied using Elixir, with practical examples based on an employee list.

We will use the following advanced employee list:

```
advanced_employees = [
  %{name: "Alice", department: "Engineering", salary: 60000, years_of_
experience: 5},
  %{name: "Bob", department: "Marketing", salary: 45000, years_of_experience: 3},
  %{name: "Carol", department: "Engineering", salary: 75000, years_of_
experience: 8},
  %{name: "Dave", department: "Sales", salary: 50000, years_of_experience: 6}
]
```

In the following examples, we will explore different ways to apply data-reducing techniques using Elixir's **Enum.reduce/3** function. Each example demonstrates a specific approach to aggregating data from a collection, whether it is calculating total values, finding the maximum, or generating summaries. These examples will help you understand how to effectively use **Enum.reduce/3** to transform a collection into a single, meaningful result in your Elixir applications:

- Calculating total salary.

  **Objective**: Aggregate the total salary of all employees:

  ```
  1. defmodule EmployeeReducer do
  2.    def total_salary(employees) do
  3.        Enum.reduce(employees, 0, fn %{salary: salary}, acc -> acc +
  ```

```
      salary end)
 4.   end
 5. end
 6.
 7. # Usage
 8. EmployeeReducer.total_salary(advanced_employees)
 9. # Returns the sum of all employees' salaries
10. 230000
```

- Finding maximum years of experience.

  **Objective**: Determine the maximum years of experience among all employees:

```
1. def max_experience(employees) do
2.    Enum.reduce(employees, 0, fn %{years_of_experience: exp}, acc
   -> max(exp, acc) end)
3. end
4.
5. # Usage
6. EmployeeReducer.max_experience(advanced_employees)
7. # Returns the highest number of years of experience
8. 8
```

- Aggregating data into a map.

  **Objective**: Create a map summarizing the total salary and average years of experience by department:

```
01. def department_summary(employees) do
02.    Enum.reduce(employees, %{}, fn %{department: dept, salary:
    salary, years_of_experience: exp}, acc ->
03.      dept_info = acc[dept] || %{total_salary: 0, total_experience:
    0, count: 0}
04.      new_total_salary = dept_info.total_salary + salary
05.      new_total_experience = dept_info.total_experience + exp
06.      new_count = dept_info.count + 1
07.      Map.put(acc, dept, %{total_salary: new_total_salary, total_
    experience: new_total_experience, count: new_count})
08.    end)
09.    |> Enum.map(fn {dept, %{total_salary: total_salary, total_
```

```
       experience: total_experience, count: count}} ->
10.          %{department: dept, total_salary: total_salary, average_
       experience: total_experience / count}
11.      end)
12. end
13.
14. # Usage
15. EmployeeReducer.department_summary(advanced_employees)
16. # Returns a summary of total salary and average experience for
    each department
17. [
18.    %{average_experience: 6.5, department: "Engineering", total_
       salary: 135000},
19.    %{average_experience: 3.0, department: "Marketing", total_
       salary: 45000},
20.    %{average_experience: 6.0, department: "Sales", total_salary:
       50000}
21. ]
```

- Calculating weighted average salary.

    **Objective**: Compute the weighted average salary based on years of experience:

```
1. def weighted_average_salary(employees) do
2.   total_exp = Enum.reduce(employees, 0, fn %{years_of_experience:
     exp}, acc -> acc + exp end)
3.   Enum.reduce(employees, 0, fn %{salary: salary, years_of_
     experience: exp}, acc -> acc + salary * exp end) / total_exp
4. end
5.
6. # Usage
7. EmployeeReducer.weighted_average_salary(advanced_employees)
8. # Returns the weighted average salary
9. 60681.818181818184
```

In each example, **Enum.reduce/3** is used to iteratively process the collection and reduce it to a single value, whether it is a numerical aggregate, a maximum value, or a more complex data structure like a map. This demonstrates the power and flexibility of data reduction in Elixir, making it an indispensable tool for collection processing and data analysis.

The complete code is given as follows:

```
01. defmodule EmployeeReducer do
02.   def total_salary(employees) do
03.     Enum.reduce(employees, 0, fn %{salary: salary}, acc -> acc + salary end)
04.   end
05.
06.   def max_experience(employees) do
07.     Enum.reduce(employees, 0, fn %{years_of_experience: exp}, acc ->
    max(exp, acc) end)
08.   end
09.
10.   def department_summary(employees) do
11.     Enum.reduce(employees, %{}, fn %{department: dept, salary: salary,
    years_of_experience: exp}, acc ->
12.       dept_info = acc[dept] || %{total_salary: 0, total_experience: 0,
    count: 0}
13.       new_total_salary = dept_info.total_salary + salary
14.       new_total_experience = dept_info.total_experience + exp
15.       new_count = dept_info.count + 1
16.       Map.put(acc, dept, %{total_salary: new_total_salary, total_
    experience: new_total_experience, count: new_count})
17.     end)
18.     |> Enum.map(fn {dept, %{total_salary: total_salary, total_
    experience: total_experience, count: count}} ->
19.         %{department: dept, total_salary: total_salary, average_
    experience: total_experience / count}
20.       end)
21.   end
22.
23.   def weighted_average_salary(employees) do
24.     total_exp = Enum.reduce(employees, 0, fn %{years_of_experience:
    exp}, acc -> acc + exp end)
25.     Enum.reduce(employees, 0, fn %{salary: salary, years_of_experience:
    exp}, acc -> acc + salary * exp end) / total_exp
26.   end
27. end
```

# Data combining

In Elixir, data combining involves merging or concatenating multiple collections to form a unified dataset. This operation is essential when you need to consolidate data from different sources or formats. Elixir's **Enum** module offers various functions that facilitate this process, enabling efficient and flexible data combinations.

Let us explore practical examples of data combining using the advanced version of the employee list, along with another list for demonstration purposes.

We will use the following advanced employee list:

```
advanced_employees = [
  %{name: "Alice", department: "Engineering", salary: 60000, projects:
["Project X", "Project Y"]},
  %{name: "Bob", department: "Marketing", salary: 45000, projects: ["Project
Z"]},
  %{name: "Carol", department: "Engineering", salary: 75000, projects:
["Project X", "Project A", "Project B"]},
  %{name: "Dave", department: "Sales", salary: 50000, projects: []}
]
```

Let us also consider a list of new hires to combine with our existing employees:

```
new_hires = [
  %{name: "Eve", department: "Engineering", salary: 65000, projects: ["Project
Y"]},
  %{name: "Frank", department: "Marketing", salary: 48000, projects: []}
]
```

In the following examples, we will explore different methods for combining and transforming data using Elixir's powerful **Enum** module. Each example demonstrates a specific technique for merging or manipulating lists of data, whether it is concatenating employee records, merging project lists, or pairing related elements from two separate lists. These examples will help you understand how to efficiently combine and transform data in your Elixir applications:

- Concatenating employee lists.

  **Objective**: Combine the list of current employees with the list of new hires:

  ```
  1. defmodule EmployeeCombiner do
  2.   def combine_employees(existing_employees, new_employees) do
  3.     Enum.concat(existing_employees, new_employees)
  4.   end
  ```

```
5. end
6.
7. # Usage
8. EmployeeCombiner.combine_employees(advanced_employees, new_hires)
9. # Returns a combined list of all employees, including new hires
```

- Merging project lists.

  **Objective**: Create a combined list of all unique projects across all employees:

```
1. def all_projects(employees) do
2.   employees
3.   |> Enum.flat_map(fn %{projects: projects} -> projects end)
4.   |> Enum.uniq()
5. end
6.
7. # Usage
8. EmployeeCombiner.all_projects(advanced_employees)
9. # Returns a list of unique projects from all employees
10. ["Project X", "Project Y", "Project Z", "Project A", "Project B"]
```

- Combining and transforming data.

  **Objective**: Combine data from two lists and transform the result (e.g., combining employee names with their respective department):

```
1. def combine_and_transform(employees, departments) do
2.   employees
3.   |> Enum.map(fn %{name: name, department: dept} ->
4.     department_name = departments[dept]
5.     "#{name} (#{department_name})"
6.   end)
7. end
8.
9. # Assuming a map of department abbreviations to names
10. departments = %{"Engineering" => "Eng", "Marketing" => "Mkt", "Sales" => "Sl"}
```

```
11.
12. # Usage
13. EmployeeCombiner.combine_and_transform(advanced_employees,
    departments)
14. # Returns a list of employees with their department abbreviations
15. ["Alice (Eng)", "Bob (Mkt)", "Carol (Eng)", "Dave (Sl)"]
```

- Zipping two lists.

    **Objective**: Pair elements from two lists based on their position:

```
1. def zip_names_and_salaries(employees) do
2.   names = Enum.map(employees, fn %{name: name} -> name end)
3.   salaries = Enum.map(employees, fn %{salary: salary} -> salary
     end)
4.   Enum.zip(names, salaries)
5. end
6. # Usage
7. EmployeeCombiner.zip_names_and_salaries(advanced_employees)
8. # Returns a list of tuples pairing each employee's name with
   their salary
9. [{"Alice", 60000}, {"Bob", 45000}, {"Carol", 75000}, {"Dave",
   50000}]
```

In these examples, we employ various Enum functions like **Enum.concat/2**, **Enum.flat_map/2**, and **Enum.zip/2** to combine data from different lists. Whether it is merging lists, extracting and unifying specific data, or pairing elements from multiple collections, Elixir provides efficient and expressive tools for data combining. This showcases the language's capability to handle complex data manipulation tasks with ease and flexibility.

The complete code is given as follows:

```
01. defmodule EmployeeCombiner do
02.   def combine_employees(existing_employees, new_employees) do
03.     Enum.concat(existing_employees, new_employees)
04.   end
05.
06.   def all_projects(employees) do
07.     employees
08.     |> Enum.flat_map(fn %{projects: projects} -> projects end)
09.     |> Enum.uniq()
```

```
10.    end
11.
12.    def combine_and_transform(employees, departments) do
13.      employees
14.      |> Enum.map(fn %{name: name, department: dept} ->
15.        department_name = departments[dept]
16.        "#{name} (#{department_name})"
17.      end)
18.    end
19.
20.    def zip_names_and_salaries(employees) do
21.      names = Enum.map(employees, fn %{name: name} -> name end)
22.      salaries = Enum.map(employees, fn %{salary: salary} -> salary end)
23.      Enum.zip(names, salaries)
24.    end
25.  end
26.
```

# Data grouping

Data grouping is a crucial operation in programming where elements of a collection are organized into groups based on specific criteria. This process is especially important for categorizing data, generating reports, or preparing data for further analysis. In Elixir, the **Enum** module offers the **Enum.group_by/3** function, which is particularly powerful for such tasks.

Let us apply data grouping to the advanced employee list by demonstrating various scenarios where grouping can provide valuable insights:

```
advanced_employees = [
  %{name: "Alice", department: "Engineering", salary: 60000, projects:
["Project X", "Project Y"]},

  %{name: "Bob", department: "Marketing", salary: 45000, projects: ["Project
Z"]},

  %{name: "Carol", department: "Engineering", salary: 75000, projects:
["Project X", "Project A", "Project B"]},

  %{name: "Dave", department: "Sales", salary: 50000, projects: []}
]
```

In the following examples, we will explore different methods for grouping data using Elixir's **Enum.group_by/3** function. Each example demonstrates how to categorize data based on specific criteria, such as grouping employees by department, project participation, or salary range. These examples will help you understand how to effectively organize and categorize your data, leveraging Elixir's powerful capabilities for data grouping to gain valuable insights and facilitate further analysis:

- Grouping by department.

  **Objective**: Group employees by their department:

```
1. defmodule EmployeeGrouper do
2.   def group_by_department(employees) do
3.     Enum.group_by(employees, fn %{department: dept} -> dept end)
4.   end
5. end
6.
7. # Usage
8. EmployeeGrouper.group_by_department(advanced_employees)
9. # Returns a map where each key is a department and each value is
   a list of employees in that department
```

- Grouping by project participation.

  **Objective**: Group employees based on the projects they are involved in:

```
1. def group_by_projects(employees) do
2.   employees
3.   |> Enum.flat_map(fn %{name: name, projects: projects} -> Enum.
   map(projects, fn project -> {project, name} end) end)
4.   |> Enum.group_by(fn {project, _name} -> project end, fn {_
   project, name} -> name end)
5. end
6.
7. # Usage
8. EmployeeGrouper.group_by_projects(advanced_employees)
9. # Returns a map where each key is a project and each value is a
   list of employees working on that project
```

- Grouping and counting employees.

  **Objective**: Count the number of employees in each department:

```
1. def count_employees_by_department(employees) do
```

```
2.   Enum.group_by(employees, fn %{department: dept} -> dept end)
3.   |> Enum.map(fn {dept, emps} -> {dept, length(emps)} end)
4. end
5.
6. # Usage
7. EmployeeGrouper.count_employees_by_department(advanced_employees)
8. # Returns a list of tuples, each containing a department and the
   count of employees in that department
```

- Grouping by salary range.

  **Objective**: Group employees into salary ranges:

```
1. def group_by_salary_range(employees, range_size) do
2.   Enum.group_by(employees, fn %{salary: salary} -> div(salary,
   range_size) * range_size end)
3. end
4.
5. # Usage
6. EmployeeGrouper.group_by_salary_range(advanced_employees, 10000)
7. # Returns a map where each key is a salary range and each value
   is a list of employees in that salary range
```

**range_size** represents the size of each salary range. For example, if **range_size** is **10000**, it means we want to group salaries in ranges of 0-9999, 10000-19999, 20000-29999, and so on.

In these examples, **Enum.group_by/3** is used to categorize the employee data based on various criteria, such as department, project participation, and salary ranges. This demonstrates Elixir's powerful capabilities in efficiently organizing and categorizing data, making it an invaluable tool for data analysis and reporting.

The complete code is given as follows:

```
01. defmodule EmployeeGrouper do
02.   def group_by_department(employees) do
03.     Enum.group_by(employees, fn %{department: dept} -> dept end)
04.   end
05.
06.   def group_by_projects(employees) do
07.     employees
08.     |> Enum.flat_map(fn %{name: name, projects: projects} ->
09.       Enum.map(projects, fn project -> {project, name} end)
```

```
10.      end)
11.      |> Enum.group_by(fn {project, _name} -> project end, fn {_project,
   name} -> name end)
12.    end
13.
14.    def count_employees_by_department(employees) do
15.      Enum.group_by(employees, fn %{department: dept} -> dept end)
16.      |> Enum.map(fn {dept, emps} -> {dept, length(emps)} end)
17.    end
18.
19.    def group_by_salary_range(employees, range_size) do
20.      Enum.group_by(employees, fn %{salary: salary} ->
21.        div(salary, range_size) * range_size
22.      end)
23.    end
24. end
25.
```

# Data sorting

Data sorting is a fundamental operation in programming that involves the arrangement of elements in a collection in a specific order based on defined criteria. In Elixir, the **Enum** module provides versatile functions like **Enum.sort/2** and **Enum.sort_by/3** for sorting collections. These functions are crucial for organizing data in a meaningful way, whether it is for display, analysis, or further processing.

Let us explore the application of data sorting using the advanced employee list, demonstrating how we can sort data in various scenarios:

```
advanced_employees = [
  %{name: "Alice", department: "Engineering", salary: 60000, projects:
["Project X", "Project Y"]},
  %{name: "Bob", department: "Marketing", salary: 45000, projects: ["Project Z"]},
  %{name: "Carol", department: "Engineering", salary: 75000, projects:
["Project X", "Project A", "Project B"]},
  %{name: "Dave", department: "Sales", salary: 50000, projects: []}
]
```

In the following examples, we will explore various methods for sorting data using Elixir's **Enum.sort/2** and **Enum.sort_by/3** functions. Each example demonstrates how to arrange employee data based on different criteria, such as sorting by name, salary, department, or the number of projects. These examples will help you understand how to effectively organize your data in a meaningful order, whether for analysis, presentation, or further processing. Sorting is a fundamental operation, and mastering these techniques will enhance your ability to manage and manipulate data in Elixir:

- Sorting by name.

  **Objective**: Sort the employees by their names in ascending order:

```
1. defmodule EmployeeSorter do
2.   def sort_by_name(employees) do
3.     Enum.sort_by(employees, &(&1.name))
4.   end
5. end
6.
7. # Usage
8. EmployeeSorter.sort_by_name(advanced_employees)
9. # Returns the employees list sorted by name
```

- Sorting by salary.

  **Objective**: Sort the employees by their salary, from highest to lowest:

```
1. def sort_by_salary_desc(employees) do
2.   Enum.sort_by(employees, &(&1.salary), &>=/2)
3. end
4.
5. # Usage
6. EmployeeSorter.sort_by_salary_desc(advanced_employees)
7. # Returns the employees list sorted by salary in descending order
```

- Sorting by multiple criteria.

  **Objective**: Sort employees first by department, and within each department, by name:

```
1. def sort_by_department_and_name(employees) do
2.   Enum.sort_by(employees, &[&1.department, &1.name])
3. end
4.
5. # Usage
6. EmployeeSorter.sort_by_department_and_name(advanced_employees)
7. # Returns the employees list sorted first by department, then by
   name within each department
```

- Custom sorting.

  **Objective**: Sort employees based on the number of projects they are involved in, with those involved in more projects listed first:

```
1. def sort_by_project_count(employees) do
2.    Enum.sort_by(employees, fn %{projects: projects} ->
      length(projects) end, :desc)
3. end
4.
5. # Usage
6. EmployeeSorter.sort_by_project_count(advanced_employees)
7. # Returns the employees list sorted by the number of projects,
      descending
```

In these examples, **Enum.sort_by/3** is extensively used to perform sorting operations. This function allows for flexible sorting based on single or multiple criteria and even supports custom sorting logic, as demonstrated in the last example. Sorting is essential for preparing data in an ordered format, which is often a prerequisite for other operations like searching or presenting data to end-users. Elixir's sorting capabilities showcase its strength in handling and organizing complex data structures effectively.

The complete code is given as follows:

```
1. defmodule EmployeeSorter do
2.    def sort_by_name(employees) do
3.       Enum.sort_by(employees, &(&1.name))
4.    end
5.
6.    def sort_by_salary_desc(employees) do
7.       Enum.sort_by(employees, &(&1.salary), &>=/2)
8.    end
9.
10.   def sort_by_department_and_name(employees) do
11.      Enum.sort_by(employees, &[&1.department, &1.name])
12.   end
13.
14.   def sort_by_project_count(employees) do
15.      Enum.sort_by(employees, fn %{projects: projects} -> length(projects)
      end, :desc)
```

```
16.    end
17. end
```

# Data enumeration

Data enumeration in programming refers to the process of iterating over each element in a collection, typically for executing an operation or a side effect, like printing or logging. In Elixir, this is commonly done using the **Enum.each/2** function from the **Enum** module, which is particularly handy for running code that affects each item in a collection without transforming the collection itself.

Let us apply data enumeration to the advanced employee list, showcasing how to use this approach in different practical scenarios:

```
advanced_employees = [
  %{name: "Alice", department: "Engineering", salary: 60000, projects:
["Project X", "Project Y"]},
  %{name: "Bob", department: "Marketing", salary: 45000, projects: ["Project
Z"]},
  %{name: "Carol", department: "Engineering", salary: 75000, projects:
["Project X", "Project A", "Project B"]},
  %{name: "Dave", department: "Sales", salary: 50000, projects: []}
]
```

In the following examples, we will explore different ways to use data enumeration in Elixir by applying the **Enum.each/2** function. Each example demonstrates how to iterate over a list of employees to perform various side effects, such as printing names, logging salaries, or listing projects. These examples will help you understand how to leverage data enumeration in scenarios where the goal is to execute operations on each element of a collection without modifying the collection itself. Mastering these techniques will enhance your ability to manage and interact with data in Elixir:

- Printing employee names.

  **Objective**: Iterate over the list of employees and print each employee's name:

  ```
  1. defmodule EmployeeEnumerator do
  2.   def print_names(employees) do
  3.     Enum.each(employees, fn %{name: name} -> IO.puts(name) end)
  4.   end
  5. end
  6.
  7. # Usage
  ```

```
8. EmployeeEnumerator.print_names(advanced_employees)
9. # Prints the name of each employee
```

- Logging employee salaries.

  **Objective**: Log the salary of each employee for auditing purposes:

```
1. def log_salaries(employees) do
2.   Enum.each(employees, fn %{name: name, salary: salary} ->
3.     IO.inspect("#{name}'s salary: $#{salary}")
4.   end)
5. end
6.
7. # Usage
8. EmployeeEnumerator.log_salaries(advanced_employees)
9. # Logs the salary of each employee
```

- Enumerating over projects.

  **Objective**: Iterate through all employees and list their projects:

```
1. def list_all_projects(employees) do
2.   Enum.each(employees, fn %{name: name, projects: projects} ->
3.     IO.puts("#{name} is working on: #{Enum.join(projects, ",
      ")}")
4.   end)
5. end
6.
7. # Usage
8. EmployeeEnumerator.list_all_projects(advanced_employees)
9. # Lists all projects for each employee
```

In these examples, **Enum.each/2** is used to perform actions on each element of the collection. The function is ideal for cases where we need to execute code for its side effects (like printing or logging) for each item in the collection. This demonstrates Elixir's capability in handling data enumeration in a concise and expressive manner, enabling clear and readable code for iterating over collections.

The complete code is given as follows:

```
01. defmodule EmployeeEnumerator do
02.   def print_names(employees) do
03.     Enum.each(employees, fn %{name: name} -> IO.puts(name) end)
```

```
04.   end
05.
06.   def log_salaries(employees) do
07.     Enum.each(employees, fn %{name: name, salary: salary} ->
08.       IO.inspect("#{name}'s salary: $#{salary}")
09.     end)
10.   end
11.
12.   def list_all_projects(employees) do
13.     Enum.each(employees, fn %{name: name, projects: projects} ->
14.       IO.puts("#{name} is working on: #{Enum.join(projects, ", ")}")
15.     end)
16.   end
17. end
18.
```

# Data streaming

Data streaming in Elixir is a powerful concept, especially useful for handling large datasets or when you want to process data lazily. Unlike immediate enumeration with the **Enum** module, the **Stream** module in Elixir allows for building composable, lazy operations that are executed only when needed. This approach can be more memory-efficient, as it processes elements one at a time rather than loading an entire collection into memory.

Let us explore how data streaming can be applied using the advanced employee list, demonstrating various scenarios where streaming is beneficial:

```
advanced_employees = [
  %{name: "Alice", department: "Engineering", salary: 60000, projects:
["Project X", "Project Y"]},
  %{name: "Bob", department: "Marketing", salary: 45000, projects: ["Project
Z"]},
  %{name: "Carol", department: "Engineering", salary: 75000, projects:
["Project X", "Project A", "Project B"]},
  %{name: "Dave", department: "Sales", salary: 50000, projects: []}
]
```

In the following examples, we will explore the concept of data streaming in Elixir using the **Stream** module. Each example demonstrates how to set up lazy operations on a collection, allowing for efficient data processing, especially when dealing with large datasets. These examples will show you how to apply streaming for tasks such as transforming data incrementally, filtering collections lazily, and combining multiple streaming operations. By understanding and utilizing data streaming, you can optimize memory usage and enhance performance in your Elixir applications, particularly when processing large or complex datasets:

- Lazy transformation of data.

  **Objective**: Incrementally increase each employee's salary by 10%, but only execute this when the final result is needed:

```
1.  defmodule EmployeeStreamer do
2.    def lazy_salary_increase(employees) do
3.      Stream.map(employees, fn %{salary: salary} = employee ->
4.        Map.update!(employee, :salary, &(&1 + &1 * 0.1))
5.      end)
6.    end
7.  end
8.
9.  # Usage
10. stream = EmployeeStreamer.lazy_salary_increase(advanced_
    employees)
11. Enum.to_list(stream)
12. # The salaries are increased, but only when the stream is
    enumerated
```

- Streaming with filtering.

  **Objective**: Create a stream to filter out employees in a specific department, executing it lazily:

```
1.  def stream_engineering(employees) do
2.    employees
3.    |> Stream.filter(fn %{department: dept} -> dept == "Engineering"
    end)
4.  end
5.
6.  # Usage
7.  stream = EmployeeStreamer.stream_engineering(advanced_employees)
8.  Enum.to_list(stream)
9.  # Returns employees in the Engineering department
```

- Combining streams.

  **Objective**: Combine multiple streaming operations, like filtering and then transforming data:

  ```
  1. def stream_transform(employees) do
  2.   employees
  3.   |> Stream.filter(fn %{department: dept} -> dept == "Engineering" end)
  4.   |> Stream.map(fn %{name: name} -> "Engineer: #{name}" end)
  5. end
  6.
  7. # Usage
  8. stream = EmployeeStreamer.stream_transform(advanced_employees)
  9. Enum.to_list(stream)
  10. # Processes the data lazily, returning names with a prefix only
     for engineering department
  ```

- Streaming for large datasets.

  **Objective**: Process a large dataset in a memory-efficient manner using streaming:

  ```
  1. def large_dataset_stream() do
  2.   1..1_000_000
  3.   |> Stream.map(fn x -> x * 2 end)
  4.   |> Stream.filter(fn x -> rem(x, 3) == 0 end)
  5. end
  6.
  7. # Usage
  8. stream = EmployeeStreamer.large_dataset_stream()
  9. Enum.take(stream, 10)
  10. # Returns the first 10 numbers that are doubled and divisible by
     3, without loading the entire range into memory
  ```

The complete code is given as follows:

```
01. defmodule EmployeeStreamer do
02.   def lazy_salary_increase(employees) do
03.     Stream.map(employees, fn %{salary: salary} = employee ->
04.       Map.update!(employee, :salary, &(&1 + &1 * 0.1))
05.     end)
```

```
06.    end
07.
08.    def stream_engineering(employees) do
09.      employees
10.      |> Stream.filter(fn %{department: dept} -> dept == "Engineering" end)
11.    end
12.
13.    def stream_transform(employees) do
14.      employees
15.      |> Stream.filter(fn %{department: dept} -> dept == "Engineering" end)
16.      |> Stream.map(fn %{name: name} -> "Engineer: #{name}" end)
17.    end
18.
19.    def large_dataset_stream() do
20.      1..1_000_000
21.      |> Stream.map(fn x -> x * 2 end)
22.      |> Stream.filter(fn x -> rem(x, 3) == 0 end)
23.    end
24. end
```

# Understanding recursion in Elixir

Recursion is a fundamental concept in functional programming, and Elixir, being a functional language, leverages recursion extensively for iteration and data processing. Unlike imperative languages, where loops are used for repetition, functional languages like Elixir rely on recursive functions to achieve similar results. This section will explore the basics of recursion in Elixir, explain how it works under the hood, and provide practical exercises to solidify your understanding.

## Recursion

Recursion occurs when a function calls itself as part of its execution. In Elixir, recursive functions typically consist of two parts:

- **Base case**: A condition that stops the recursion. Without a base case, the recursion would continue indefinitely, leading to a stack overflow.
- **Recursive case**: The part of the function where it calls itself with modified arguments, moving closer to the base case with each call.

# Working of recursion in Elixir

Elixir, like other functional languages, optimizes recursion through a technique known as **tail call optimization (TCO)**. This optimization allows recursive functions to reuse stack frames, preventing stack overflow and making recursion efficient even for large datasets.

**Example 3.1**: Factorial function.

A classic example of recursion is the factorial function, which multiplies a number by every positive integer less than itself. Here is how you can implement it in Elixir:

```
1.  defmodule Math do
2.    def factorial(0), do: 1 # Base case
3.    def factorial(n) when n > 0 do
4.      n * factorial(n - 1)  # Recursive case
5.    end
6.  end
7.
8.  # Usage
9.  Math.factorial(5)
10. # Output: 120
```

In this example:

The base case is when **n** equals **0**, where the function returns **1**.

The recursive case multiplies n by the result of **factorial(n - 1)** until n reaches **0**.

**Example 3.2**: Sum of a list.

Another common use of recursion is summing the elements of a list. Here is how it is done in Elixir:

```
1.  defmodule ListOperations do
2.    def sum([]), do: 0 # Base case: an empty list
3.    def sum([head | tail]) do
4.      head + sum(tail)   # Recursive case: add the head to the sum of the tail
5.    end
6.  end
7.
8.  # Usage
9.  ListOperations.sum([1, 2, 3, 4, 5])
10. # Output: 15
```

In this example:

The base case handles an empty list, returning **0**. The recursive case splits the list into a head and a tail, adds the head to the sum of the tail, and continues until the list is empty.

## Tail recursion

Tail recursion is a special form of recursion where the recursive call is the last operation in the function. Elixir can optimize tail-recursive functions to prevent stack overflow by reusing the current function's stack frame.

**Example 3.3**: Tail-recursive factorial.

Here is how to rewrite the factorial function using tail recursion:

```
1.  defmodule Math do
2.    def factorial(n), do: factorial(n, 1)
3.
4.    defp factorial(0, acc), do: acc # Base case
5.    defp factorial(n, acc) when n > 0 do
6.      factorial(n - 1, acc * n) # Tail-recursive call
7.    end
8.  end
9.
10. # Usage
11. Math.factorial(5)
12. # Output: 120
```

In this version:

- The accumulator acc carries the intermediate result, making the function tail-recursive.
- The recursive call **factorial(n - 1, acc * n)** is the last operation, allowing Elixir to optimize it efficiently.

Understanding recursion is crucial for mastering Elixir and functional programming. Recursion allows you to break down complex problems into simpler subproblems and solve them elegantly. By practicing with the examples and exercises provided, you will develop a strong grasp of how recursion works in Elixir and how to apply it effectively in your code.

# Pattern matching and guards

In Elixir, pattern matching is a distinctive and powerful tool. We will explore the concept of pattern matching in Elixir, understand the use of guards, and provide practical examples to illustrate these concepts.

# Understanding pattern matching in Elixir

At its core, pattern matching in Elixir is about matching the shape of data. It is a powerful feature that allows you to check, destructure, and extract values from complex data structures based on their form rather than just their value. Unlike traditional conditional checks, pattern matching in Elixir lets you concisely express and decompose data, making your code more readable and expressive.

Pattern matching is ubiquitous in Elixir, and it is used in a variety of contexts, from simple variable assignments to function definitions, case statements, and even in data structures like lists and tuples. This feature allows you to write cleaner, more declarative code, enabling you to focus on what the data looks like rather than how to access it. By mastering pattern matching, you will unlock a fundamental aspect of Elixir's expressiveness, leading to more intuitive and maintainable code.

## Basics of pattern matching

Pattern matching is often seen in variable assignments. When you write:

```
1. {a, b} = {1, 2}
```

Here, you are telling Elixir to match the left-hand side (**{a, b}**) with the right-hand side (**{1, 2}**). After this operation, **a** will be **1**, and **b** will be **2**.

## Pattern matching with lists

Pattern matching works wonderfully with lists. Consider the following:

```
1. [head | tail] = [1, 2, 3]
```

Here, the head will be assigned **1**, and the **tail** will get **[2, 3]**. This is extremely handy in recursive functions.

# Guards in pattern matching

Guards add another level of sophistication to pattern matching in Elixir. They allow you to specify additional, more precise conditions that must be met for a pattern to match. While basic pattern matching works by comparing the structure of data, guards enable you to enforce constraints based on the values within that structure. This means you can refine your matches by checking for specific conditions, such as ensuring a number is positive, a list is not empty, or a value falls within a particular range.

Guards are commonly used in function clauses, case expressions, and conditional statements, allowing you to handle complex logic with clarity and precision. By using guards, you can avoid deeply nested conditionals and make your code more readable and expressive. This makes guards an essential tool in Elixir, especially when you need to manage complex control flows or validate data in a concise and declarative way.

# Using guards

Here is a basic example:

```
01. defmodule Greeter do
02.    def greet(age) when age < 12 do
03.      "Hello, kid!"
04.    end
05.
06.    def greet(age) when age < 20 do
07.      "What's up, teen?"
08.    end
09.
10.    def greet(age) do
11.      "Greetings, adult!"
12.    end
13. end
14.
```

In the preceding snippet, the **greet** function uses guards (when **age < 12**, when **age < 20**) to differentiate responses based on age.

# Combining pattern matching with guards

Elixir works best when pattern matching is combined with guards. Consider a function that processes a list of tuples representing people and their ages:

```
01. defmodule AgeProcessor do
02.    def process([]), do: :done
03.
04.    def process([{name, age} | tail]) when age >= 18 do
05.      IO.puts "#{name} is an adult."
06.      process(tail)
07.    end
08.
09.    def process([{name, _age} | tail]) do
10.      IO.puts "#{name} is a minor."
11.      process(tail)
12.    end
13. end
14.
```

Imagine you have a list of tuples with names and scores. For example:

```
students = [
  {"Alice", 88},
  {"Bob", 47},
  {"Charlie", 95},
  {"Diana", 67},
  {"Eve", 42}
]
```

In this example, we will create a function that processes a list of tuples, where each tuple contains a student's name and their score. The function will first filter out any students who scored below **50**, and then sort the remaining students by their scores in ascending order. This will allow us to easily identify the students with the highest scores.

```
1. defmodule StudentProcessor do
2.   def filter_and_sort(students) do
3.     students
4.     |> Enum.filter(fn {_name, score} -> score >= 50 end)
5.     |> Enum.sort_by(fn {_name, score} -> score end)
6.   end
7. end
```

This example uses pattern matching in the anonymous functions within **Enum.filter** and **Enum.sort_by**. If you call **StudentProcessor.filter_and_sort(students)**, it would return:

```
[
  {"Diana", 67},
  {"Alice", 88},
  {"Charlie", 95}
]
```

**Example 3.5**: Extracting and summing values.

Suppose you have a list of maps representing different fruits and their quantities. For example:

```
fruits = [
  %{name: "Apple", quantity: 10},
  %{name: "Banana", quantity: 5},
  %{name: "Orange", quantity: 8},
  %{name: "Strawberry", quantity: 15}
]
```

In this example, we will create a function that processes this list of maps to calculate the total quantity of all the fruits combined. The function will extract the quantity from each map and then sum these values to get the total quantity:

```
1. defmodule FruitCalculator do
2.   def total_quantity(fruits) do
3.     fruits
4.     |> Enum.map(fn %{quantity: qty} -> qty end)
5.     |> Enum.sum()
6.   end
7. end
```

In this example, pattern matching is used to extract the quantity from each map in the list. If you call **FruitCalculator.total_quantity(fruits)**, it would return: **38**

In conclusion, Elixir's pattern matching and guards offer a concise and expressive way to write code. By matching the structure of data and using guards for additional conditions, you can write more readable and maintainable Elixir code. Remember, the key is to practice and experiment with these features in various scenarios to fully grasp their power and utility.

# Conclusion

This chapter is dedicated to Elixir collections and processing, focusing on how the language elegantly handles collections of lists, tuples, and maps as fundamental data structures. A major part of the discussion centers on the Enum module, a powerful tool in Elixir's standard library for transformation, aggregation, finding, and filtering data within these collections. Core concepts explored include data transformation, with examples showing how to modify and reformat data using functions like Map and Map_join. This leads into data aggregation, the process of combining collection data into a single summary result, such as calculating Total salary or average experience. The chapter also details data finding, which involves locating elements that meet specific criteria, and data filtering, the technique of selecting a subset of elements based on a condition. Finally, data reducing is covered, the process of transforming a collection into a single value, often used for complex summaries. The Stream module is introduced to complement Enum, allowing for the lazy processing of large datasets.

The next chapter chapter explores the core of Elixir's concurrent programming capabilities

# Practical exercises

Now that we have explored Elixir's handling of collections, recursion, and pattern matching with guards in this chapter, it is time for some hands-on work.

Try solving the following exercises by yourself. Let us assume an advanced employee list for these exercises:

```
advanced_employees = [
  %{name: "Alice", department: "Engineering", salary: 60000, projects:
["Project X", "Project Y"]},
  %{name: "Bob", department: "Marketing", salary: 45000, projects: ["Project Z"]},
  %{name: "Carol", department: "Engineering", salary: 75000, projects:
["Project X", "Project A", "Project B"]},
  %{name: "Dave", department: "Sales", salary: 50000, projects: []}
]
```

**Exercise 3.1**: Find the most frequent item:

1.  **Objective**: Determine the most frequently occurring item in a list.
2.  **Enum functions**: `Enum.frequencies/1`, `Enum.max_by/2`
3.  **Problem type**: Frequency analysis.

**Exercise 3.2**: Extracting nested data:

1.  **Objective**: Given a list of maps, extract a certain nested value from each map.
2.  **Enum functions**: `Enum.map/2`, `Enum.filter/2`
3.  **Problem type**: Data extraction and transformation.

**Exercise 3.3**: Merging and summarizing data:

1.  **Objective**: Merge two lists of maps based on a common key and summarize a value.
2.  **Enum functions**: `Enum.group_by/3`, `Enum.reduce/3`
3.  **Problem type**: Data merging and aggregation.

**Exercise 3.4**: Flattening and unique filtering:

1.  **Objective**: Flatten a list of lists and then filter out duplicate items.
2.  **Enum functions**: `Enum.flat_map/2`, `Enum.uniq/1`
3.  **Problem type**: Data flattening and deduplication.

**Exercise 3.5**: Pairwise differences:

1.  **Objective**: Compute the pairwise difference between successive elements in a list.
2.  **Enum functions**: `Enum.chunk_every/2`, `Enum.map/2`
3.  **Problem type**: Sequential data processing.

Each exercise is designed to tackle a particular type of problem using a combination of Enum functions in Elixir. These exercises cover a wide range of scenarios, from data analysis and processing, offering a practical approach to learning Elixir's powerful enumerable capabilities.

The solutions are as follows:

1. **Exercise 3.1:**

```
1.  def most_frequent_department(employees) do
2.    employees
3.    |> Enum.map(& &1.department)
4.    |> Enum.frequencies()
5.    |> Enum.max_by(fn {_dept, count} -> count end)
6.  end
```

2. **Exercise 3.2:**

```
1.  def names_in_department(employees, dept) do
2.    employees
3.    |> Enum.filter(&(&1.department == dept))
4.    |> Enum.map(& &1.name)
5.  end
```

3. **Exercise 3.3:**

```
1.  def summarize_salaries_by_department(employees) do
2.    employees
3.    |> Enum.group_by(& &1.department)
4.    |> Enum.map(fn {dept, emps} ->
5.        {dept, Enum.reduce(emps, 0, fn %{salary: s}, acc -> acc
   + s end)}
6.      end)
7.  end
```

4. **Exercise 3.4:**

```
1.  def unique_projects(employees) do
2.    employees
3.    |> Enum.flat_map(& &1.projects)
4.    |> Enum.uniq()
5.  end
```

6. **Exercise 3.5:**

```
1.  def sequential_salary_differences(employees) do
2.    employees
3.    |> Enum.map(& &1.salary)
4.    |> Enum.chunk_every(2, 1, :discard)
```

```
5.        |> Enum.map(fn [first, second] -> abs(second - first) end)
6.    end
```

# Points to remember

- **Understanding Elixir collections**: Elixir provides various types of collections, such as lists, tuples, and maps, each serving different purposes and use cases. Lists are linked lists, ideal for sequential access, whereas tuples are stored contiguously in memory and are suitable for fixed-size collections. Maps are key-value stores used for fast data retrieval by key.

- **Power of the Enum module**: The Enum module is a cornerstone in Elixir for processing collections, offering a wide array of functions for data transformation, filtering, reduction, and more. Functions like Enum.map/2, Enum.filter/2, and Enum.reduce/3 are fundamental for iterating over and manipulating collections.

- **Data transformation**: Transformation involves modifying each element of a collection, often using functions like Enum.map/2.

- **Data aggregation and reduction**: Aggregation is the process of combining elements of a collection to produce a single summarized result, which is typically achieved using Enum.reduce/3. Reduction often involves more complex operations where elements are transformed before being aggregated.

- **Data finding and filtering**: Finding and filtering are crucial for extracting specific elements from collections based on given conditions, using functions like Enum. find/3 and Enum.filter/2.

- **Data grouping and sorting**: Grouping and sorting are used to organize data into meaningful structures or orders. Enum.group_by/3 is used for grouping data based on specified criteria, while Enum.sort/2 and Enum.sort_by/3 are used for sorting.

- **Data streaming for efficiency**: The Stream module allows for lazy data processing, which is particularly useful for large collections or for more memory-efficient data handling.

- **Pattern matching and guards**: Elixir's pattern matching and guards are not just tools for conditional logic; they play a significant role in the effective processing of collections.

# CHAPTER 4

# Concurrent Programming in Elixir

## Introduction

In the fast-evolving world of software development, concurrency has become a cornerstone for building efficient and responsive applications. Elixir is a dynamic, functional language designed for building scalable and maintainable applications, and excels in this domain. This chapter explores the core of Elixir's concurrent programming capabilities, an area where it particularly shines due to its Erlang roots.

Concurrent programming in Elixir is not just about running code simultaneously; it is about creating robust applications that can handle multiple Tasks in an efficient and fault-tolerant manner. This chapter will guide you through the intricacies of Elixir's approach to concurrency, exploring its processes, the nuances of inter-process communication, and the **Open Telecom Platform** (OTP), which is pivotal in providing robustness and concurrency to Elixir applications.

## Structure

This chapter will cover the following topics:

- Elixir processes
- Inter-process communication

- Introduction to Open Telecom Platform in Elixir

- GenServer in Elixir

- Supervisor

- Tasks

- Agents

- Fault tolerance and crash handling

# Objectives

This chapter aims to provide a comprehensive understanding of concurrent programming in Elixir, starting with the fundamentals of Elixir processes, their creation, and management. You will learn how these lightweight processes serve as the foundation for building concurrent applications. The chapter then explores inter-process communication, detailing how Elixir processes exchange messages to coordinate Tasks and share data efficiently. Following this, we introduce the OTP, a powerful set of libraries and design principles that enhance the development of robust and scalable applications. You will gain insights into various OTP components such as GenServer, Supervisor, DynamicSupervisor, Tasks, and Agents, each playing a crucial role in maintaining state, managing concurrency, and handling failures. A key focus of this chapter is Elixir's fault tolerance and crash-handling mechanisms, demonstrating strategies to build resilient applications that recover seamlessly from failures. To reinforce these concepts, the chapter concludes with hands-on practical exercises that will enable you to apply what you have learned, giving you real-world experience in designing and implementing concurrent applications in Elixir.

# Elixir processes

In Elixir, a process is a lightweight thread of execution. Unlike operating system processes, Elixir processes are extremely lightweight in terms of memory and CPU usage. They run concurrently and are isolated from each other, ensuring that a failure in one does not directly impact another. These processes are the heart of concurrent programming in Elixir and are managed by the Erlang Virtual Machine (BEAM).

## Characteristics of Elixir processes

The characteristics of Elixir processes are given as follows:

- **Isolation**: Each process has its own separate memory space and cannot directly access the memory of other processes. This isolation provides a strong fault tolerance as failures are contained within a single process.

- **Message passing**: Processes communicate via message passing, making them loosely coupled and easier to maintain.

- **Concurrency**: Processes can run simultaneously, and the BEAM scheduler efficiently handles the distribution of these processes across multiple CPUs.

# Creating and managing processes

Elixir provides straightforward functions to create and manage processes. The most basic way to create a process is to use the **spawn** function.

**Example 4.1**: Creating a process:

```
01. iex> # 1 - Define a simple function
02. iex> defmodule MyModule do
03. ...>    def say_hello do
04. ...>      IO.puts("Hello, World!")
05. ...>    end
06. ...> end
07. :ok
08.
09. iex> # 2 - Spawn a new process to run that function
10. iex> pid = spawn(MyModule, :say_hello, [])
11. #PID<0.123.0> # prints "Hello, World!" and the child exits
12.
13. iex> # 3 - Confirm what a PID looks like
14. iex> pid
15. #PID<0.123.0>
16.
17. iex> # 4 - Ask whether that PID is still alive
18. iex> Process.alive?(pid)
19. false # the process finished as soon as it printed
20.
```

In this example, we define a module **MyModule** with a function **say_hello**. We then create a new process using **spawn**, which runs **say_hello** in that process.

# Inter-process communication

**Inter-process communication** (**IPC**) in Elixir is a fundamental concept that allows processes to communicate with each other. Since Elixir processes are isolated, they do not share memory and cannot directly access each other's state. Therefore, IPC is achieved through message passing, which is a core feature of the Erlang VM (BEAM) on which Elixir runs. This message-passing mechanism is robust and forms the basis of creating fault-tolerant and distributed systems in Elixir.

# Basics of message passing

In Elixir, each process has a mailbox that stores incoming messages. Messages are stored in the order they are received. The mailbox is unique to each process and is not shared with others.

When a process wants to communicate with another, it sends a message to the target process's mailbox. These messages are queued and retrieved asynchronously by the receiving process.

**Example 4.2**: Basic message passing:

```
01. defmodule Communicator do
02.    def send_message(pid, msg) do
03.       send(pid, {:my_message, self(), msg})
04.    end
05.
06.    def receive_message do
07.       receive do
08.          {:my_message, sender_pid, msg} ->
09.             IO.puts("Received message from #{inspect(sender_pid)}: #{msg}")
10.             send(sender_pid, {:ack, self(), "Message received"})
11.       end
12.    end
13. end
14.
15. # Creating two processes
16. sender_pid = spawn(Communicator, :receive_message, [])
17. receiver_pid = spawn(Communicator, :receive_message, [])
18.
19. # Sending messages between them
20. Communicator.send_message(sender_pid, "Hello from receiver to sender")
21.
```

In this example, the **Communicator** module defines **send_message** and **receive_message** functions. We spawn two processes and use **send_message** to send messages between them. Each process receives and acknowledges the message.

# Handling asynchronous messages

Elixir processes handle messages asynchronously. The messages sent to a process are stored in its mailbox and processed one by one. If a process receives a message it does not expect or handle, it remains in the mailbox and can be processed later.

**Example 4.3**: Asynchronous message handling:

```
01. defmodule Communicator do
02.   def send_message(pid, msg) do
03.     send(pid, {:my_message, self(), msg})
04.   end
05.
06.   def receive_message do
07.     receive do
08.       {:my_message, sender_pid, msg} ->
09.         IO.puts("Received message from #{inspect(sender_pid)}: #{msg}")
10.         send(sender_pid, {:ack, self(), "Message received"})
11.     end
12.   end
13. end
14.
15. # Creating two processes
16. sender_pid = spawn(Communicator, :receive_message, [])
17. receiver_pid = spawn(Communicator, :receive_message, [])
18.
19. # Sending messages between them
20. Communicator.send_message(sender_pid, "Hello from receiver to sender")
21. Communicator.send_message(receiver_pid, "Hello from sender to receiver")
```

In this example, **AsyncHandler** waits for messages and prints them out. Messages are handled based on their pattern and importance, demonstrating asynchronous processing.

# Process linking and monitoring

Elixir allows processes to monitor and link to each other, which is crucial for fault tolerance. When a process dies, linked processes can be notified, or they can crash as well, depending on the desired behavior.

**Example 4.4**: Process monitoring:

```
01. defmodule Watcher do
02.   def start_watching do
03.     spawn(fn -> monitor_process end)
04.   end
05.
06.   defp monitor_process do
07.     # Spawning a process to watch
08.     pid = spawn(fn -> run_task end)
09.
10.     # Monitoring the spawned process
11.     Process.monitor(pid)
12.
13.     receive do
14.       {:DOWN, _ref, :process, _pid, _reason} ->
15.         IO.puts("The watched process has terminated")
16.     end
17.   end
18.
19.   defp run_task do
20.     # Simulating a task
21.     :timer.sleep(1000)
22.     IO.puts("Task completed")
23.   end
24. end
25.
26. # Starting the watcher
27. Watcher.start_watching()
```

In this example, the **Watcher** module spawns a process and monitors it. When the monitored process dies or completes its task, the watcher receives a message indicating this.

IPC in Elixir, primarily through message passing, is a powerful mechanism for building concurrent and distributed applications. It allows processes to communicate in a decoupled manner, enhancing fault tolerance and system resilience. The examples above illustrate basic communication patterns, asynchronous message handling, and process linking and monitoring, which are key components in Elixir's approach to IPC. As you progress, you will encounter more complex patterns and use cases that leverage these fundamentals to build robust applications.

**Note: For readers focusing on OTP abstractions over raw Elixir processes, as you embark on the journey of learning concurrent programming in Elixir, it is important to understand the relationship between raw Elixir processes and the abstractions provided by the OTP.**

# Power of open telecom platform

Elixir is built on top of the Erlang VM (BEAM), and one of its most powerful features is the OTP framework. OTP provides high-level abstractions that simplify the creation and management of processes in Elixir. While it is certainly possible to write concurrent code using raw Elixir processes, OTP abstractions like GenServer, Supervisor, Task, and Agent bring several advantages, which are as follows:

- **Simplicity and readability**: OTP abstractions allow you to write concise and readable code. They handle the complexities of process management, enabling you to focus on business logic.

- **Fault tolerance**: OTP's Supervisor and GenServer are designed for fault tolerance. They provide mechanisms for error recovery and process supervision, which are essential for building robust applications.

- **Standardization**: Using OTP abstractions promotes standardization in your code, making it easier to understand, maintain, and modify.

- **Built-in features**: OTP components come with many built-in features, such as state management, message passing, and asynchronous calls, reducing the need to implement these functionalities from scratch.

# Using raw processes

While OTP covers a wide range of use cases, there might be situations where you need the fine-grained control offered by raw Elixir processes. Such cases are, however, more of an exception than the rule. In general, OTP abstractions should be your go-to choice for most concurrent programming Tasks in Elixir.

As you progress through the chapters, focus on understanding and leveraging the power of OTP. Remember that OTP's high-level abstractions are designed to make your life easier as a developer, providing a robust, fault-tolerant, and efficient way to handle concurrency in Elixir. There is usually no need to understand the lower-level details of raw Elixir processes unless you have a very specific requirement that OTP cannot fulfill.

# Introduction to Open Telecom Platform in Elixir

OTP is not just a telecom solution, as its name might suggest. It is a collection of libraries and design principles for Erlang, upon which Elixir is built. OTP transforms Elixir from a simple functional programming language into a powerful tool for building scalable, distributed, and fault-tolerant applications.

OTP comprises several components, but the most crucial ones are:

- **GenServer**: A generic server implementation that abstracts the common functionalities of a server, making it easier to implement server-like processes.

- **Supervisor**: Supervisors are responsible for starting, stopping, and monitoring their child processes. They play a pivotal role in building fault-tolerant systems through their ability to restart child processes in case of failures.

- **Application**: In OTP, an application is a component that packages related functionalities. It provides a standardized approach to configuring and running functional blocks.

- **Erlang Term Storage (ETS)**: A powerful in-memory database for storing and retrieving data efficiently.

- **Other behaviors**: Such as Task (for short-lived processes) and Agent (for maintaining state).

# GenServer in Elixir

GenServer stands for a **generic server** in the Elixir ecosystem. It is one of the most important and frequently used components of the OTP. It abstracts the functionalities required for implementing a server in a concurrent, fault-tolerant manner. GenServer is used to maintain state, handle synchronous and asynchronous requests, and implement server-like behavior in a standardized way.

The key concepts of GenServer are as follows:

- **State management**: GenServer can maintain state across multiple interactions.

- **Synchronous and asynchronous requests**: It handles synchronous (call) and asynchronous (cast) requests. A call is used when the caller expects a response, while a cast is used when no response is needed.

- **Callbacks:** GenServer uses a callback mechanism where specific functions are invoked in response to various messages and events.

# Implementing a GenServer

To implement a GenServer, you define a module that uses GenServer behavior and implements various callback functions.

**Example 4.5**: Basic GenServer implementation:

```elixir
01. defmodule MyGenServer do
02.   use GenServer
03.
04.   # Starting the GenServer
05.   def start_link(initial_value) do
06.     GenServer.start_link(__MODULE__, initial_value)
07.   end
08.
09.   # Server initialization
10.   def init(initial_value) do
11.     {:ok, initial_value}
12.   end
13.
14.   # Handling synchronous calls
15.   def handle_call(:get_value, _from, state) do
16.     {:reply, state, state}
17.   end
18.
19.   # Handling asynchronous casts
20.   def handle_cast({:set_value, new_value}, state) do
21.     {:noreply, new_value}
22.   end
23.
24.   # Client API
25.   def get_value(pid) do
26.     GenServer.call(pid, :get_value)
27.   end
28.
29.   def set_value(pid, value) do
```

```
30.      GenServer.cast(pid, {:set_value, value})
31.   end
32. end
33.
34. # Using the GenServer
35. {:ok, pid} = MyGenServer.start_link(0)
36. MyGenServer.set_value(pid, 10)
37. current_value = MyGenServer.get_value(pid)
38. IO.puts("Current Value: #{current_value}")
```

In this example, **MyGenServer** maintains an integer state. It provides functions to set this value asynchronously and get the value synchronously.

# Advanced features

GenServer also supports more advanced features like handling timeouts, managing a global state, and integrating with supervisors for fault tolerance.

**Example 4.6**: Handling timeouts:

```
01. defmodule TimeoutGenServer do
02.    use GenServer
03.
04.    def start_link(_) do
05.      GenServer.start_link(__MODULE__, :ok)
06.    end
07.
08.    def init(:ok) do
09.      # Set a timeout of 1000 milliseconds
10.      {:ok, :ok, 1000}
11.    end
12.
13.    def handle_info(:timeout, _state) do
14.      IO.puts("Timeout occurred")
15.      {:stop, :normal, :no_state}
16.    end
17. end
18.
```

```
19.  # Starting the GenServer
20.  {:ok, pid} = TimeoutGenServer.start_link(nil)
21.
```

In this advanced example, **TimeoutGenServer** uses a timeout to perform an action (printing a message) after a specified period.

**GenServer** is a powerful tool in Elixir for creating servers that are concurrent, fault-tolerant, and efficient. It simplifies the complexities of process management and communication, allowing developers to focus on the business logic of their applications. Through practical examples, we see how **GenServer** can be utilized for various purposes, from simple state management to handling timeouts and asynchronous operations. As you explore further into Elixir and OTP, the understanding and use of GenServer will be crucial in building robust applications.

# Supervisor

Supervisor is a specialized process that monitors child processes and implements strategies to handle their failures. It is a crucial component of the fault-tolerance model provided by the OTP. Supervisors ensure that an application remains functional, even in the face of errors and crashes, by restarting child processes according to predefined rules.

The key concepts of Supervisors are explained as follows:

- **Child process management**: Supervisors manage child processes, which can be workers (like GenServers) or other supervisors, creating a hierarchical process structure.
- **Restart strategies**: Supervisors define how to restart child processes. Some common strategies include:
    - o **:one_for_one**: If a child process terminates, only that process is restarted.
    - o **:one_for_all**: If a child process terminates, all other child processes are terminated and restarted.
    - o **:rest_for_one**: If a child process terminates, the rest of the child processes started after it are terminated and restarted.
- **Fault tolerance**: Supervisors are the cornerstone of building fault-tolerant applications in Elixir.

# Implementing a supervisor

To use a Supervisor, you need to define a module that uses the Supervisor behavior and sets up child processes and restart strategies.

**Example 4.7**: Basic **Supervisor** implementation:

```
01. defmodule MySupervisor do
02.   use Supervisor
03.
04.   def start_link(opts) do
05.     Supervisor.start_link(__MODULE__, :ok, opts)
06.   end
07.
08.   def init(:ok) do
09.     children = [
10.       {MyWorker, []}
11.     ]
12.
13.     Supervisor.init(children, strategy: :one_for_one)
14.   end
15. end
16.
17. defmodule MyWorker do
18.   use GenServer
19.
20.   # GenServer implementation...
21. end
22.
23. # Starting the Supervisor
24. {:ok, sup_pid} = MySupervisor.start_link(name: MySupervisor)
25.
```

In this example, **MySupervisor** starts with a single child process, **MyWorker**, a **GenServer**. If **MyWorker** crashes, **MySupervisor** will restart it based on the **:one_for_one** strategy.

Supervisors in Elixir are a fundamental part of building resilient applications that can withstand failures. By effectively managing child processes and defining restart strategies, supervisors help in maintaining the overall integrity and availability of the application. The examples demonstrate static management of child processes, illustrating the flexibility and power of supervisors in the Elixir OTP environment. As you progress in Elixir application development, understanding and utilizing supervisors will be key to ensuring robust and fault-tolerant applications.

# DynamicSupervisor

The DynamicSupervisor is a specialized type of supervisor in Elixir's OTP framework designed to supervise a dynamic set of child processes. Unlike a regular Supervisor, where the children are known and started at initialization, a DynamicSupervisor can start children dynamically at runtime.

The key characteristics of DynamicSupervisor are:

- **Flexibility**: It can start and stop child processes on demand.

- **Fault tolerance**: Like regular supervisors, DynamicSupervisors provide fault tolerance. If a child process crashes, it can be restarted according to the defined strategy.

- **Simplicity**: It simplifies scenarios where the number of processes is not known upfront or can change over time.

## Implementing a DynamicSupervisor

To use a DynamicSupervisor, you define a module that uses the DynamicSupervisor behavior and starts children dynamically.

**Example 4.8**: Basic DynamicSupervisor:

```
01. defmodule MyDynamicSupervisor do
02.    use DynamicSupervisor
03.
04.    def start_link(opts \\ []) do
05.       DynamicSupervisor.start_link(__MODULE__, :ok, opts)
06.    end
07.
08.    def init(:ok) do
09.       DynamicSupervisor.init(strategy: :one_for_one)
10.    end
11.
12.    def start_child(module, args) do
13.       spec = {module, args}
14.       DynamicSupervisor.start_child(__MODULE__, spec)
15.    end
16. end
17.
```

```
18.  # Starting the DynamicSupervisor
19.  {:ok, sup_pid} = MyDynamicSupervisor.start_link()
20.
21.  # Dynamically starting a child
22.  {:ok, child_pid} = MyDynamicSupervisor.start_child(MyWorker, [arg1,
     arg2])
23.
```

In this example, **MyDynamicSupervisor** is set up with a **:one_for_one** restart strategy. Child processes can be started dynamically using the **start_child** function, which delegates to **DynamicSupervisor.start_child**.

# Advanced usage

DynamicSupervisors are particularly useful in systems where workloads are dynamic in nature, such as a web server handling incoming requests.

**Example 4.9**: DynamicSupervisor in a web server context:

```
01. defmodule RequestHandler do
02.   use GenServer
03.
04.   def start_link(request) do
05.     GenServer.start_link(__MODULE__, request)
06.   end
07.
08.   def init(request) do
09.     # Handle the request
10.     {:ok, request}
11.   end
12. end
13.
14. defmodule WebServerSupervisor do
15.   use DynamicSupervisor
16.
17.   def start_link do
18.     DynamicSupervisor.start_link(__MODULE__, :ok, name: __MODULE__)
19.   end
```

```
20.
21.    def init(:ok) do
22.      DynamicSupervisor.init(strategy: :one_for_one)
23.    end
24.
25.    def handle_request(request) do
26.      DynamicSupervisor.start_child(__MODULE__, {RequestHandler, re-
       quest})
27.    end
28. end
29.
30. # Starting the Web Server Supervisor
31. {:ok, _sup_pid} = WebServerSupervisor.start_link()
32.
33. # Handling a new request
34.    WebServerSupervisor.handle_request(%{path: "/home", method: "GET"})
```

In this example, **WebServerSupervisor** manages **RequestHandler** processes. Each incoming web request starts a new **RequestHandler** process, which allows handling each request concurrently and independently.

DynamicSupervisors provide a robust and flexible way to manage a dynamic set of processes. They are particularly useful in scenarios where you need to start and stop child processes on the fly, such as in response to external events or incoming requests. By combining DynamicSupervisors with other OTP features like *GenServers* and *Agents*, you can build highly concurrent, fault-tolerant applications that can adapt to changing workloads dynamically.

# Task

Elixir's Task module is a powerful tool for spawning background processes and performing asynchronous operations. It allows you to execute functions asynchronously, making it easier to perform concurrent operations that can run parallel to your main program flow. This is particularly useful in input or output-bound or computationally intensive Tasks that you do not want to block your application's execution.

## Understanding Tasks

A Task in Elixir is built on top of Erlang's processes, providing a more straightforward abstraction for concurrency. When you start a task, it runs a given function in a new process, allowing your application to continue executing other operations concurrently.

The key features of Tasks are:

- **Simplicity**: Tasks provide a simple interface for asynchronous execution.
- **Concurrency**: They allow you to easily run multiple operations at the same time, leveraging Elixir's powerful concurrency model.
- **Error handling**: Tasks can be linked to the calling process, so if a Task crashes, the calling process can be notified, ensuring better fault tolerance.
- **Return value**: You can retrieve the return value of a Task, making it suitable for scenarios where you need to process results from asynchronous operations.

**Example 4.10**: Basic usage of a Task:

```
01. defmodule BasicTask do
02.   def long_running_task do
03.     :timer.sleep(3000) # Simulates a long-running task by sleeping for 3000ms
04.     "Task completed"
05.   end
06.
07.   def run do
08.     task = Task.async(&long_running_task/0) # Starts the task asynchronously
09.     IO.puts("Doing some work...") # Simulate doing some other work
10.     result = Task.await(task) # Waits for the task to complete
11.     IO.puts("Async task result: #{result}")
12.   end
13. end
14.
15. BasicTask.run()
16.
```

In this example, **long_running_task** simulates a time-consuming operation. We run this task asynchronously with **Task.async** and then proceed to do some other work (printing **"Doing some work..."**). After that, we wait for the task to finish with **Task.await** and print its result.

Suppose you have a list of items that you want to process in parallel. You can use **Task.async_stream** to map over the collection concurrently.

**Task.async_stream** is a powerful function for processing collections concurrently. It allows you to execute a given function over each item in an enumerable, running multiple operations in parallel and collecting the results. Here is an example of how you can use it:

```
01. defmodule ParallelTask do
02.    def expensive_computation(x) do
03.       :timer.sleep(2000) # Simulates an expensive computation by sleeping
       for 2000ms
04.       x * x
05.    end
06.
07.    def run(list) do
08.       list
09.       |> Task.async_stream(&expensive_computation/1)
10.       |> Enum.to_list() # Collects the results into a list
11.    end
12. end
13.
14. result = ParallelTask.run(1..5)
15. IO.inspect(result)
```

This example takes a list of numbers, applies an *expensive computation* to each in parallel using Tasks, and then collects the results. **Task.async_stream** is more suited for this scenario as it automatically handles both async execution and awaiting results.

The output of **IO.inspect(result)** will be a list of **{:ok, value}** tuples for successful computations or **{:error, reason}** tuples if any errors occurred during the Tasks' execution. This makes **Task.async_stream** particularly useful for error handling and concurrent processing in Elixir applications.

Using **Task.async_stream** like this significantly improves performance for I/O-bound or CPU-intensive operations. It allows the work to be done concurrently, utilizing the available system resources more efficiently.

# Handling timeouts

It is important to handle timeouts properly when using **Task.await**, the default timeout is 5000 milliseconds (or 5 seconds). This default behavior ensures that your application does not wait indefinitely for a task to complete, potentially leading to a deadlock or a poor user experience due to long response times.

**Example 4.11**: Handling Task Timeouts with **Task.await**:

```
01. defmodule TaskTimeout do
02.    def long_task do
```

```
03.        :timer.sleep(5000) # Simulates a long task
04.        "Done"
05.      end
06.
07.    def run do
08.      task = Task.async(&long_task/0)
09.
10.      case Task.await(task, 2000) do
11.        {:ok, result} -> IO.puts("Task completed: #{result}")
12.        :error -> IO.puts("Task timed out")
13.      end
14.    end
15.  end
16.
17.  TaskTimeout.run()
18.
```

In this example, if the task is not completed within **2000** milliseconds, **Task.await** returns **:error**, allowing you to handle the timeout case.

Tasks in Elixir provide a convenient way to perform asynchronous operations, offering powerful constructs for concurrency with minimal boilerplate. Whether you are making HTTP requests, accessing a database, or performing heavy computations, leveraging Tasks can significantly improve the responsiveness and throughput of your Elixir applications.

# Agents

Elixir's Agent module provides a simple abstraction around state management, allowing you to maintain state in a separate process that can be accessed and updated concurrently by other processes. Agents are a straightforward means to achieve statefulness in an otherwise stateless environment, making them ideal for scenarios where you need to store and manipulate state across different parts of your application.

## Understanding Agents

An Agent is essentially a process that encapsulates state with the ability to modify and query that state via functions. They are built on top of Erlang's process model and provide a simpler interface for state management compared to directly using processes and messages. Agents can be used for various purposes, such as storing configuration, caching values, or maintaining counters.

The key features of Agents are as follows:

- **State management**: Agents provide an easy way to keep and manage the state.
- **Simplicity**: They offer a simpler alternative to GenServers for state management without the need to implement multiple callback functions.
- **Concurrency**: Like other Elixir processes, Agents run concurrently and are isolated, making them a robust choice for storing state in a concurrent application.

# Using Agents

Agents are typically used to store state that needs to be accessed or modified by different parts of an application.

**Example 4.12**: Basic usage of an Agent:

```
01. defmodule Counter do
02.   def start_link(default_value) do
03.     Agent.start_link(fn -> default_value end, name: __MODULE__)
04.   end
05.
06.   def get_value do
07.     Agent.get(__MODULE__, fn state -> state end)
08.   end
09.
10.   def update_value(fun) do
11.     Agent.update(__MODULE__, fun)
12.   end
13. end
14.
15. # Start an agent with initial state
16. {:ok, _pid} = Counter.start_link(0)
17.
18. # Get the current state
19. IO.puts("Current value: #{Counter.get_value()}")
20.
21. # Update the state
22. Counter.update_value(fn state -> state + 1 end)
23.
```

```
24. # Get the updated state
25. IO.puts("Updated value: #{Counter.get_value()}")
```

In this example, **MyAgent** encapsulates a simple integer state. It provides functions to get and update this state. **Agent.get** and **Agent.update** are used to read and modify the state, respectively.

**Example 4.13**: Sharing state across process.

Agents can be used to share state across multiple processes in a controlled manner:

```
01. defmodule Counter do
02.   def start_link do
03.     Agent.start_link(fn -> 0 end, name: :shared_counter)
04.   end
05.
06.   def increment do
07.     Agent.update(:shared_counter, &(&1 + 1))
08.   end
09.
10.   def get_value do
11.     Agent.get(:shared_counter, & &1)
12.   end
13. end
14.
15. # Starting the agent
16. Counter.start_link()
17.
18. # Increment the counter from different processes
19. spawn(fn -> Counter.increment() end)
20. spawn(fn -> Counter.increment() end)
21.
22. # Getting the value
23. IO.puts("Counter value: #{Counter.get_value()}")
```

This example demonstrates an agent (**:shared_counter**) used to keep a shared counter. Multiple processes can safely increment the counter, illustrating how Agents can manage shared state in a concurrent application.

# Storing and retrieving complex state

Agents are not limited to simple data types; they can store any Elixir data structure. Here is an example of using an agent to store and manipulate a map:

```elixir
01. defmodule Store do
02.   def start_link do
03.     Agent.start_link(fn -> %{} end, name: __MODULE__)
04.   end
05.
06.   def put(key, value) do
07.     Agent.update(__MODULE__, fn state -> Map.put(state, key, value) end)
08.   end
09.
10.   def get(key) do
11.     Agent.get(__MODULE__, fn state -> Map.get(state, key) end)
12.   end
13. end
14.
15. # Start the agent with an empty map
16. {:ok, _pid} = Store.start_link()
17.
18. # Store some key-value pairs
19. Store.put(:a, 1)
20. Store.put(:b, 2)
21.
22. # Retrieve a value
23. value = Store.get(:a)
24. IO.puts("Value of :a is #{value}")
```

In this example, the **Store** module uses an agent to manage a map. We provide functions to start the agent, add key-value pairs to the map, and retrieve values by key.

Agents in Elixir are a straightforward and efficient way to manage state within an application. Their simplicity makes them an excellent choice for scenarios where all you need is to store and retrieve state without the need for the more complex functionalities of a GenServer. As seen in the examples, Agents can be used for various purposes, such as maintaining counters, caching data, or storing application configuration. Understanding and using Agents is essential for

Elixir developers looking to implement state management in a concurrent and fault-tolerant environment.

The following table lists the differences between Agents and GenServers:

| Feature | Agents | GenServers |
| --- | --- | --- |
| Simplicity | Designed for simplicity, primarily used for state management. | More powerful and flexible, used for complex state management and communication. |
| State focus | Stores state that can be retrieved or updated by other processes, acting as a wrapper for state. | Manages state while also handling different types of synchronous and asynchronous requests. |
| Logic complexity | Minimal logic, best suited for simple shared state management. | Allows defining custom behaviors, handling incoming messages, and executing background Tasks. |
| Communication mechanism | Supports basic synchronous (`Agent.get/3`, `Agent.get_and_update/3`) and asynchronous (`Agent.update/3`, `Agent.cast/2`) operations. | Provides built-in support for message passing via synchronous (`GenServer.call/3`) and asynchronous (`GenServer.cast/2`) communication. |
| Fault tolerance and supervision | Less fault-tolerant, not directly supervised in a supervision tree. | Fits well into OTP's supervision tree, supports fault tolerance and automatic recovery. |
| Scalability and performance | Suitable for lightweight state storage, but lacks advanced features for scalability. | Ideal for building scalable and performant applications requiring concurrency, background jobs, and robust workflows. |

*Table 4.1: Difference between Agents and GenServers*

Use Agents when your primary need is simple state management without the need for handling complex behaviors or custom message processing. They are ideal for scenarios where you simply need to read and write some shared state across processes.

Use GenServers when you need to manage state in conjunction with complex interactions, custom request handling, or when building services that require more than just simple state access. GenServers are suitable for applications requiring full control over message processing, task execution, and interaction with other processes or services.

While both Agents and GenServers are powerful tools for building concurrent applications in Elixir, the choice between them depends on the complexity of the task at hand. Agents are best for straightforward state management, while GenServers offer more flexibility and control for managing state, handling messages, and implementing complex interactions within an application.

# Fault tolerance and crash handling

Built on the Erlang VM (BEAM), Elixir is designed with fault tolerance at its core. This design philosophy is encapsulated in the *Let it crash* principle, emphasizing building resilient systems that can recover from failures automatically. Elixir and Erlang achieve fault tolerance through a combination of lightweight process isolation, supervision trees, and the principles of the OTP.

## Process isolation

In Elixir, every task is executed in a separate process. These processes are lightweight, with their own garbage collection and stack. They are completely isolated from one another, which means that if one process crashes, it does not directly affect others. This isolation is the first step towards fault tolerance.

**Example 4.14**: Process isolation:

```
1.  defmodule IsolatedProcess do
2.    def start do
3.      spawn(fn -> raise "Oops, I crashed" end)
4.    end
5.  end
6.
7.  # Starting the isolated process
8.  IsolatedProcess.start()
9.
10. IO.puts("The main process continues running.")
```

In this example, even though the spawned process crashes, the main process continues running unaffected.

## Supervision trees

Supervision trees are hierarchical structures of processes where Supervisor processes monitor worker processes (and possibly other Supervisors). If a worker process crashes, its Supervisor is notified and can take action, such as restarting the worker process.

**Example 4.15**: Basic Supervisor:

```
01. defmodule MyWorker do
02.   use GenServer
03.
```

```
04.    def start_link(_) do
05.      GenServer.start_link(__MODULE__, :ok, name: __MODULE__)
06.    end
07.
08.    def init(:ok) do
09.      {:ok, :ok}
10.    end
11. end
12.
13. defmodule MySupervisor do
14.    use Supervisor
15.
16.    def start_link do
17.      Supervisor.start_link(__MODULE__, [], name: __MODULE__)
18.    end
19.
20.    def init(_) do
21.      children = [
22.        {MyWorker, []}
23.      ]
24.
25.      Supervisor.init(children, strategy: :one_for_one)
26.    end
27. end
28.
29. # Starting the supervisor, which in turn starts the worker
30. MySupervisor.start_link()
```

Here, **MySupervisor** supervises **MyWorker**. If **MyWorker** crashes, **MySupervisor** will automatically restart it.

# Role of OTP

OTP provides a set of behaviors and conventions for building fault-tolerant applications. GenServer for stateful servers, Supervisor for supervision, and application for starting the supervision tree are core components of OTP that facilitate building resilient systems.

**Practical example**: Fault tolerance in a web application

Imagine a web application with a background job system. Jobs can occasionally fail due to temporary issues like network timeouts.

```
01. defmodule BackgroundJob do
02.   use GenServer
03.
04.   def start_link(job_data) do
05.     GenServer.start_link(__MODULE__, job_data)
06.   end
07.
08.   def init(job_data) do
09.     Process.send_after(self(), :process_job, 1_000) # Delay job
       processing for demonstration
10.     {:ok, job_data}
11.   end
12.
13.   def handle_info(:process_job, %{type: :success} = state) do
14.     IO.puts("Job #{inspect(state)} completed successfully.")
15.     {:stop, :normal, state}
16.   end
17.
18.   def handle_info(:process_job, %{type: :fail} = state) do
19.     IO.puts("Job #{inspect(state)} failed. Crashing for restart...")
20.     raise "Job failed"
21.   end
22. end
23.
24. defmodule JobSupervisor do
25.   use Supervisor
26.
27.   def start_link(opts) do
28.     Supervisor.start_link(__MODULE__, :ok, opts)
29.   end
30.
```

```
31.    def init(:ok) do
32.       children = [
33.          Supervisor.child_spec({BackgroundJob, %{type: :success, id: 1}},
      id: :success_job),
34.          Supervisor.child_spec({BackgroundJob, %{type: :fail, id: 2}}, id:
      :fail_job)
35.       ]
36.
37.       strategy = :one_for_one
38.       options = [strategy: strategy, max_restarts: 10, max_seconds: 60] #
      Adjusted restart intensity
39.
40.       Supervisor.init(children, options)
41.    end
42. end
43.
44.
45. # Starting the Job Supervisor
46. {:ok, sup_pid} = JobSupervisor.start_link(name: :job_supervisor)
```

In this setup, **JobSupervisor** supervises **BackgroundJob**. If a job fails, it gets restarted, assuming the failure might be temporary. This allows the application to recover from transient errors without manual intervention automatically.

In OTP, the default restart strategy parameters are:

- **:max_restarts**: The maximum number of restarts allowed within a time frame, defaulting to 3.

- **:max_seconds**: The time frame in seconds within which the restarts are counted, defaulting to 5 seconds.

If a child process crashes and is restarted more times than **:max_restarts** within **:max_seconds**, the Supervisor itself will terminate. This behavior is intended to prevent situations where a child process is constantly failing and being restarted, which could lead to instability in the system.

In this example, the **JobSupervisor** is configured to allow up to 10 restarts within 60 seconds before it considers the failure rate too high and stops attempting to restart its children.

Fault tolerance and crash handling in Elixir leverage the BEAM's process model, supervision trees, and OTP behaviors to build resilient systems. By embracing the *Let it crash* philosophy, developers can create applications that self-heal from failures, enhancing reliability and uptime. Through careful design of supervision trees and appropriate crash handling strategies, complex systems can maintain high levels of availability and robustness.

# Conclusion

This chapter has taken you through an exploration into concurrent programming in Elixir, covering the powerful abstractions provided by OTP, including processes, GenServers, Supervisors, DynamicSupervisors, Tasks, and Agents. By understanding these components, you are now equipped to build robust, scalable, and fault-tolerant applications that can handle the complexities of modern software requirements.

Remember that the key to mastering concurrent programming in Elixir lies in practicing and applying these concepts to real-world problems. Experiment with creating your own processes, managing state with GenServers, orchestrating process lifecycles with Supervisors, and leveraging Tasks and Agents for specific use cases. Embrace the *Let it crash* philosophy to design systems that are not just fault-tolerant but also self-healing and resilient.

As you continue your journey in Elixir, keep exploring and experimenting with the concepts discussed in this chapter. The ability to think concurrently and manage state and processes effectively will be invaluable skills as you tackle more advanced topics and build sophisticated applications in Elixir.

Now that you understand how Elixir handles multiple Tasks at once, we will discuss how it works across multiple computers. In the next chapter, you will learn how Elixir makes distributed systems easier by allowing different machines to communicate and work together. We will cover distributed OTP applications, how processes talk to each other across nodes, and how to handle network issues. This will help you build strong, reliable systems that scale easily.

# Practical exercises

**Exercise 4.1**

**Objective**: Create a **GenServer** that periodically refreshes its data from an external source:

```
01. defmodule RefreshingServer do
02.   use GenServer
03.
04.   def start_link(opts \\ []) do
05.     GenServer.start_link(__MODULE__, %{data: :none}, opts)
06.   end
07.
```

```elixir
08.    def init(state) do
09.      schedule_refresh(10) # Schedule first refresh in 10 seconds
10.      {:ok, state}
11.    end
12.
13.    def get_data(pid) do
14.      GenServer.call(pid, :get_data)
15.    end
16.
17.    def handle_call(:get_data, _from, state) do
18.      {:reply, state.data, state}
19.    end
20.
21.    def handle_info(:refresh, state) do
22.      new_data = fetch_external_data()
23.      schedule_refresh(10) # Schedule next refresh
24.      {:noreply, %{state | data: new_data}}
25.    end
26.
27.    defp fetch_external_data do
28.      # Simulate fetching data from an external source
29.      external_data = :rand.uniform(100)
30.      :timer.sleep(1000) # Delay to simulate data fetching
31.      {:some, :external, external_data}
32.    end
33.
34.    defp schedule_refresh(interval) do
35.      Process.send_after(self(), :refresh, interval * 1000)
36.    end
37. end
38.
39. # Starting the Refreshing Server
40. {:ok, pid} = RefreshingServer.start_link()
41.
```

```
42. # Getting refreshed data
43. IO.inspect(RefreshingServer.get_data(pid))
```

This **GenServer**, **RefreshingServer**, refreshes its internal state by fetching external data at regular intervals. The **handle_info** callback handles the **:refresh** message, which triggers data fetching and reschedules the next refresh.

## Exercise 4.2

**Objective**: Implement a **GenServer** that acts as a rate limiter, allowing a certain number of requests within a time frame.

```
01. defmodule RateLimiterServer do
02.    use GenServer
03.
04.    def start_link(request_limit, time_window) do
05.       GenServer.start_link(__MODULE__, {request_limit, time_window, %{}},
       name: __MODULE__)
06.    end
07.
08.    def init({request_limit, time_window, requests}) do
09.       state = %{request_limit: request_limit, time_window: time_window,
       requests: requests}
10.       {:ok, state}
11.    end
12.
13.    def check_rate(client_id) do
14.       GenServer.call(__MODULE__, {:check_rate, client_id})
15.    end
16.
17.    def handle_call({:check_rate, client_id}, _from, %{request_limit:
       limit, time_window: window, requests: reqs} = state) do
18.       current_time = :erlang.system_time(:millisecond)
19.       valid_time = current_time - window * 1000
20.
21.       requests = Enum.filter(reqs[client_id] || [], fn {timestamp, _} ->
       timestamp > valid_time end)
22.       if length(requests) < limit do
23.          {:reply, :allow, %{state | requests: Map.update(reqs, client_id,
```

```
       [{current_time, :allow} | requests], fn req -> [{current_time, :allow} |
       req] end)}}
24.     else
25.        {:reply, :deny, state}
26.     end
27.   end
28. end
29.
30. # Starting the Rate Limiter Server
31. {:ok, pid} = RateLimiterServer.start_link(5, 60) # Allow 5 requests in
       60 seconds
32.
33. # Checking the rate
34. Enum.each(1..6, fn _ ->
35.   result = RateLimiterServer.check_rate(:client_1)
36.   IO.puts("Request result: #{result}")
37. end)
```

**RateLimiterServer** maintains a request log for each client ID. The **check_rate** function checks if adding another request would exceed the limit within the time window. It filters out old requests and then decides to allow or deny the new request.

**Exercise 4.3**

**Objective**: Use Task Streams to process a large list of data in parallel without overwhelming the system:

```
01. defmodule ParallelDataStream do
02.   def process_item(item) do
03.     # Simulate some processing
04.     :timer.sleep(1000)
05.     IO.puts("Processed: #{item}")
06.     item * 2
07.   end
08.
09.   def run(data_list) do
10.     data_list
11.     |> Task.async_stream(&process_item/1, max_concurrency: 4)
12.     |> Enum.to_list()
```

```
13.    end
14. end
15.
16. # Running the parallel data processing
17. results = ParallelDataStream.run(1..10)
18. IO.inspect(results)
```

**ParallelDataStream** uses **Task.async_stream** to process each item in the **data_list** in parallel. **max_concurrency:  4** limits the number of concurrently running Tasks to avoid overloading the system.

### Exercise 4.4

**Objective**: Read and process multiple files asynchronously using Tasks:

```
01. defmodule AsyncFileReader do
02.   def read_and_process_file(file_path) do
03.     # Simulate reading and processing a file
04.     :timer.sleep(2000)
05.     IO.puts("Processed file: #{file_path}")
06.   end
07.
08.   def read_files(file_paths) do
09.     file_paths
10.     |> Enum.map(&Task.async(AsyncFileReader, :read_and_process_file,
    [&1]))
11.     |> Enum.map(&Task.await/1)
12.   end
13. end
14.
15. # Running the async file processing
16. file_paths = ["file1.txt", "file2.txt", "file3.txt"]
17. AsyncFileReader.read_files(file_paths)
```

In this example, **AsyncFileReader** reads and processes a list of file paths asynchronously. Each file is processed in a separate Task, allowing for concurrent processing of multiple files.

### Exercise 4.5

**Objective**: Implement a **GenServer** that keeps a counter and periodically saves its state to an Agent as a backup:

```
01. defmodule BackupAgent do
02.   def start_link do
03.     Agent.start_link(fn -> nil end, name: :backup_agent)
04.   end
05.
06.   def fetch_current_value() do
07.     Agent.get(:backup_agent, fn state -> state end)
08.   end
09.
10.   def backup(state) do
11.     Agent.update(:backup_agent, fn _ -> state end)
12.   end
13. end
14.
15. defmodule AdvancedGenServer do
16.   use GenServer
17.
18.   def start_link do
19.     GenServer.start_link(__MODULE__, 0, name: __MODULE__)
20.   end
21.
22.   def init(state) do
23.     schedule_backup()
24.     {:ok, state}
25.   end
26.
27.   def handle_info(:backup, state) do
28.     BackupAgent.backup(state)
29.     schedule_backup()
30.     {:noreply, state}
31.   end
32.
33.   def increment do
34.     GenServer.cast(__MODULE__, :increment)
```

```
35.    end
36.
37.    defp schedule_backup do
38.       Process.send_after(self(), :backup, 10_000) # 10 seconds
39.    end
40.
41.    def handle_cast(:increment, state) do
42.       {:noreply, state + 1}
43.    end
44. end
45.
46. # Starting the services
47. BackupAgent.start_link()
48. {:ok, _pid} = AdvancedGenServer.start_link()
49.
50. # Incrementing the counter
51. AdvancedGenServer.increment()
52.
53. # Fetching the current value from the BackupAgent
54. current_backup = BackupAgent.fetch_current_value()
55. IO.puts("Current backup value: #{inspect(current_backup)}")
```

This **GenServer, AdvancedGenServer**, maintains a counter and periodically backs up its state to an **Agent, BackupAgent**. The backup is scheduled using **Process.send_after**.

# Points to remember

- **Elixir processes**: It is important to understand that Elixir processes are lightweight and isolated. They enable concurrent execution without shared state, which forms the foundation of fault tolerance in Elixir applications.

- **IPC**: In Elixir, IPC is done through message passing. Remember that processes communicate by sending and receiving messages asynchronously, which decouples the processes and enhances fault tolerance.

- **OTP fundamentals**: The OTP is a set of libraries and design principles that provide a robust framework for building concurrent, scalable, and fault-tolerant applications in Elixir.

- **GenServer**: Grasp the importance of GenServer for managing state, handling synchronous and asynchronous requests, and implementing server logic in a fault-tolerant way.

- **Supervisors**: Recognize the role of Supervisors in managing the lifecycle of worker processes, including starting, stopping, and restarting processes in response to failures based on predefined strategies.

- **DynamicSupervisor**: Understand the use cases for DynamicSupervisor, which allows for starting and stopping child processes dynamically, providing flexibility for applications with variable workloads.

- **Tasks and Agents**: Learn when to use Tasks for asynchronous operations and Agents for simple state management, and how they compare to GenServers in terms of functionality and use cases.

- **Fault tolerance and crash handling**: Embrace the *Let it crash* philosophy, focusing on building systems that automatically recover from failures rather than trying to prevent them at all costs.

# Join our Discord space

Join our Discord workspace for latest updates, offers, tech happenings around the world, new releases, and sessions with the authors:

https://discord.bpbonline.com

# CHAPTER 5

# Understanding Distributed Systems

## Introduction

In this chapter, we welcome you to our comprehensive journey into the world of distributed systems using Elixir. In today's technology-driven landscape, the need for robust, scalable, and fault-tolerant applications is more crucial than ever. Elixir, a dynamic, functional language built on the Erlang VM, is known for its prowess in handling the complexities of distributed computing. This chapter explore Elixir's capabilities, exploring how its features and design principles make it a prime candidate for building and managing distributed systems. From the foundational concepts of distributed computing to the intricacies of Elixir's OTP framework, we will uncover the elements that make Elixir an exceptional choice for distributed application development.

## Structure

This chapter will cover the following topics:

- Understanding distributed systems
- Elixir for disturbed systems
- Distributed Open Telecom Platform applications
- Handling network partitions and failures
- Node liveness and heartbeat management

# Objectives

Our objective is to provide a thorough understanding of distributed systems through the lens of Elixir, a dynamic, functional language renowned for its suitability in building scalable and fault-tolerant applications. We aim to explore the fundamental concepts of distributed computing and explore why Elixir, with its robust concurrency model and **Open Telecom Platform (OTP)** framework, stands out as a powerful tool for this purpose. A significant focus will be on learning how to construct and manage distributed OTP applications, alongside gaining insights into handling network partitions and system failures. Moreover, we intend to bring these concepts to life with practical implementations and real-world case studies. This exploration is designed not only to impart theoretical knowledge but also to equip you with the practical skills necessary for designing and operating distributed systems in Elixir.

# Understanding distributed systems

Distributed systems operate as coordinated networks of independent computing units, each executing specific tasks while collectively contributing to a unified objective. These systems enable seamless collaboration between multiple machines, ensuring efficiency, scalability, and fault tolerance. At their core, distributed systems are designed to function cohesively, with each component communicating and synchronizing operations to maintain overall system integrity. Understanding the mechanisms that drive these systems is essential to developing reliable, high-performance applications capable of handling complex workloads across multiple nodes.

The following are some key characteristics that define the world of distributed computing:

- **Concurrency and parallelism**: Distributed systems enable multiple processes to run simultaneously across different machines, efficiently handling tasks in parallel. This approach improves performance, supports heavier workloads, and ensures system resilience by maintaining operations even if one process fails.

- **Resource sharing:** Distributed systems optimize resource utilization by allowing shared access to storage, data, and computing power. This minimizes redundancy and ensures that critical information and resources remain readily available to all connected nodes, enhancing overall efficiency.

- **Scalability**: These systems are designed to accommodate increasing workloads by dynamically adding more nodes as demand grows. This adaptability allows for seamless expansion, ensuring that the system can efficiently handle varying levels of user traffic and data processing requirements.

- **Fault tolerance**: Failures, such as hardware crashes or network disruptions, are inevitable in distributed environments. However, fault tolerance mechanisms enable automatic process monitoring, restarts, and failover strategies, ensuring continuous operation and minimizing system downtime.

- **Transparency**: A well-architected distributed system conceals its internal complexities from end-users, presenting itself as a unified entity. The intricate network of interconnected nodes, processes, and communication protocols operates seamlessly in the background, providing users with a smooth and uninterrupted experience.

- **Heterogeneity**: Distributed systems support diverse hardware, software, and network configurations. This flexibility enables different nodes to perform specialized tasks while maintaining interoperability. By leveraging heterogeneous components, these systems achieve optimal resource allocation and efficiency.

- **Security**: Robust security measures, including encryption, access control, and authentication protocols, are essential in distributed systems to safeguard sensitive data and prevent unauthorized access. These mechanisms ensure data integrity, confidentiality, and protection against potential threats.

- **Complexity**: Designing and maintaining distributed systems involves significant complexity due to the need for process coordination, reliable communication, and data consistency across multiple nodes. Effective planning, rigorous testing, and strategic architectural decisions are required to manage these challenges and ensure seamless operation.

Distributed systems play a critical role in modern computing by enabling collaboration, resilience, and scalability. Understanding their core characteristics provides valuable insight into how these systems function and the challenges they address. While distributed computing introduces complexities, its benefits in efficiency, fault tolerance, and adaptability make it indispensable in today's digital landscape.

# Elixir for distributed systems

Elixir, known for its functional design and expressive syntax, demonstrates its true potential in the realm of distributed systems. This chapter explores how Elixir's specialized features enable developers to build resilient and scalable applications capable of meeting the demands of complex, distributed environments.

In the following sections, we examine Elixir's distinguishing traits such as concurrency, fault tolerance, message passing, immutability, OTP, distribution, and best practices, each of which contributes to overcoming the challenges inherent in distributed computing:

- **Built for concurrency**: Elixir's concurrency model is rooted in the Erlang Virtual Machine (BEAM), renowned for efficiently handling lightweight processes. These processes run concurrently with minimal overhead, facilitating the execution of numerous asynchronous operations. This architecture is particularly advantageous in distributed systems that require robust parallel processing and rapid state updates.

- **Fault tolerance**: Resilience in the face of failure. Elixir employs supervision trees to monitor processes and automatically restart them when crashes occur. By quickly isolating failures and recovering from them, Elixir minimizes downtime and prevents localized issues from escalating into system-wide breakdowns. This fault-tolerant approach ensures the application remains operational and dependable under adverse conditions.

- **Message passing**: Streamlined communication. Instead of sharing mutable state directly, Elixir processes communicate through asynchronous message passing. This design eliminates many of the synchronization issues common in concurrent environments, as no two processes operate on the same shared data. Clear boundaries and explicit messaging facilitate more predictable behavior and simplify the implementation of distributed system features.

- **Immutable data**: Consistent and predictable operations. Immutability in Elixir ensures that data cannot be altered after creation. Functions produce new data structures rather than modifying existing ones, reducing the risk of unexpected changes and data corruption. This principle is particularly critical in distributed contexts where simultaneous updates and complex interactions can easily lead to inconsistent states in mutable systems.

- **OTP**: Comprehensive tools for distributed applications. OTP provides a suite of libraries and frameworks that streamline the development of fault-tolerant and highly available applications. Components such as GenServers, supervision trees, and state machines form the backbone of robust Elixir services, while OTP's design encourages best practices that address the complexity of managing distributed tasks and states.

- **Clustered Erlang distribution protocol (Cerd)**: Expanding capacity, Elixir supports horizontal scalability through the clustered Erlang distribution protocol. By enabling processes to run seamlessly across multiple nodes, applications can dynamically adjust to growing workloads or user demands. This distributed approach allows organizations to expand capacity by simply adding additional nodes to the cluster.

- **Challenges and best practices**: Despite Elixir's strong concurrency and fault tolerance, distributed systems still face challenges such as network partitions and synchronization overhead. Strategies like leader-based consensus algorithms, partition-tolerant design, and eventual consistency can mitigate these issues. Proactive monitoring and thorough testing are also essential to maintain system stability and integrity in the face of unpredictable network conditions.

- **Building resilient, scalable applications**: Overall, Elixir provides a powerful set of tools and methodologies for constructing distributed systems that can handle complex communication patterns, maintain high availability, and recover gracefully from failures. By leveraging concurrency, immutability, OTP frameworks, and careful architectural choices, developers can create systems that deliver consistent performance and reliability even under growing demands. While network partitions and other challenges remain, Elixir's capabilities, combined with strategic design and continuous monitoring, enable the development of robust, scalable services that excel in modern distributed environments.

# Distributed Open Telecom Platform applications

In Elixir, the OTP provides a foundational framework for building fault-tolerant, distributed applications. OTP's structures and design principles, including GenServers, Supervisors, and Applications, offer a structured approach to concurrency and resilience. When creating distributed OTP applications, each node in the system can host various supervised processes, ensuring that failures remain isolated and that affected processes are automatically restarted. By deploying these supervised processes across multiple nodes, developers can distribute workloads effectively, maintain service availability, and scale the application as user demands grow.

The following are the key points:

- **GenServers**: Abstract stateful processes, providing a clean interface for sending and handling messages.

- **Supervisors**: Monitor worker processes, restarting them based on pre-defined strategies if failures occur.

- **Applications**: Serve as the entry point for starting supervision trees and overall application configuration in a distributed environment.

# Handling network partitions and failures

In distributed systems, network partitions and failures are not just possible; they are practically inevitable. Network partitions arise when communication between nodes is disrupted, leaving parts of the system unable to exchange data. Failures may involve anything from temporary process malfunctions to permanent hardware breakdowns. Elixir, running on the Erlang VM (BEAM), provides a set of robust tools and design patterns that enable developers to build resilient systems capable of enduring these disruptions with minimal impact on availability and data integrity.

## Nature and causes of network partitions

A network partition occurs when the network infrastructure fails to deliver messages between subsets of nodes. Possible causes include:

- **Hardware malfunctions**: Broken routers, switches, or damaged network cables.

- **Software issues**: Bugs within networking protocols, misconfigurations, or driver problems.

- **Temporary overloads**: High traffic causing packet loss or timeouts.

- **External events**: Power failures, natural disasters, or other unforeseen disruptions.

When nodes in a distributed system lose connectivity, they may continue to operate independently, leading to potential data conflicts or inconsistencies. Handling partitions effectively requires strategies to detect, mitigate, and recover from these communication breakdowns.

# Fault tolerance in Elixir

Building robust and resilient applications goes beyond simply handling everyday traffic; it also involves preparing for unexpected crashes, network disruptions, and unforeseen performance bottlenecks. The following are some mechanisms provided by Elixir that help ensure your system continues to run smoothly, even in the face of errors and failures:

- **Lightweight processes**: Elixir processes are designed to be isolated and inexpensive. This architecture ensures that failures within individual processes do not necessarily affect the entire node. When paired with supervision trees, processes can be quickly restarted without causing a cascade of failures.

- **Supervision trees**: A key feature inherited from Erlang/OTP, supervision trees monitor and manage processes. If a process fails, whether due to a crash or a network-induced exception, the supervisor determines the recovery strategy, such as restarting the process or escalating the failure. This design confines issues, preventing a localized failure from spreading throughout the system.

- **Message passing model**: Elixir's processes communicate solely through asynchronous message passing, eliminating the need for shared mutable state. This design prevents many concurrency conflicts and allows each process to continue running even when other parts of the system are temporarily unreachable.

# Strategies for handling network partitions

The following are several approaches you can adopt to detect, manage, and recover from network partitions in Elixir-based systems. Each point includes a brief explanation to clarify its significance:

- **Detection and monitoring**: Ensuring data integrity and availability during partitions often involves strategic replication and consistency decisions, balancing performance against the possibility of temporary inconsistency:
  - **Heartbeats and timers**: Processes or nodes regularly send heartbeat messages to detect failures. If a heartbeat is not received within a specified timeframe, the application can assume that a node is unreachable.

- **Node discovery tools**: Libraries such as libcluster can be configured to check node availability and update cluster membership automatically.

- **Graceful degradation**: When certain nodes or services become unavailable, gracefully reducing functionality helps the rest of the system remain partially operational without a total shutdown:
  - **Reduced functionality**: If a node becomes unreachable, the system may downgrade to a subset of functionalities that can continue without that node's data.
  - **Fallback or circuit breakers**: Services might route requests to backup nodes or alternate services if the primary node is partitioned.

- **Data replication and consistency models:** Building redundancy into the architecture ensures that even if one node fails or becomes isolated, the overall system continues to function with minimal disruption:
  - **Eventual consistency**: Nodes temporarily store updates locally, reconciling data once the partition is resolved. This approach avoids blocking operations but may allow brief inconsistencies.
  - **Quorum-based writes**: Requiring a majority of nodes to confirm a write can maintain a higher level of consistency, though availability might be reduced during partitions.
  - **Conflict resolution**: When connectivity returns, reconciling divergent data may involve strategies like last write wins, manual merges, or more sophisticated consensus algorithms such as *Raft* or *Paxos*.

- **Resilience through redundancy**: Building redundancy into the architecture ensures that even if one node fails or becomes isolated, the overall system continues to function with minimal disruption:
  - **Replica nodes**: Hosting duplicate instances of critical processes or data across multiple nodes ensures that a failure in one part of the system does not result in downtime:
  - **Load balancing**: Distributing requests across multiple nodes can reduce the impact of any single node's failure.

- **Recovery and reconciliation**: After the partition is resolved or a failed node returns online, the system must synchronize data and restore full functionality, often with minimal manual intervention:
  - **Automated restart**: OTP supervision automatically restarts failed processes, returning them to a stable state.

o **Data synchronization**: Once the partition is resolved, nodes synchronize their data. This can involve conflict resolution logic if updates were made on both sides during the downtime.

# Node liveness and heartbeat management

In distributed computing, especially when using Elixir, understanding how each node (an individual server or machine participating in your system) is managed and monitored is critical. A fundamental concept in managing distributed nodes is determining which nodes are operational and reachable; this is known as **node liveness**.

Elixir relies on Erlang's built-in distribution system, commonly referred to as the **Erlang distribution protocol (EDP)**.

# Erlang distribution protocol

The Erlang distribution protocol enables multiple Erlang (and thus Elixir) nodes to connect and communicate seamlessly, allowing them to behave as a single cohesive unit. EDP handles:

- **Node discovery**: Identifying new nodes joining the cluster.
- **Node communication**: Sending messages and commands between nodes.
- **Node monitoring (Liveness)**: Continuously checking if nodes are alive and responsive.

## Working of node liveness monitoring

Node liveness monitoring involves each node regularly sending small, periodic signals called **heartbeats** to its connected peers. Think of heartbeats as simple: *Are you alive?* Messages are exchanged frequently to ensure all nodes remain responsive:

- **Heartbeat frequency**: By default, Erlang nodes send heartbeat messages approximately every **15 seconds**. This timing is determined by a configuration setting called **net_ticktime**. The default value of **net_ticktime** is 60 seconds, and heartbeats occur every quarter of this interval (thus, every 15 seconds).

- **Detecting failures**: If a node misses **four consecutive heartbeat signals** (meaning it has not responded for around 60 seconds under default settings), the node is considered down or unreachable. At this point, the system generates a special message called {:nodedown, node} to notify other processes within the system about the node's status.

## Setting heartbeat frequency in Elixir

To configure the heartbeat frequency in an Elixir application, you typically set the **net_ticktime** value in the VM arguments or configuration files:

- **Using VM arguments**: Create or modify a file such as vm.args:

1. `-name node@host`
2. `-setcookie mycookie`
3. `-kernel net_ticktime 120`

This sets the heartbeat interval to 120 seconds, thus heartbeats occur every 30 seconds (a quarter of the **net_ticktime** value).

- **Using Mix configuration**: You can configure your Elixir application's heartbeat frequency in the configuration files as follows:

  1. `config :kernel, net_ticktime: 120`

Adjust the **net_ticktime** value based on your network environment, balancing rapid node detection with network overhead considerations.

Imagine a distributed Elixir system with three nodes: Node A, Node B, and Node C. Each node sends heartbeat messages to the others regularly:

- If Node B stops responding (due to network issues or hardware failure), after approximately 60 seconds (assuming the default settings), Nodes A and C both independently conclude that Node B is down.

- Processes running on Node A or Node C can then respond to this event, for example, by redistributing Node B's tasks to ensure minimal disruption.

The following are the limitations and practical considerations:

- **Balance between frequency and load**:

  - Frequent heartbeats provide quick failure detection but increase network overhead.

  - Less frequent heartbeats reduce network traffic but delay failure detection.

- **Split-brain scenarios**: EDP alone does not fully prevent *split-brain* issues (where two groups of nodes mistakenly operate independently). Additional libraries like **libcluster** or **Partisan** can help manage more robust node membership and avoid inconsistencies.

- **Scalability concerns**:

  - For systems with numerous nodes (hundreds or thousands), EDP's heartbeat mechanism alone might become inefficient.

  - Specialized libraries or advanced strategies (such as gossip protocols or quorum-based systems) are recommended to efficiently manage large clusters.

# Extending node management with libcluster

Elixir developers often use additional tools like **libcluster** to improve cluster management. libcluster helps nodes discover each other dynamically and maintain an accurate view of node membership through enhanced heartbeat strategies and automatic reconnection logic.

In summary, understanding node liveness through heartbeat management is essential for building reliable and robust distributed Elixir applications. Configuring heartbeat intervals carefully and considering advanced clustering tools like libcluster enables efficient node management and improved fault tolerance in your distributed systems.

# Practical considerations

When building reliable distributed systems, it is essential to go beyond architectural principles and focus on how those ideas translate into day-to-day operational choices and strategies. In the following are some key aspects of system performance, testing, and teamwork that can help your Elixir applications gracefully handle network partitions and other unpredictable conditions:

- **Performance versus consistency**: The **consistency, availability, partition tolerance (CAP)** theorem reminds us that in the presence of a network partition, a system must choose between strict consistency and continued availability. Elixir's concurrency features can facilitate both approaches, but developers must carefully weigh trade-offs.

- **Testing partition scenarios**: It is crucial to test how the system behaves under simulated partitions. Tools that introduce network latency or drop connections can validate whether the system's partition-handling logic performs as expected.

- **Monitoring and alerting**: Integrating monitoring solutions (such as Grafana, Prometheus, or ELK stack) allows developers to track node health, process uptime, and network usage. Alerting mechanisms can promptly notify operators of node outages or abnormally high error rates.

- **Documentation and collaboration**: Clearly documenting failure-handling strategies ensures that every team member understands recovery procedures. Consistent communication among team members and cross-training on distributed systems principles also reduces the risk of misconfiguration or oversight.

Network partitions and failures are unavoidable in distributed systems, but Elixir's design, from lightweight processes and supervision trees to robust message passing, minimizes their impact. By proactively detecting disruptions, employing resilient architectures, and carefully balancing consistency with availability, developers can build systems that continue operating reliably under adverse conditions. Through thorough testing and iterative refinement, Elixir-based applications can achieve high levels of fault tolerance and deliver stable services despite the uncertainties inherent in any distributed environment.

# Conclusion

As we conclude this chapter on distributed systems with Elixir, we have explored how Elixir's robust features and the Erlang VM's capabilities address the inherent complexities of distributed computing. From concurrency management with lightweight processes to fault tolerance via supervision trees, Elixir stands out not just as a language, but as an ecosystem well-suited for modern, distributed applications.

Our practical examples and the exploration of GenServer and libcluster provided hands-on insights into implementing and managing distributed services. We observed how Elixir's environment simplifies development and operations, making it accessible even to those new to the concept of distributed computing. In essence, this chapter is a stepping stone to more advanced distributed designs, whether for building highly available web applications, large-scale data processing systems, or real-time communication platforms. Elixir offers the tools and paradigms to bring these visions to life, efficiently and reliably.

In the next chapter, we will discuss the Elixir build tool, Mix. You will learn how Mix facilitates project creation, compilation, and dependency management. We will also explore ExUnit for testing your Elixir code, along with debugging tools that help identify and resolve issues in your projects. This set of essential skills will further equip you to develop high-quality, maintainable Elixir applications.

# Practical exercises

Demonstrating how Elixir works in a distributed environment can be quite insightful. A practical way to do this is by showing a simple distributed application using GenServer and libcluster.

This example will illustrate how Elixir nodes can discover each other and communicate in a distributed setting:

1. **Setting up the project**: To get started, we first need to set up a new Elixir project that will serve as our distributed application:

    a.  Create a new Elixir project:
    ```
    mix new my_distributed_app --sup
    ```

    b.  Change into the project directory:
    ```
    cd my_distributed_app
    ```

    c.  Add libcluster to your dependencies in mix.exs:
    ```
    defp deps do
      [
        {:libcluster, "~> 3.3"}
      ]
    end
    ```

d.  Run mix deps.get to fetch the new dependency.

2.  **Implementing a distributed GenServer:** Create a simple GenServer that holds and modifies a state, such as a counter.

Create a GenServer module (**lib/counter.ex**):

```
01. defmodule MyDistributedApp.Counter do
02.   use GenServer
03.
04.   def start_link(_) do
05.     GenServer.start_link(__MODULE__, 0, name: {:global, __MODULE__})
06.   end
07.
08.   def increment do
09.     GenServer.cast({:global, __MODULE__}, :increment)
10.   end
11.
12.   def get_count do
13.     GenServer.call({:global, __MODULE__}, :get_count)
14.   end
15.
16.   @impl true
17.   def init(initial_count), do: {:ok, initial_count}
18.
19.   @impl true
20.   def handle_cast(:increment, count) do
21.     {:noreply, count + 1}
22.   end
23.
24.   @impl true
25.   def handle_call(:get_count, _from, count) do
26.     {:reply, count, count}
27.   end
28. end
```

**3.** **Configuring libcluster for node discovery:** Set up libcluster for automatic node discovery in your application:

    a.  Configure **libcluster** in **config/config.exs**:

```
01.    import Config
02.
03.    config :libcluster,
04.      topologies: [
05.        example: [
06.          strategy: Cluster.Strategy.Epmd,
07.          config: [
08.            # Make sure these hostnames match how you name or
      sname your nodes
09.            hosts: [:"node1@127.0.0.1", :"node2@127.0.0.1"]
10.          ]
11.        ]
12.      ]
```

    b.  Start libcluster in your application start function (**lib/my_distributed_app/application.ex**):

```
01.    defmodule MyDistributedApp.Application do
02.      use Application
03.
04.      def start(_type, _args) do
05.        children = [
06.          # Start the cluster supervisor
07.          {Cluster.Supervisor, [topologies(), [name:
      MyDistributedApp.ClusterSupervisor]]},
08.          # Start a GenServer, for example:
09.          MyDistributedApp.Counter
10.        ]
11.
12.        opts = [strategy: :one_for_one, name: MyDistributedApp.
      Supervisor]
13.        Supervisor.start_link(children, opts)
14.      end
```

```
15.
16.    defp topologies do
17.        Application.get_env(:libcluster, :topologies) || []
18.    end
19.  end
```

4. **Running the distributed application**: Now that everything is set up, we can test the distributed nature of our Elixir application:

   a. **Start multiple nodes**: Open two terminal windows or tabs. In each, navigate to your project directory.

   b. **Run the first node**:

   ```
   1. iex --name node1@127.0.0.1 -S mix
   ```

   c. **Run the second node**:

   ```
   1. iex --name node2@127.0.0.1 -S mix
   ```

   d. **Test the distributed counter**: On node1, run:

   ```
   1. MyDistributedApp.Counter.increment()
   ```

   On node2, run:

   ```
   1. MyDistributedApp.Counter.get_count()
   ```

   You should see the updated count, indicating that the state is shared across the nodes.

This setup demonstrates a basic distributed Elixir application using GenServer and libcluster. The libcluster library facilitates the discovery and connection of different nodes, allowing them to communicate and share state. This example can serve as a foundational model for understanding how distributed systems can be built and managed in Elixir.

# Points to remember

When building and maintaining distributed systems, developers often face a range of challenges, from coordinating multiple processes to handling network partitions and ensuring fault tolerance. The following outlines some common hurdles and how Elixir's unique features and philosophies help overcome them:

- **Concurrency and parallelism:**
  o **Challenge**: Managing concurrent operations and parallel processing efficiently across multiple nodes can be complex and error-prone.

- o **Elixir's solution**:

  - **Lightweight processes**: Elixir uses lightweight processes managed by the BEAM (Erlang VM) that can handle millions of concurrent processes with minimal overhead.

  - **Message passing**: Communication between processes is done through message passing, which avoids shared-state issues and simplifies concurrent programming.

- **Fault tolerance:**

  - o **Challenge**: Ensuring the system remains operational even when parts of it fail.

  - o **Elixir's solution**:

    - **Supervision trees**: Elixir has built-in constructs for fault tolerance, most notably supervision trees, which automatically restart failed processes based on predefined strategies.

    - **Let it crash philosophy**: Elixir encourages a design approach where processes are allowed to fail and restart gracefully, rather than trying to catch and handle every exception.

- **Scalability:**

  - o **Challenge**: Effectively scaling the system to handle increased load without significant reconfiguration or downtime.

  - o **Elixir's solution**:

    - **Distribution transparency**: Elixir facilitates the distribution of tasks across multiple nodes with minimal changes to the codebase, making scaling more straightforward.

    - **Load balancing**: The ability to spawn numerous processes allows for effective load distribution and balancing across the system.

- **Network partitions and communication:**

  - o **Challenge**: Handling network partitions and ensuring reliable communication in a distributed environment.

  - o **Elixir's solution**:

    - **Resilient communication**: Elixir's message-passing model is inherently resilient. Messages are queued when a process is unavailable, ensuring delivery once the process or node is back online.

    - **Cluster management**: Tools like libcluster aid in managing clusters of Elixir nodes, handling node discovery and automatic reformation of clusters after partitions.

- **Data consistency:**
  - o **Challenge**: Maintaining data consistency across multiple nodes, especially in the face of network partitions or concurrent updates.
  - o **Elixir's solution**:
    - ▪ **Mnesia database**: Elixir can leverage Mnesia, a distributed database built into Erlang, designed to handle data replication and consistency across nodes.
    - ▪ **Conflict resolution**: Elixir's functional nature and process isolation help in implementing conflict resolution logic effectively.
- **System maintenance and upgrades:**
  - o **Challenge**: Updating and maintaining the system without causing downtime or service interruptions.
  - o **Elixir's solution**:
    - o **Hot code swapping**: The Erlang VM, on which Elixir runs, supports hot code swapping, allowing updates to be made on the fly without stopping the system.
    - o **Immutable data**: Elixir's immutable data structures prevent side effects during updates, making maintenance tasks less risky.

# Join our Discord space

Join our Discord workspace for latest updates, offers, tech happenings around the world, new releases, and sessions with the authors:

https://discord.bpbonline.com

# CHAPTER 6

# Mix Tooling, Testing, and Debugging in Elixir

## Introduction

Elixir is a dynamic, functional language designed for building scalable and maintainable applications and offers a rich set of tools for developers to enhance productivity and ensure code quality. In this chapter, we will understand the world of Mix, Elixir's build tool, and explore its capabilities in project management, compilation, and testing. We will also explore how to leverage ExUnit for testing and the various debugging tools at your disposal. By mastering these tools, you will be well-equipped to build robust, error-free applications in Elixir.

## Structure

This chapter will cover the following topics:

- Mix overview and benefits
- Managing dependencies with Mix
- Generating documentation with Mix
- Testing with ExUnit
- Debugging tools in Elixir
- Best practices for debugging in Elixir

# Objectives

The primary goal of this chapter is to provide you with a comprehensive understanding of Mix tooling, testing with ExUnit, and debugging in Elixir. By the end of this chapter, you should be able to effectively utilize Mix for various development tasks, write and manage tests using ExUnit, and employ effective debugging strategies to maintain high-quality, reliable Elixir applications. Whether you are a beginner or an experienced Elixir developer, this chapter aims to enhance your skills and knowledge, making your development process more efficient and your applications more robust.

# Mix overview and benefits

Developing an Elixir application can be compared to a strategic process where efficiency and organization play a crucial role. While you focus on implementing innovative ideas, a reliable tool is required to manage essential but repetitive tasks. This is where Mix comes in. Mix is Elixir's built-in build tool and task runner, integral to managing the life-cycle of your projects. It is an essential part of the Elixir ecosystem, combining project compilation, dependency management, running tests, task automation, and more. Think of Mix as your project's manager; it keeps track of tasks and resources, ensuring everything runs smoothly and consistently.

The following are the works of Mix:

- **Manages dependencies efficiently**: Mix helps identify, retrieve, and maintain the necessary tools and libraries for your project, ensuring they remain up to date.

- **Builds and compiles your application**: Once all dependencies are in place, Mix compiles your code and transforms it into a functional Elixir application.

- **Facilitates robust testing**: Mistakes are inevitable, but Mix streamlines the testing process through seamless integration with ExUnit, ensuring code reliability.

- **Generates comprehensive documentation**: Mix enables the creation of clear and structured documentation, making it easier for others to understand and contribute to your project.

- **Automates repetitive tasks**: With the ability to execute custom scripts, Mix automates mundane development tasks, allowing developers to focus on core functionality.

The following are the reasons to Mix essentials:

- **Enhances developer productivity**: By automating tedious tasks, Mix allows developers to dedicate more time to writing efficient and high-quality Elixir code.

- **Ensures project consistency**: Mix organizes dependencies and development tools, ensuring that all team members work within a unified and stable environment.

- **Accelerates development workflow**: Experimenting with new features and ideas becomes more efficient, enabling rapid iterations and testing.

- **Supports high-quality applications**: With built-in tools for testing, documentation, and project management, Mix helps create well-structured, maintainable, and production-ready applications.

Let us discuss the harnessing power of Mix. Mix is more than just a build tool; it is an essential companion in Elixir development. By leveraging its capabilities, you can streamline your workflow, build robust applications, and refine your expertise in Elixir. With Mix as an integral part of your development process, you can efficiently manage projects, automate tasks, and ensure high-quality code, ultimately enhancing your proficiency as an Elixir developer.

# Managing dependencies with Mix

Managing dependencies is a crucial aspect of Elixir development, ensuring that external libraries are seamlessly integrated and properly maintained within a project. Mix provides a structured approach to handling dependencies, allowing developers to declare, fetch, update, and clean dependencies efficiently. Follow the given steps to build a simple Elixir app:

1. **Declaring dependencies**: To include an external library in an Elixir project, it must be specified in the **mix.exs** file. For instance, if an application requires an email-sending library, the dependency is declared as follows:

   ```
   1. def deps do
   2.   [{:phoenix_mailer, "~> 3.3.0"}]
   3. end
   ```

   This informs Mix to locate and install the **phoenix_mailer** library, ensuring it is compatible with version **3.3.0** or later.

2. **Fetching dependencies**: Run **mix deps.get** to fetch the library and all its dependencies. Mix stores them in a special folder, keeping your project organized.

3. **Utilizing dependencies**: After installation, the functions provided by the dependency become available for use within the project. For instance, the **phoenix_mailer** library can now be used to send emails, attach documents, and perform related tasks.

4. **Managing and updating dependencies**: As your app grows, you might need other libraries. Mix lets you add and update them easily in **mix.exs**, ensuring everything stays compatible and organized.

Let us expand on some of those Mix commands that help keep your dependencies organized and up-to-date:

- **mix deps.update:** This updates specific dependencies to their latest compatible versions:
  - o **Basic usage:** `mix deps.update [dependency_name]` (for example, `mix deps.update phoenix_mailer`)
  - o **Updating all:** `mix deps.update all` updates all the dependencies in your **mix.exs** file.
  - o **Safe updates:** Use `mix deps.update patch` or `minor` to update only patch or minor versions, minimizing potential breaking changes.
- **mix deps.unlock:** This unlocks dependencies, allowing you to update them before re-locking:
  - o **Usage:** `mix deps.unlock`
- **mix deps.clean:** This removes downloaded dependencies and archives, potentially freeing up disk space:
  - o **Caution:** Use with care, as it requires re-downloading everything later.

# Generating documentation with Mix

Good documentation is vital for the maintainability and understandability of software projects. In Elixir, Mix offers a powerful tool for generating documentation directly from the codebase. This functionality is primarily provided through ExDoc, a tool that creates beautiful, readable, and searchable documentation for Elixir projects.

Mix generates documentation by:

- **ExDoc integration:** ExDoc is seamlessly integrated with Mix. It works by parsing inline documentation and code annotations to produce comprehensive and navigable HTML documentation.

- **Setting up ExDoc:** To use ExDoc, you need to add it as a dependency in your mix.exs file. This is typically done under the :dev environment since you only need it during development.

- **Writing documentation comments:** Elixir has first-class support for inline documentation. The documentation for functions is written directly above the function using Elixir's docstring syntax.

# Practical example of generating documentation

Let us go through a step-by-step example of adding ExDoc to your project and generating documentation:

1. **Adding ExDoc dependency:** Open your **mix.exs** file and add ExDoc to your dependencies:

```
1. defp deps do
2.   [
3.     {:ex_doc, "~> 0.25", only: :dev, runtime: false}
4.   ]
5. end
```

Here, **{:ex_doc, "~> 0.25", only: :dev, runtime: false}** tells Mix to use ExDoc version compatible with **0.25**, but only in the development environment.

2. **Fetching and compiling ExDoc**: Run the following in your terminal:

```
1. mix deps.get
2. mix deps.compile
```

This will download and compile ExDoc.

3. **Writing documentation**: Add documentation to your functions using docstrings. For example:

```
1. defmodule MyModule do
2.   @doc """
3.   Adds two numbers.
4.
5.   ## Examples
6.
7.       iex> MyModule.add(2, 3)
8.       5
9.   """
10.  def add(a, b), do: a + b
11. End
```

4. **Generating documentation**: Run the following command:

```
1. mix docs
```

This will generate HTML documentation for your project in the **doc/** directory.

5. **Viewing the documentation**: Open the **doc/index.html** file in a web browser to view your project's documentation.

By integrating ExDoc with Mix, Elixir makes it straightforward to generate detailed and user-friendly documentation for your projects. This approach not only helps in maintaining the code but also ensures that other developers, or even a future you, can quickly understand and use your modules and functions. Good documentation is a hallmark of a mature, maintainable project, and Mix, in tandem with ExDoc, provides an excellent platform for achieving this.

# Testing with ExUnit

ExUnit is the test framework that ships with Elixir, designed specifically for testing Elixir code. It is a feature-rich framework that makes it easy to write and organize tests for your Elixir projects. With ExUnit, you can write unit tests, integration tests, and even perform **test-driven development (TDD)**.

The key features of ExUnit include:

- **Simple test syntax**: ExUnit tests are Elixir scripts, making them easy to write and understand. Tests are defined within test blocks.

- **Setup blocks**: It provides setup blocks to prepare the test context, allowing common setup tasks to be executed before each test or once before all tests.

- **Assertions**: ExUnit comes with various assertions to check different conditions in your tests.

- **Test tags and exclusions**: You can tag tests and use these tags to include or exclude certain tests from the test run.

- **Async testing**: ExUnit supports running tests asynchronously to speed up the test suite.

Consider a hypothetical Elixir module named **MyCalculator**, which implements various arithmetic functions. The following sections demonstrate how this module works and how it can be tested using ExUnit.

# MyCalculator module

The **MyCalculator** module defines basic arithmetic operations such as addition, subtraction, and division. It also includes functionality for handling division by zero and printing a welcome message. Follow the codes:

```
1. defmodule MyCalculator do
2.    def add(a, b), do: a + b
3.    def subtract(a, b), do: a - b
4.    def divide(a, 0), do: {:error, "Cannot divide by zero"}
5.    def divide(a, b), do: a / b
6.    def print_welcome_message(), do: IO.puts "Welcome to MyCalculator!"
7. end
```

# MyCalculatorTest module

The **MyCalculatorTest** module is responsible for verifying the correctness of the **MyCalculator** module. It demonstrates several ExUnit functionalities, including assertions, setup blocks, grouped test cases, and capturing IO output. Follow the commands:

```
01. defmodule MyCalculatorTest do
02.   use ExUnit.Case, async: true
03.
04.   # Setup block for shared context
05.   setup do
06.     {:ok, base_number: 10}
07.   end
08.
09.   # Grouping tests with describe
10.   describe "Arithmetic functions" do
11.     test "add/2 function", context do
12.       assert MyCalculator.add(context[:base_number], 5) == 15
13.     end
14.
15.     test "subtract/2 function", context do
16.       assert MyCalculator.subtract(context[:base_number], 5) == 5
17.     end
18.
19.     test "divide/2 function with zero", context do
20.       assert_raise RuntimeError, "Cannot divide by zero", fn ->
21.         MyCalculator.divide(context[:base_number], 0)
22.       end
23.     end
24.
25.     test "divide/2 function" do
26.       assert {:ok, result} = {:ok, MyCalculator.divide(10, 2)}
27.       assert result == 5
28.     end
29.   end
30.
```

```
31.    # Testing IO output
32.    test "print_welcome_message/0 outputs correct message" do
33.      assert capture_io(fn -> MyCalculator.print_welcome_message() end) ==
       "Welcome to MyCalculator!\n"
34.    end
35. end
```

A detailed explanation of functions is as follows:

- **async: true**: This enables tests to run concurrently, improving test suite performance. It is particularly useful for independent tests.

- **setup**: Here, we set up a shared context for our tests. The **base_number** is made available to each test, demonstrating how you can prepare common data for multiple tests.

- **describe**: This block groups related tests, in this case, arithmetic functions. It helps to organize tests logically.

- **test with context**: Within each test block, we assert the behavior of our functions. The context variable, originating from the setup block, provides shared data (**base_number**).

- **assert_raise**: This assertion checks if a specific exception is raised. Here, it is used to ensure **divide/2** raises an error when dividing by zero.

- **assert with pattern matching**: We use pattern matching in our assert statement to both destructure a tuple and assert its values. This demonstrates the power of Elixir's pattern matching in testing.

- **capture_io**: This is used to test functions that output to the console. We capture the IO output of **print_welcome_message** and assert it is what we expect.

Testing is a crucial aspect of software development, and ExUnit provides a robust, easy-to-use framework for writing tests in Elixir. By leveraging its features, such as setup blocks, assertions, and async testing, you can ensure your Elixir code is reliable, bug-free, and maintainable. Whether you are doing TDD or simply writing tests for existing code, ExUnit is an invaluable tool in the Elixir developer's toolkit.

# Debugging tools in Elixir

Debugging is a crucial part of the software development process, and Elixir provides a variety of tools to help identify and fix bugs in your code. Understanding and effectively using these tools can significantly enhance your productivity and improve the reliability of your applications.

The key debugging tools in Elixir are listed as follows:

- **Interactive Elixir (IEx):**
  - o **Description**: IEx is Elixir's interactive shell, which can be extremely helpful for debugging. It allows you to run Elixir code in a live, interactive environment and is great for experimenting with code snippets, testing functions, and exploring libraries.
  - o **Usage**: Start IEx in the context of your project by running:

    ```
    1. iex -S mix
    ```

In your project directory, this loads your project and its dependencies, allowing you to interact directly with your project's modules and functions.

- **IO.inspect:**
  - o **Description**: `IO.inspect` is a simple yet powerful tool for debugging. It prints the value of the variable or expression passed to it, without affecting the program's flow.
  - o **Usage**: **Place `IO.inspect(variable)`** in your code where you want to check the value of the variable. It is especially useful for inspecting values in a pipeline, e.g:

    ```
    1. Users
    2. |> Enum.map(& &1.age)
    3. |> IO.inspect(label: "Ages")
    4. |> Enum.sum()
    ```

- **dbg():**
  - o **Description**: Introduced in Elixir 1.13, **dbg/1** is a built-in macro that prints both the expression and its resulting value, along with file and line number, without interrupting execution. It returns the original value, making it perfect for inline debugging.
  - o **Usage**: Insert **dbg(expr)** anywhere in your code or pipeline. For example:

    ```
    1. Users
    2. |> Enum.filter(&(&1.active))
    3. |> dbg(label: "Active users")
    4. |> Enum.count()
    ```

- **Logger module:**
  - o **Description**: Elixir's **Logger** module provides a way to output structured debugging information. It supports multiple log levels (such as **:debug**, **:info**, **:warn**, **:error**) and is configurable to suit various environments.

    o   **Usage**: Add log statements like:

```
1. require Logger
2.
3. Logger.debug("Debug info: #{inspect(variable)}")
```

- **Mix tasks:**

    o   **Description**: Mix, Elixir's build tool, offers several tasks that can aid in debugging, such as mix xref for finding cross-references in code, and mix compile with flags for warnings and errors.

    o   **Usage**:

```
1. mix xref graph        # shows module/function dependency graph

2. mix compile --warnings-as-errors
```

- **The debugger (Erlang's Debugger):**

    o   **Description**: Elixir also has access to Erlang's graphical debugger, which can set breakpoints and step through code execution.

    o   **Usage**:

```
1. :debugger.start()

2. :int.ni(MyModule)

3. :int.break(MyModule, 42)   # set breakpoint at line 42
```

- **Observer tool:**

    o   **Description**: The Observer is a graphical tool that provides detailed information about your Erlang/Elixir system: process lists, applications, and metrics—ideal for performance debugging and system monitoring.

    o   **Usage**:

```
1. :observer.start()
2.
```

# Best practices for debugging in Elixir

Some best practices for debugging in Elixir are as follows:

- **Start simple**: Begin with **IO.inspect** and Logger statements to understand the problem.

- **Incremental testing**: Use IEx to test small parts of your code independently.

- **Use Mix tasks effectively**: Regularly use Mix tasks to identify and fix compilation and dependency issues.

- **Step-by-step debugging**: Use the graphical debugger for complex issues where you need to inspect the program's state at specific points.

- **Performance analysis**: Utilize the Observer tool for memory and performance-related issues, especially in a live system.

- **Logs analysis**: Regularly review logs for warnings, errors, or unusual patterns.

# Conclusion

This chapter has equipped you with an understanding of Mix tooling, managing dependencies, generating documentation, testing with ExUnit, and using various debugging tools in Elixir. These components are crucial in crafting efficient, reliable, and high-quality Elixir applications. By integrating these practices into your development workflow, you can enhance the quality of your code along with your productivity and problem-solving skills. Remember that effective development in Elixir is not just about writing code; it is about leveraging the ecosystem's tools to write better code. As you continue to explore and build with Elixir, keep experimenting with these tools and techniques to master the art of Elixir programming.

In the next chapter, we will explore Elixir's metaprogramming, an advanced feature that allows you to write code that can generate or modify other code dynamically. You will learn how macros work, the differences between compile-time and run-time execution, and how to manipulate Elixir's abstract syntax tree using quoting and unquoting. Mastering metaprogramming will enable you to write more expressive and flexible code, taking your Elixir expertise to the next level.

# Practical exercises

1. **Using Mix for a new project:**

    a. Create a new Elixir project with mix new practice_app.

    b. Explore the folder structure and identify the role of mix.exs.

    c. Add a simple module and run it using iex -S mix.

2. **Managing dependencies:**

    a. Add the jason dependency (for JSON handling) to your mix.exs.

    b. Run mix deps.get and confirm that the package has been fetched.

    c. Write a short script to encode and decode JSON using Jason.

3. **Generating documentation:**

    a. Add @moduledoc and @doc attributes to one of your modules and functions.

    b. Run mix docs to generate HTML documentation.

    c. Open the generated documentation in your browser and verify your annotations appear.

4. **Testing with ExUnit:**

    a. Create a new test file in test/practice_app_test.exs.

    b. Write a simple test for a function in your project (e.g., adding two numbers).

    c. Run mix test and check that your tests pass.

5. **Debugging with IEx and IO.inspect/2:**

    a. Write a function with a small bug (e.g., incorrectly summing a list).

    b. Use IO.inspect/2 inside the function to inspect intermediate values.

    c. Run the function in iex and trace the problem step by step.

# Points to remember

- **Mix tooling**: Mix is a powerful build tool in Elixir for project creation, compilation, and task automation. It streamlines the development process and enforces best practices.

- **Managing dependencies**: Utilize Mix for efficient dependency management. Remember to declare your dependencies in the mix.exs file and use mix deps.get and mix deps.compile to manage them.

- **Generating documentation**: Leverage ExDoc with Mix to generate comprehensive documentation. Ensure your code is well-documented to maintain readability and ease of use.

- **Testing with ExUnit**: Write tests using ExUnit to ensure your code works as expected. Utilize its features like setup blocks, describe groupings, and various assertions to write robust tests.

- **Debugging tools**: Familiarize yourself with debugging tools like IEx, IO.inspect, Logger, Mix tasks, Erlang's debugger, and the Observer tool for effective problem-solving.

- **Asynchronous testing**: Take advantage of ExUnit's async: true for faster test execution but use it judiciously to avoid issues with shared state.

- **Mocking and external services**: Use tools like Mox for mocking external services or APIs in your tests.

- **Performance analysis**: Use the Observer tool for in-depth performance analysis and to monitor system resources.

- **Regular code refactoring**: Regularly refactor your code to improve efficiency and maintainability. Use Mix tasks like mix xref to identify areas that need refactoring.

- **Continuous learning**: Elixir and its ecosystem are continuously evolving. Stay updated with the latest tools and practices for optimal development.

# CHAPTER 7
# Elixir Metaprogramming

## Introduction

Metaprogramming in Elixir is the process of writing code that can generate or transform other code at compile-time. This powerful feature enables you to extend the language's capabilities, reduce boilerplate, and create more expressive APIs. By learning metaprogramming, you gain the ability to harness Elixir's macro system for tasks ranging from code generation to **domain-specific language (DSL)** design.

This chapter will discuss the fundamental concepts of metaprogramming in Elixir, covering why metaprogramming is useful, what macros are, how compile-time logic differs from run-time logic, and how quoting or unquoting works under the hood.

## Structure

The following topics are discussed in the chapter:

- Metaprogramming
- Understanding macros
- Compile-time vs. run-time
- Quoting and unquoting

# Objectives

In this chapter, we aim to guide you through the core principles and techniques of Elixir's metaprogramming, empowering you to write code that can generate or transform other code. By exploring why metaprogramming is valuable, how macros operate at compile-time, and the mechanisms of quoting and unquoting, you will gain the ability to craft more elegant, flexible, and expressive Elixir applications. By the end of this chapter, you will not only understand the distinction between compile-time and run-time but also be capable of leveraging macros to eliminate boilerplate, create DSLs, and extend Elixir's functionality in powerful ways.

# Metaprogramming

Metaprogramming is the practice of writing code that can inspect, generate, or modify other code at compile-time. In Elixir, this is primarily done through macros, which allow you to shape the final compiled code in ways that normal functions cannot. While this might sound complicated at first, think of metaprogramming as a powerful tool that can save you from repetitive work and enable you to write more expressive, domain-specific code.

The following is a step-by-step explanation of why metaprogramming is valuable, especially for beginners:

1. **Eliminate boilerplate**: Boilerplate refers to repetitive code that does not vary much from one place to another. For instance, you might find yourself writing similar functions or patterns across multiple modules:

```
01. # Example of potential boilerplate in a Phoenix context
02. defmodule MyApp.Users do
03.   alias MyApp.User
04.
05.   def create_user(attrs) do
06.     # Some repetitive code
07.   end
08.
09.   def get_user(id) do
10.     # Some repetitive code
11.   end
12.
13.   def update_user(id, attrs) do
14.     # Some repetitive code
15.   end
16. End
```

If you have many modules like **Users**, **Products**, **Orders**, etc., you might repeat similar **create, read, update, delete** (**CRUD**) logic over and over.

By using a macro, you could write the logic for these CRUD operations once, then generate the module functions automatically. For example:

```
01. defmodule MyMacros do
02.   defmacro generate_crud_functions(schema) do
03.     quote do
04.       def create(unquote(schema), attrs) do
05.         # Insert into DB
06.       end
07.
08.       def get(unquote(schema), id) do
09.         # Get from DB
10.       end
11.
12.       def update(unquote(schema), id, attrs) do
13.         # Update DB
14.       end
15.
16.       def delete(unquote(schema), id) do
17.         # Delete from DB
18.       end
19.     end
20.   end
21. end
22.
23. defmodule MyApp.Users do
24.   import MyMacros
25.
26.   # This single macro call could replace 4 repeated functions
27.   generate_crud_functions(:users)
28. End
```

With this approach, you can avoid writing the same code multiple times, making your project easier to maintain and less error-prone.

2. **Create domain-specific languages**: A DSL is a special way of writing code that closely resembles the language of a particular domain or area of expertise. Instead of using generic Elixir functions, a DSL allows you to write code that feels more natural to the problem you are solving.

   For instance, if you are building a web framework, you might want to define routes like this:

   ```
   01. get "/", PageController, :index
   02. post "/signup", UserController, :create
   ```

   These look like simple lines, but under the hood, they might expand into complex Elixir functions and pattern matches. Thanks to metaprogramming, frameworks like Phoenix can provide a DSL that makes routing code much more readable and declarative.

   This DSL approach can also be used in other domains, such as:

   a. **Configuration**: Defining config rules in a project.

   b. **Testing**: Creating custom test assertions that read like English sentences.

   c. **Data modeling**: Specifying schema definitions in a concise and readable form.

3. **Extend language features**: Elixir has powerful base features, but sometimes you need to extend or tweak them to fit your application's needs. With metaprogramming:

   a. You can add new compile-time checks or behaviors.

   b. You can transform code before it is run, injecting additional functionality or validations.

   For example, if you wanted to enforce certain naming conventions in your code, you might write a macro that checks function names at compile-time and raises a warning or error if they do not follow a certain format.

4. **Gain compile-time guarantees**: When you use macros, the transformations happen at compile-time. This can bring several benefits:

   a. **Performance**: If you generate complex code at compile-time, you do not pay a performance penalty at run-time for building that code dynamically.

   b. **Early error detection**: Errors in macro-generated code often surface during compilation, saving you from discovering them later in production.

5. **Real-world framework examples**: Metaprogramming in Elixir is not just an academic exercise; it powers some of the most widely used frameworks and libraries in the ecosystem. By examining the following projects, you will see metaprogramming in action and understand how macros enable developers to write minimal, expressive code that accomplishes a great deal under the hood:

   a. **Phoenix**: Uses macros to define routing, controllers, channels, and more. Instead of manually wiring up everything, you write concise DSL-style code and let Phoenix generate the details behind the scenes.

   b. **Ecto**: The schema macro in Ecto transforms declarations of fields into functions and metadata that Elixir uses to perform database operations.

   c. **ExUnit**: Elixir's testing framework uses macros to define test blocks (test **description** do end) that transform your test code into the structures needed to run them.

By examining these projects, you will see metaprogramming in action and understand how macros allow developers to write minimal, expressive code that does a lot under the hood.

6. **Potential pitfalls**: While metaprogramming is powerful, it is not always the right solution:

   a. **Complexity**: Macros can make code harder to read if overused. Newcomers might struggle with following the flow of code that is generated at compile-time.

   b. **Debugging**: Tracing errors in macro-generated code can be more challenging. You have to think in terms of **Abstract Syntax Trees** (**ASTs**) and how code is transformed.

   c. **Maintainability**: A macro that generates thousands of lines of code in multiple modules can become a maintenance nightmare if not well-documented and properly understood.

7. **Rule of thumb**: The following are the rules:

   a. Use macros when you truly benefit from compile-time generation or transformations.

   b. If a plain function can solve the problem, it is usually better to stick with the simpler approach.

# Understanding macros

Macros are one of the most powerful features in Elixir, serving as the foundation of metaprogramming within the language. For new Elixir developers, grasping macros is not just about learning how to use them, but also understanding their implications and how they can be harnessed to write more dynamic and efficient code.

# Macros

In Elixir, a macro is a special kind of function that is called at compile time and operates on the abstract syntax tree of the code. Unlike regular functions, which execute at runtime and work with data, macros execute at compile time and work with Elixir code itself.

The following figure illustrates the lifecycle of a macro in Elixir, showing how source code is transformed during compilation before execution:

Elixir Code ⟶ Compile Time ⟶ AST Generation ⟶ Macro Execution ⟶ Code Transformation ⟶ New Elixir Code

*Figure 7.1: Flow of a macro in Elixir*

The primary purpose of macros is to extend the language's capabilities without modifying its source code, allowing developers to introduce new syntactic features and domain-specific languages.

# Working with macros

Macros work by receiving Elixir code as their input and producing code as their output, which is then inserted back into the program. This process is facilitated by two key mechanisms: quoting and unquoting, which respectively transform code into ASTs and inject evaluated expressions back into code.

The following is a simple example to illustrate the definition and use of a macro in Elixir:

```
01. defmodule MyHelper do
02.   defmacro multiply_by_two(expr) do
03.     quote do
04.       2 * unquote(expr)
05.     end
06.   end
07. end
08.
09. defmodule MyProgram do
10.   require MyHelper
11.   def run do
12.     MyHelper.multiply_by_two(3)  # This will be replaced by 2 * 3 at
       compile time
13.   end
14. end
```

In this example, **multiply_by_two** is a macro that takes an expression, multiplies it by two, and then includes this computation back into the place where the macro is called. This transformation happens during compile time.

# Benefits of using macros

By harnessing macros in Elixir, developers can unlock a range of advantages that go beyond simple code transformations. The following highlights some of the most notable benefits:

- **Code generation**: Macros can dynamically generate code based on complex conditions or configurations. This is particularly useful for creating APIs or frameworks that need to provide a flexible interface to the users.

- **Code reuse**: By abstracting repetitive patterns into macros, developers can significantly reduce the amount of boilerplate code in their applications.

- **Performance optimization**: Since macros execute at compile time, they can pre-compute results or simplify expressions before the code is run, potentially enhancing the application's performance.

- **Extending the language**: Macros allow developers to add new constructs and syntactic sugar to Elixir, making the language more expressive and tailored to specific problems.

## Considerations when using macros

While macros are powerful, they should be used judiciously:

- **Debugging difficulty**: Since macros can transform the code significantly, they can make debugging more challenging. The source code that a developer sees is not what gets executed.

- **Overuse**: Overusing macros can make the code hard to understand and maintain, especially for those not familiar with the transformations happening at compile time.

- **Learning curve**: Understanding how macros work and how to use them effectively requires a solid understanding of Elixir's compilation process and its syntax.

Therefore, macros in Elixir are a potent tool for metaprogramming, enabling developers to write more concise, expressive, and efficient applications. However, they come with responsibilities and should be approached with care, especially by new developers who are still familiarizing themselves with the language's core principles.

# Compile-time vs. run-time

One of the most important concepts to grasp in Elixir, especially when discussing metaprogramming, is the distinction between compile-time and run-time. In Elixir, code goes through several phases before your application starts executing in earnest. Understanding what happens before (compile-time) and what happens during your program's execution (run-time) clarifies why macros can do things that normal functions cannot.

The following is a concise overview of each step in Elixir's journey from reading your source files to running your application, illustrating where macros fit into the process and how compile-time transformations differ from run-time behaviors:

1. **The Elixir compilation pipeline**: Consider the following step-by-step process that Elixir code undergoes before it runs:

    a. **Parsing**: Your code (**.ex** or **.exs** files) is read and converted into an abstract syntax tree (AST).

    b. **Macro Expansion**: During this phase, Elixir encounters macro calls. These macros execute at compile-time and can modify the AST before it is fully compiled.

    c. **Compilation**: The final AST, complete with any code injected by macros, is converted into Erlang bytecode.

    d. **Run-time**: The compiled bytecode is then loaded and executed in the BEAM (Erlang VM).

    The following are the quick takeaways:

    a. **Compile-time**: Where macros do their work, rewriting code.

    b. **Run-time**: Where your application logic happens, interacting with users, files, databases, etc.

2. **Compile-time involves**: Compile-time is all about preparing your code to be executed efficiently. Elixir can:

    a. **Expand macros**: Macros are special **compile-time functions** that return Elixir AST instead of normal values.

    b. **Perform validations**: Certain validations (syntax, references, etc.) are done before the code even runs.

    c. **Optimize**: Elixir may optimize the code, sometimes inlining or removing unneeded parts.

**Example 7.1**: A macro printing at compile-time.

Let us illustrate a macro that prints a message when it is expanded (that is, at compile-time):

```
01. defmodule MyMacros do
02.   defmacro compile_time_message do
03.     IO.puts("Macro is being expanded at compile-time!")
04.     quote do
```

```
05.          IO.puts("Hello from the injected run-time code!")
06.      end
07.    end
08. end
09.
10. defmodule Example do
11.    require MyMacros
12.
13.    def test do
14.      MyMacros.compile_time_message()
15.    end
16. End
```

When you compile this code (for example, by running **iex -S mix**), you will see:

   a.  Macro is being expanded at compile-time (Printed during compilation, before your program even runs.)

   b.  No other output at this point.

When you call **Example.test()** at run-time:

   a.  Hello from the injected run-time code. (Printed during the actual execution of the function.)

   b.  This example shows that macros can do work (like printing) at compile-time and also inject code that will run later.

3.  **Run-time involves**: Run-time is when your compiled code is actually executed. This is where:

   a.  Functions process data, respond to user requests, read files, interact with databases, etc.

   b.  Side effects (for example, printing to the console, sending network requests) take place.

   c.  Your application logic comes to life.

Normal function versus macro at run-time:

   a.  **A normal function**: Will be called many times at run-time, recalculating its logic each time.

   b.  **A macro**: Injects code once at compile-time. That code is still executed at run-time, but the generation of that code happened earlier.

**Example 7.2:** Observe the following code snippet, which demonstrates how macros inject code at compile-time but execute it at run-time:

```
01. defmodule Calculator do
02.   def multiply_runtime(x, y) do
03.     x * y
04.   end
05.
06.   defmacro multiply_compiletime(x, y) do
07.     # This happens at compile-time
08.     quote do
09.       # This multiplication happens at run-time, but the structure
10.       # of the function call was generated at compile-time.
11.       unquote(x) * unquote(y)
12.     end
13.   end
14. end
15.
16. defmodule Demo do
17.   require Calculator
18.
19.   def run do
20.     # 1) Normal function call (run-time)
21.     IO.puts("Runtime: #{Calculator.multiply_runtime(2, 3)}")
22.
23.     # 2) Macro call triggers code injection at compile-time,
24.     # but the multiplication also happens at run-time.
25.     IO.puts("Compile-time generated code at run-time: #{Calculator.multiply_compiletime(2, 3)}")
26.   end
27. End
```

In the macro case:

a. The shape of the code (that is, 2 * 3) is decided at compile-time.

b. The execution of the multiplication (2 * 3) occurs at run-time.

4. **Benefits of compile-time logic**: Keep these advantages in mind when deciding if compile-time operations are right for your scenario:

   a. **Performance**: Some work done during compilation means less overhead during execution (for instance, inlined code or constant folding).

   b. **Eliminate boilerplate**: You can generate repetitive code structures at compile-time, so you do not have to write them by hand.

   c. **DSLs**: Domain-specific languages become easier to implement since you can tailor the language at compile-time.

   d. **Error checking**: Mistakes are often caught early, preventing run-time failures.

   **Example 7.3**: If you have many similar schemas in Ecto, you can write a macro that defines fields for each schema. Those fields become part of the final modules at compile-time, reducing duplication and potential human error.

5. **When to use run-time logic**: While compile-time transformations are powerful, many tasks are more naturally suited to run-time:

   a. **Dynamic data**: If you need to handle user input, do I/O operations, or react to changing external conditions, these happen at run-time.

   b. **Simpler control flow**: Macros can make logic more complicated if overused. A normal function might be more straightforward to maintain and debug if your requirement does not need code injection.

   c. **Testing and debugging**: Plain run-time functions are generally easier to test and debug compared to macros.

   The key insight is that if you do not need to transform your code structure or do something that must happen at compile-time, stick to run-time functions.

6. **Quick compare and contrast**: The following table is a side-by-side comparison of key differences between compile-time and run-time in Elixir. This table highlights how macros (which operate at compile-time) contrast with normal functions (which operate at run-time), helping clarify when each approach is most appropriate:

| Aspect | Compile-time | Run-time |
|---|---|---|
| Execution phase | During code compilation (macro expansion) | While the program is actively running |
| Primary mechanism | Macros (**defmacro**) | Functions (**def**) |
| Input and output | Input: AST/code, Output: AST/code | Input: Data, Output: Processed data or side effects |

| Aspect | Compile-time | Run-time |
|---|---|---|
| Use cases | DSL creation, code generation, validations | Business logic, I/O, user interaction |
| Performance | Potentially faster final code | Normal code, typically simpler to reason about. |
| Debugging complexity | Higher (two-phase thinking) | Lower (single-phase thinking) |

*Table 7.1: A high-level overview of compile-time vs. run-time*

# Quoting and unquoting

In Elixir, quoting and unquoting let you treat code as data, giving you the ability to manipulate Elixir's AST directly. These concepts are at the heart of metaprogramming because they enable macros to generate or transform code before it is compiled. Understanding how quoting and unquoting work will help you write more powerful and flexible macros.

# Quoting

When you quote code in Elixir, you convert that code into an abstract syntax tree. An AST is a data structure (often made up of nested tuples and lists) that represents your code in a form the compiler can process:

```
01. ast = quote do
02.    1 + 2
03. end
04.
05. IO.inspect(ast)
06. # Output: {:+, [context: Elixir, import: Kernel], [1, 2]}
```

The following is the breakdown of the codes:

- **quote do ...** end takes the expression **1 + 2** and converts it into a tuple: **{:+, [context: Elixir, import: Kernel], [1, 2]}**.

- This tuple is Elixir's internal representation of the code **1 + 2**.

# Quote code

The following are the reasons for the quote code:

- **AST manipulation**: You can store and manipulate pieces of code as data (e.g., transform it, combine it with other code).

- **Macro writing**: Macros often need to produce or alter code, which is done by returning an AST.

# Unquoting

Unquoting is how you inject or splice values (or entire ASTs) back into a quoted expression. You use the unquote/1 function inside a quote block to place a variable or expression inside the AST you are building:

```
01. x = 10
02.
03. ast = quote do
04.   unquote(x) + 2
05. end
06.
07. IO.inspect(ast)
08. # Output: {:+, [context: Elixir, import: Kernel], [10, 2]}
```

The following is the breakdown of the codes:

- **unquote(x)** takes the value of **x** (which is 10) and inserts it into the AST at the appropriate spot.

- The resulting AST represents **10 + 2**.

## Use case for unquoting

Whenever you need to create a dynamic piece of code inside a quoted expression, you will reach for unquote/1. This is especially common in macros, where the input parameters get transformed into parts of the resulting code.

# Quoting complex expressions

Quoting is not limited to simple arithmetic. You can quote entire blocks of code, including function definitions and control structures:

```
01. ast = quote do
02.   def say_hi(name) do
03.     IO.puts("Hi, #{name}!")
04.   end
05. end
06.
```

```
07. IO.inspect(ast)
08. # This will be a nested tuple describing the 'def' of a function 'say_
    hi'
```

Inside such a quoted block, you can unquote variables to inject dynamic content:

```
01. function_name = :say_bye
02. message = "Bye, friend!"
03.
04. ast = quote do
05.   def unquote(function_name)(name) do
06.     IO.puts("#{unquote(message)}, #{name}!")
07.   end
08. End
```

In this example:

- We are injecting **:say_bye** as the function name.

- We are injecting **Bye, friend!** into the body.

# Handling abstract syntax tree directly

Sometimes, you will want to modify an AST without using quote/unquote directly in a macro. For instance, you might have a function that receives an AST (quoted expression) and transforms it.

The following example illustrates how you can directly manipulate an Elixir AST by pattern-matching on its structure. Instead of using quote and unquote within a macro, this approach relies on a function that receives a quoted expression, walks the AST, and performs targeted transformations:

```
01. defmodule ASTTransformer do
02.   def replace_add_with_sub(ast) do
03.     # A simple pattern match to find addition operations and replace them
         with subtraction
04.     case ast do
05.       {:+, meta, args} ->
06.         {:-, meta, args}
07.
08.       {op, meta, args} when is_list(args) ->
09.         {op, meta, Enum.map(args, &replace_add_with_sub/1)}
```

```
10.
11.        other ->
12.          other
13.      end
14.    end
15.  end
16.
17.  input_ast = quote do
18.    1 + 2 + 3
19.  end
20.
21.  IO.inspect(ASTTransformer.replace_add_with_sub(input_ast))
22.  # This transforms {:+, _, [1, {:+, _, [2, 3]}]]} into
23.  # {:-, _, [1, {:-, _, [2, 3]}]]}
```

Keep the following key insights in mind whenever you work with AST transformations in Elixir, as they can help you build more robust and maintainable metaprogramming logic:

- **Pattern matching on AST**: You can recursively walk the AST, changing parts as needed.
- **Custom transformations**: This is how you can implement complex logic or optimizations at compile-time.

# Potential pitfalls and best practices

Metaprogramming can unlock powerful capabilities in Elixir, but it also carries a unique set of challenges that can lead to confusing or difficult-to-maintain code. In the following are some common pitfalls to watch out for, along with best practices to help ensure your macros remain both effective and readable:

- **Overly complex quoting**: When crafting macros, it is essential to keep your quoting blocks manageable and comprehensible. Otherwise, debugging and collaboration can become significantly more challenging:
  - o Keep your macro logic clear by minimizing how much you quote and unquote.
  - o Nested, complicated quotes can be hard to read and debug.
- **Variable capture**: Although capturing variables from the macro's calling environment can be powerful, it also has the potential to create unexpected behavior or confusion if used haphazardly:
  - o Be aware that unquoted variables in macros can capture variables from the macro's calling environment.

- o    This can be powerful, but also lead to confusing variable scoping issues.

- **Use helpers:** Elixir provides several helper functions that streamline the macro-writing process, making it safer and easier to handle complex quoting scenarios:
  - o    Elixir provides functions like `Macro.escape/1` to make certain quoting scenarios (like embedding structs or non-literal values) safer.
  - o    Use `Macro.expand/2` or `Macro.to_string/1` for debugging.

- **Performance considerations**: It is because macros run at compile-time; overly expensive operations in your macros can slow down the entire build process:
  - o    Quoting and unquoting themselves are fast, but remember that macros always run at compile-time.
  - o    Do not do expensive operations there unnecessarily.

# Simple demonstration

In the following, there is a small macro example that demonstrates both quoting and unquoting in a concise way:

```
01. defmodule MyMacros do
02.   defmacro repeat_times(times, expr) do
03.     quote do
04.       for _ <- 1..unquote(times) do
05.         unquote(expr)
06.       end
07.     end
08.   end
09. end
10.
11. defmodule Demo do
12.   import MyMacros
13.
14.   def test do
15.     repeat_times(3, IO.puts("Hello!"))
16.   end
17. end
18.
19. # Explanation:
```

```
20. # 1) 'repeat_times/2' receives an AST for '3' and an AST for 'IO.
    puts("Hello!")'.
21. # 2) We quote a 'for' comprehension, unquoting 'times' for 1..times, and
    the expression for the loop body.
22. # 3) The macro expands into the code:
23. #
24. #    for _ <- 1..3 do
25. #      IO.puts("Hello!")
26. #    end
```

When **Demo.test()** runs, it prints:

```
01. Hello!
02. Hello!
03. Hello!
```

# Conclusion

Metaprogramming is one of Elixir's most empowering features, letting you shape code in ways that go beyond ordinary functions. By learning how macros work, distinguishing between compile-time and run-time, and mastering the art of quoting and unquoting, you now possess the tools to eliminate boilerplate, craft domain-specific languages, and inject advanced compile-time validations into your Elixir code. These techniques can greatly enhance both the expressiveness and maintainability of your projects provided you use them judiciously and document them well.

As you continue to explore the Elixir ecosystem, remember to experiment, read existing libraries, and engage with the community. Metaprogramming becomes more intuitive with practice, and real-world examples often provide the best insights into effective macro design. Even a small amount of metaprogramming experience can rapidly expand your coding horizons.

In the next chapter, we will discuss web development with Phoenix, Elixir's modern web framework. It will guide you through building your first Phoenix application, showing you how to structure routes, controllers, and views. From there, we will discuss Ecto, a powerful database wrapper that integrates seamlessly with Phoenix. By following along with a practical exercise, you will gain hands-on experience with the concepts introduced, setting a solid foundation for full-stack Elixir application development.

# Practical exercises

**Exercise 7.1:** Create a custom assertion macro

**Description**:

1.  Write a macro called **assert_equal** that takes two arguments, expected and actual.

2.  The macro should compare the two values, and if they are not equal, it should raise an **AssertionError** with a message indicating what the expected and actual values were.

3.  Use this macro in a test module to assert various equalities:

```
1.  defmodule MyAssertions do
2.    defmacro assert_equal(expected, actual) do
3.      quote do
4.        unless unquote(expected) == unquote(actual) do
5.          raise "Assertion failed! Expected:
    #{inspect(unquote(expected))}, but got:
    #{inspect(unquote(actual))}"
6.        end
7.      end
8.    end
9.  end
10.
11. defmodule TestModule do
12.   require MyAssertions
13.   def check_assertions do
14.     MyAssertions.assert_equal(1 + 1, 2)   # Should pass
15.     MyAssertions.assert_equal(3 * 3, 10) # Should raise an error
16.   end
17. end
18.
19. # To test the assertions, you can run TestModule.check_
    assertions()
```

**Exercise 7.2**: Macro for logging

**Description:**

1.  Create a macro **log_execution** that wraps any function call with logging statements that report the function's execution time.

2. The log should show when the function starts and ends, and how long it took to execute.

3. Apply this macro to several functions and observe the output when these functions are called:

```
01. defmodule ExecutionLogger do
02.   defmacro log_execution(func) do
03.     quote do
04.       start_time = :erlang.monotonic_time()
05.       result = unquote(func)
06.       end_time = :erlang.monotonic_time()
07.       IO.puts("Function executed in #{end_time - start_time} nanoseconds")
08.       result
09.     end
10.   end
11. end
12.
13. defmodule Usage do
14.   require ExecutionLogger
15.
16.   def slow_function do
17.     :timer.sleep(1000)
18.     "Done"
19.   end
20.
21.   def test_logging do
22.     ExecutionLogger.log_execution(slow_function())
23.   end
24. end
25.
26. # Usage.test_logging()
```

# Points to remember

- **Understand the purpose of metaprogramming**: Before exploring Elixir's metaprogramming, recognize how this technique can streamline your code and offer capabilities that go beyond traditional function calls:
    - o Metaprogramming allows you to write code that generates or modifies other code.
    - o It is particularly useful for reducing boilerplate, extending the language, and creating domain-specific languages within Elixir.

- **Mastery of macros is crucial**: At the heart of Elixir's metaprogramming lies the macro system, which operates at compile-time to reshape or generate code. Knowing how these macros work is essential for harnessing Elixir's full power:
    - o Macros operate at compile-time, meaning they modify or generate code before the program is run.
    - o Understanding how to write and use macros effectively is essential for leveraging the full power of Elixir's metaprogramming capabilities.

- **Distinguish between compile-time and run-time**: Being aware of which parts of your application occur at compile-time versus those that happen at run-time can optimize your application and prevent misunderstandings about code behavior:
    - o Compile-time is when code is transformed by the compiler (for example, macros are expanded).
    - o Run-time is when the compiled code is executed. Understanding the distinction is vital for optimizing performance and ensuring correct application behavior.

- **Proper use of quoting and unquoting**: Quoting and unquoting form the backbone of macro creation, enabling you to manipulate Elixir code as data structures before ultimately injecting it back into your program:
    - o Quoting converts code into its abstract syntax tree, allowing it to be manipulated as data.
    - o Unquoting injects evaluated expressions back into a quoted expression. Mastery of these is necessary for effective macro creation.

- **Be cautious with metaprogramming**: Although metaprogramming can significantly reduce boilerplate and boost flexibility, overuse or misuse can complicate your codebase and obscure intent:
    - o While powerful, metaprogramming can make code more complex and harder to understand.
    - o Use metaprogramming judiciously and only when it provides a clear benefit over traditional coding approaches.

- **Debugging and maintenance**: As soon as metaprogramming enters the picture, debugging may require deeper knowledge of Elixir's compile-time processes. Keep this in mind as you design macros:
    - Code that relies heavily on metaprogramming can be challenging to debug and maintain, especially for those not familiar with its intricacies.
    - Ensure that your use of metaprogramming enhances, rather than complicates, the readability and maintainability of your code.

- **Documentation and comments:** Providing thorough explanations for why and how macros operate is crucial, so future maintainers (or even you, months later) can easily follow the logic:
    - Given the complexity that metaprogramming can introduce, thorough documentation and comments are crucial.
    - Explain why metaprogramming is used and how the macros function to help future maintainers of the code.

- **Learn from existing libraries**: Real-world examples of metaprogramming can illustrate best practices and common pitfalls better than any theory alone:
    - Many Elixir libraries use metaprogramming extensively. Studying these can provide insights into practical uses and best practices.
    - Look at open-source projects and libraries to see how experienced developers utilize Elixir's metaprogramming features.

- **Continuous learning**: Mastering Elixir's metaprogramming features is an ongoing journey that benefits from consistent practice and community engagement:
    - Elixir's metaprogramming is a deep topic that can take time to master fully.
    - Engage with the community, participate in forums, and keep experimenting with new patterns and techniques to strengthen your understanding.

# Join our Discord space

Join our Discord workspace for latest updates, offers, tech happenings around the world, new releases, and sessions with the authors:

https://discord.bpbonline.com

# CHAPTER 8

# Working with Phoenix and Ecto

## Introduction

In this chapter, we will explore the two powerful tools in the Elixir ecosystem: the Phoenix framework and Ecto. Phoenix is a modern web framework designed for building scalable and maintainable applications with ease. It leverages the Elixir language to provide a robust platform for web development. Ecto, on the other hand, is a database wrapper that simplifies data interaction in Elixir applications. This chapter aims to introduce you to these technologies and guide you through the process of building a web application using Phoenix, along with integrating Ecto for database interactions.

## Structure

In this chapter, we will cover the following topics:

- Introduction to Phoenix
- Installing Phoenix
- Core web development
- Controllers
- Data management and security

# Objectives

The objective of this chapter is to provide a deep understanding and practical experience with using the Phoenix framework alongside Ecto for web application development. This chapter aims to equip you with the essential skills to appreciate Phoenix's core principles and its role in the Elixir ecosystem, from initial setup and configuration of a new project to mastering core web development practices. You will learn about routing, controllers, views, and templates, and real-time communication with WebSockets. It also covers robust data management and security practices, including how to organize code and manage data using Ecto, perform CRUD operations, and implement secure authentication and authorization systems. Practical examples throughout the chapter help reinforce these concepts, preparing you to develop scalable and maintainable web applications effectively. This foundational knowledge paves the way for advancing to more complex features and optimizing your web applications for production.

# Introduction to Phoenix

Phoenix is a web development framework built for the Elixir programming language. It is designed to make the development of web applications more efficient and enjoyable, leveraging the power of Elixir to provide high performance and scalability. It is built on top of the Erlang VM (BEAM), inheriting its strengths in handling concurrent and distributed systems.

# Philosophy of Phoenix

The philosophy behind Phoenix is centered around productivity, maintainability, and performance. The framework follows a set of conventions and provides a set of tools that help developers write clean and maintainable code while keeping the development process straightforward and enjoyable. The key aspects of Phoenix's philosophy include:

- **Convention over configuration**: Phoenix favors convention over configuration, meaning that it provides sensible defaults and conventions for common tasks, reducing the amount of configuration needed to get started.

- **Productivity**: Phoenix aims to increase developer productivity by providing features like code generators, LiveView for real-time interactions, and a powerful routing system.

- **Performance**: Leveraging the concurrency and fault-tolerance of the Erlang VM, Phoenix is built to handle high levels of traffic and complex operations efficiently.

- **Maintainability**: The framework encourages a modular and well-structured codebase, making it easier to maintain and extend applications over time.

## Place in the Elixir ecosystem

Phoenix holds a prominent place in the Elixir ecosystem as the go-to framework for web development. It integrates seamlessly with other Elixir libraries, such as Ecto for database interactions and Plug for creating composable web modules. The framework benefits from the vibrant Elixir community, which contributes to its development and provides a wealth of resources for learning and support.

## Core components of Phoenix

In a typical Phoenix application, the flow of a request from the client to the server involves several core components, which are explained as follows:

- **Endpoint**: The entry point for all requests to the web application. It starts with the request processing pipeline, including routing and other plug-in middleware.

- **Router**: Defines the routes of the application and maps incoming requests to the appropriate controller and action.

- **Controller**: Handles the requests, interacting with models and views to perform the necessary operations and prepare data for rendering.

- **View**: Renders the data prepared by the controller into a format suitable for the client, typically HTML or JSON.

- **Template**: Used by views to generate the final output, containing the HTML structure and embedded Elixir code for dynamic content.

Phoenix provides a well-structured and efficient framework for building web applications, emphasizing performance, maintainability, and developer productivity. Its integration with the Elixir ecosystem and the Erlang VM makes it a powerful choice for modern web development.

# Installing Phoenix

Since we have Elixir and Erlang installed, you can proceed with installing Phoenix. Follow the steps explained here:

1. **Install the Phoenix archive**: The Phoenix archive includes the `mix phx.new` task, which is used to generate a new Phoenix project. Install it by running:

   ```
   1. mix archive.install hex phx_new
   ```

   This command will fetch and install the latest version of the Phoenix project generator.

2. **Create a new Phoenix project**: To create a new Phoenix project, use the `mix phx.new` task followed by the name of your project. For example, to create a project named `my_app`, run:

   ```
   1. mix phx.new my_app
   ```

This will generate a new Phoenix project in a directory called **my_app** with all the necessary files and directories.

3. **Install dependencies**: Navigate to your new project directory and install the dependencies by running:

   1. `cd my_app`

   2. `mix deps.get`

   This command fetches and compiles all the dependencies specified in your **mix.exs** file.

# Setting up your development environment

Setting up your development environment correctly is crucial for a successful Phoenix project. It involves configuring your database settings and ensuring that your system has the necessary database installed. The following are the steps to get started:

1. **Configure your database**: Start by configuring your database in the **config/dev.exs** file. This file typically sets up Ecto to interact with PostgreSQL, but you can adjust the settings to connect to a different database. Ensure that the database service is running on your local machine. Here is an example configuration:

   ```
   1.  # Configure your database
   2.  config :my_app, MyApp.Repo,
   3.    username: "postgres",
   4.    password: "postgres",
   5.    hostname: "localhost",
   6.    database: "my_app_dev",
   7.    show_sensitive_data_on_connection_error: true,
   8.    pool_size: 10
   ```

   Make sure you have the specified database installed and running on your system.

2. **Create and migrate your database**: Run the following commands to create your database and run any migrations:

   1. `mix ecto.create`

   2. `mix ecto.migrate`

3. **Running your Phoenix application**: Follow the steps:

   a. **Start the Phoenix server**: To start your Phoenix application, run:

   `mix phx.server`

Alternatively, you can use `iex -S mix phx.server` to start the server within an interactive Elixir shell.

b. **Access your application**: Open your web browser and navigate to `http://localhost:4000`. You should see the Phoenix welcome page, indicating that your application is running successfully.

With this, you have successfully installed and set up a new Phoenix project. You are now ready to start building your web application with Phoenix.

# Core web development

Before diving into the specifics of routing, it is crucial to understand its place within Phoenix's core web development framework. Routing in Phoenix is central to how the application handles incoming web requests, directing them to the appropriate controller and action based on the URL and HTTP method.

# Routing

In Phoenix, routing is a mechanism that maps incoming requests to the appropriate controller and action. Routes are defined in the **router.ex** file, typically located in the `lib/my_app_web/router.ex` directory. The following steps are how you can define and utilize routing effectively:

1. **Defining routes**: To define a route, you need to specify the HTTP method, the path, and the controller action that should handle the request. For example:

```
1. scope "/", MyAppWeb do
2.   pipe_through :browser
3.
4.   get "/", PageController, :index
5. End
```

In this example, a **GET** request to the root path (**/**) is routed to the index action of the **PageController**.

2. **Route parameters**: Routes can also include parameters, which are captured and passed to the controller action. For example:

```
1. get "/users/:id", UserController, :show
```

In this route, **:id** is a parameter that will match any value and pass it to the show action of the **UserController** as the **id** parameter.

3. **Scopes**: They are used to group routes under a common path prefix. They can also be used to specify a pipeline of plugs that should be applied to all routes within the scope. For example:

```
1. scope "/api", HelloWeb do
2.   pipe_through :api
3.   resources "/users", UserController
4. end
```

4. **Resources**: The resources macro is a convenient way to define standard CRUD routes for a resource. For example:

```
1. resources "/users", UserController
```

This will generate routes for actions like index, show, new, create, edit, update, and delete.

5. **Pipelines**: They are a series of plugs applied to requests before they reach the controller. They are defined in the router and can be used for tasks like parsing request formats, fetching sessions, or enforcing authentication. For example:

```
1. pipeline :browser do
2.   plug :accepts, ["html"]
3.   plug :fetch_session
4.   plug :protect_from_forgery
5. end
```

6. **Nested resources**: Phoenix supports nesting resources to represent hierarchical relationships. For example:

```
1. resources "/users", UserController do
2.   resources "/posts", PostController
3. end
```

7. **Scoped routes**: Scopes can also be used to group routes under a common set of plugs or a namespace, which is useful for organizing routes for different parts of an application, such as admin interfaces or APIs.

Here is an example that includes scopes for both admin and API:

```
01. pipeline :browser do
02.   plug :accepts, ["html"]
03.   plug :fetch_session
04.   plug :protect_from_forgery
05.   plug :put_secure_browser_headers
06. end
07.
```

```
08. pipeline :api do
09.   plug :accepts, ["json"]
10. end
11.
12. pipeline :authenticate_admin do
13.   plug MyAppWeb.Plugs.AuthenticateAdmin
14. end
15.
16. scope "/admin", MyAppWeb.Admin, as: :admin do
17.   pipe_through [:browser, :authenticate_admin]
18.   resources "/users", UserController
19.   resources "/posts", PostController
20. end
21.
22. scope "/api", MyAppWeb.API, as: :api do
23.   pipe_through :api
24.   scope "/v1" do
25.     resources "/users", UserAPIController, only: [:index, :show]
26.   end
27. end
```

In this example, the **/admin** scope is for the admin interface, with routes for users and posts. The **/api/v1** scope is for the API, with routes for users. Each scope has its own set of plugs and namespaces.

In this example, the **:browser** pipeline is applied to the admin routes, while the **:api** pipeline is applied to the API routes. The **:authenticate_admin** pipeline is also applied to the admin routes to ensure only authenticated admins can access them.

For scoped routes in Phoenix, you can also use multiple scopes to organize routes for different parts of your application. Here is an example:

```
1. scope "/api", MyAppWeb do
2.   pipe_through :api
3.
4.   scope "/v1" do
5.     resources "/users", UserController, only: [:index, :show]
6.   end
```

```
7.
8.    scope "/v2" do
9.      resources "/users", UserControllerV2, only: [:index, :show]
10.   end
11. end
```

In this example, there are two scopes nested under the **/api** scope: **/v1** and **/v2**. Each version has its own set of routes for the **UserController** and **UserControllerV2**, respectively. This allows you to version your API and organize routes accordingly.

## Understanding mix phx.routes in Phoenix

The **mix phx.routes** task is a developer-friendly CLI tool provided by Phoenix to help you inspect and understand your application's routes. It lists all the available routes defined in your **router.ex** file, including HTTP methods, paths, controller actions, and route helper names.

**Usage**: In your Phoenix project directory, run:

```
1. mix phx.routes
```

This will output a table similar to:

```
1. page_path  GET    /             MyAppWeb.PageController :index
2. user_path  GET    /users        MyAppWeb.UserController :index
3. user_path  GET    /users/:id    MyAppWeb.UserController :show
4. user_path  POST   /users        MyAppWeb.UserController :create
5. ...
```

# Controllers

In the Phoenix framework, controllers play a crucial role in handling and responding to incoming web requests. They act as the intermediaries between the user interface and application logic. Controllers are responsible for interpreting user inputs delivered via HTTP requests, making decisions based on those inputs by communicating with models, and then preparing and sending an appropriate response back to the client. This can involve rendering HTML, redirecting to another resource, or responding with JSON or XML in the case of APIs. Essentially, controllers manage the flow of data in Phoenix applications, ensuring that user interactions are translated into actions that the system can process and respond to appropriately.

Here is a practical example of a controller in a Phoenix application:

```
1. defmodule MyAppWeb.PageController do
2.   use MyAppWeb, :controller
3.
```

```
4.    def hello(conn, _params) do
5.      text(conn, "Hello, world!")
6.    end
7. end
```

In this example, **PageController** includes a function **hello** that returns a plain text response saying **"Hello, world!"** when accessed. It demonstrates how a controller action can handle a request (**conn**) and use it to send a response. Controllers in Phoenix are typically placed in the **lib/my_app_web/controllers/** directory and are a fundamental part of routing and handling the HTTP lifecycle within a Phoenix application.

In Phoenix, the **conn** parameter (short for **connection**) is a fundamental part of handling web requests. It represents the state throughout the lifecycle of a request. This struct includes data about the HTTP request, such as headers, method, path, and body. It also includes response data that will eventually be sent back to the client, such as status codes and response headers.

Throughout its journey in a Phoenix application, the **conn** struct is transformed and manipulated to prepare the final response. This includes reading request data, modifying it inside controller actions, and appending response data. For example, you can directly modify the response using functions like **send_resp** or indirectly by passing the **conn** to views and templates that generate the response body.

Here is a simple use case illustrating how **conn** is typically used in a controller action:

```
1.  defmodule MyAppWeb.ExampleController do
2.    use MyAppWeb, :controller
3.
4.    def show(conn, %{"id" => id}) do
5.      case MyApp.get_item(id) do
6.        nil ->
7.          send_resp(conn, 404, "Item not found")
8.        item ->
9.          render(conn, "show.html", item: item)
10.     end
11.   end
12. end
```

In this example, the **show** function receives the **conn** struct and a map of parameters from the request URL. It tries to fetch an item by its ID, either sending a **404** response directly through conn or rendering a view if the item is found. This illustrates how **conn** is used to manage both request input and response output, forming a bridge between incoming HTTP requests and outgoing responses in Phoenix.

Therefore, controllers in the Phoenix framework are pivotal for managing the flow of data between the server and the client. They handle incoming requests, interact with models to process data, and determine the appropriate output to render, often coordinating with views for HTML responses or returning JSON or XML for APIs. Developers can maintain clean, manageable, and efficient codebases by keeping controllers slim and delegating business logic to context modules or using Plugs for reusable code. This design promotes scalability and maintainability in web applications developed with Phoenix.

# Views and templates

In the Phoenix framework, views and templates are essential components for rendering the user interface of a web application.

**Views** in Phoenix are modules that compile and render templates. They encapsulate and manage presentation logic, helping to keep templates simple and focused solely on markup. Views transform data from the controller into output formats like HTML or JSON, and they can include helper functions to handle formatting tasks or complex logic.

**Templates** are files containing HTML and **embedded Elixir** (EEx) used to dynamically generate content. They describe how data should be presented in the browser or to other clients. Templates are usually structured around views, with each view corresponding to a particular template or set of templates.

Phoenix 1.7 has introduced significant changes to its template system by adopting HEEx (HTML+EEx) as the primary template language. HEEx stands for HTML Embedded Elixir, and is an extension of the standard EEx template engine, which has been the backbone of Phoenix's templating capabilities in earlier versions.

The key features of HEEx in Phoenix 1.7 are:

- **HTML-aware extensions**: HEEx templates are designed to be aware of HTML syntax, providing safety features to prevent common issues like HTML injection. When dynamic content is interpolated into a template using `<%= %>`, any characters that might compromise HTML integrity (like `<` or `>`) have automatically escaped. This means you do not have to worry about HTML injection attacks as HEEx handles them gracefully.

- **Compile-time checks**: Development is enhanced by performing HTML validation at compile time. This means syntax errors or mismatched HTML tags are caught early in the development process, making templates more robust and reducing runtime errors.

- **Enhanced syntax for dynamic attributes**: This allows a more concise syntax for dynamic attributes in HTML elements. For instance, if you have conditional attributes or classes that depend on some Elixir expression, you can seamlessly integrate these using a simplified `{}` syntax without cluttering your template code.

- **Integration with function components**: HEEx supports using function components directly within templates, which can either be locally defined in the same module or imported from other modules. This feature allows you to encapsulate reusable pieces of your user interface as function components, promoting reusability and modularity.

The importance of views and templates in MVC architecture:

- **Understanding the role of views and templates**: In the **Model-View-Controller (MVC)** architecture, views and templates are essential for separating the presentation layer from the business logic. This separation enhances manageability and scalability by allowing changes to the website's design or layout without affecting the underlying code that handles business operations.

- **Advantages of separation**: By maintaining this separation, applications become easier to manage and scale. It promotes code reusability and improves readability. Developers can utilize partial templates and view helpers to minimize code duplication, ensuring that the codebase remains clean and well-organized. This approach not only simplifies updates and maintenance but also enhances the overall development workflow. Here is a practical example to illustrate how views and templates work together in Phoenix:

**Example 8.1**: Rendering a user profile page.

Follow these steps explained here:

1. **The controller**: First, you have a controller that fetches user data and passes it to the view:

```
1. defmodule MyAppWeb.UserController do
2.   use MyAppWeb, :controller
3.
4.   def show(conn, %{"id" => id}) do
5.     user = MyApp.Accounts.get_user(id)
6.     render(conn, "show.html", user: user)
7.   end
8. end
```

In this example, the **show** function in **UserController** retrieves a user based on the ID and uses the **render** function to display the user data using the **show.html** template.

2. **The view**: The view module may include helper functions to manipulate or format the data:

```
1. defmodule MyAppWeb.UserView do
2.   use MyAppWeb, :view
3.
```

```
4.    def full_name(user) do
5.       "#{user.first_name} #{user.last_name}"
6.    end
7. end
```

This **UserView** defines a helper function **full_name** to concatenate first and last names.

3.  **The template**: The corresponding template (**show.html.eex**) uses the view's function to render the data:

```
1. <!-- lib/my_app_web/templates/user/show.html.heex -->
2. <h1>Welcome, <%= full_name(@user) %></h1>
3. <p>Your email: <%= @user.email %></p>
```

Using HEEx templates allows for a more robust, secure, and developer-friendly experience when building HTML with embedded Elixir.

This separation allows the controller to focus solely on fetching and passing data, the view handles all presentation logic, and the template deals only with markup. Changes to the website's look and feel can be made in the templates without altering the backend logic, ensuring that the application remains easy to manage and update.

Together, views and templates provide a powerful system that supports dynamic content rendering while promoting code reusability and separation of concerns. This approach not only simplifies development and testing but also enhances collaboration among developers working on different aspects of the application, such as styling, interactivity, and data management. By leveraging Phoenix's powerful templating features, developers can build rich, interactive web applications efficiently.

# Phoenix Channels

Phoenix Channels are a feature of the Phoenix framework that enables real-time communication between clients and servers. They are particularly useful for applications that require interactive features such as live messaging, real-time notifications, gaming, and collaborative editing environments.

Phoenix Channels primarily use WebSockets for real-time communication, allowing persistent connections between the client and server. This enables messages to be pushed to clients in real-time, which is essential for features like chats, live notifications, or any interactive, real-time application.

The following is leveraging WebSockets with Phoenix Channels:

*   **Persistent connection**: Unlike traditional HTTP requests, which close the connection after each request, WebSockets maintain an open connection, allowing for full-duplex

communication. This means both the server and client can send messages at any time, independently.

- **Real-time data**: This ongoing connection enables the server to send real-time updates to the client without the client needing to request them periodically. This is particularly useful for applications that need to display real-time data, such as scores, stock updates, or dynamic content changes.

- **Efficient resource usage**: WebSockets significantly reduce the overhead of HTTP headers and the process of establishing a connection, providing a more efficient way to communicate small amounts of data frequently.

- **Fall-back transport mechanisms**: While WebSockets are the preferred transport, Phoenix Channels are designed to be transport-agnostic. If WebSockets are not available, they can fall back to other methods like long polling. This ensures that the application remains functional across a variety of browsers and network conditions.

The necessity of Phoenix Channels for modern web applications is as follows:

- **Real-time web applications**: Channels allow developers to build highly interactive and responsive applications by facilitating real-time communication. This is essential for features like live chat, live updates of content, and push notifications.

- **Scalability**: Phoenix Channels are built on top of the Erlang Virtual Machine (BEAM), known for its excellent support for handling large numbers of simultaneous connections with low latency and high fault tolerance. This makes them ideal for applications that need to scale to support many concurrent users.

- **Efficiency**: Channels that use WebSockets are used by default to maintain a persistent connection between the client and server. This is more efficient than traditional HTTP polling, as it reduces the overhead of repeatedly opening connections and allows for faster communication.

- **Flexibility**: Phoenix Channels support multiple transport mechanisms, not just WebSockets, and can fall back to long polling if WebSockets are not available. They also provide easy-to-use mechanisms for broadcasting messages to multiple clients and handling different topics and subtopics efficiently.

- **Simplified state management**: These Channels can manage the state more effectively within a connection. They allow the server to keep track of the state of its communications with various clients, which simplifies the development of complex interactive features.

Let us explore a practical example of using Phoenix Channels for a real-time chat application. This example will cover setting up the channel, handling client-server communication, and broadcasting messages to all connected clients.

1. **Create the channel**: First, you need to define a new channel. In your Phoenix application, you can create a **channel** module under **lib/my_app_web/channels**:

```
1. defmodule MyAppWeb.ChatChannel do
2.   use Phoenix.Channel
3.
4.   def join("room:lobby", _payload, socket) do
5.     {:ok, socket}
6.   end
7.
8.   def handle_in("new_msg", %{"body" => body}, socket) do
9.     broadcast!(socket, "new_msg", %{body: body})
10.    {:noreply, socket}
11.  end
12. end
```

In this example:

- The **join** function allows clients to join a specific topic, here **room:lobby**.

- The **handle_in** function listens to incoming events of type **new_msg** (a new message), takes the message from the payload, and broadcasts it to all clients connected to the **room:lobby**.

2. **Update the router**: You need to mount the channel in your application's socket router. This is typically done in **lib/my_app_web/channels/user_socket.ex**:

```
1. defmodule MyAppWeb.UserSocket do
2.   use Phoenix.Socket
3.
4.   channel "room:*", MyAppWeb.ChatChannel
5.
6.   def connect(_params, socket) do
7.     {:ok, socket}
8.   end
9.
10.  def id(_socket), do: nil
11. end
```

This configuration allows the socket connection to route any topics that **match room:*** to **MyAppWeb.ChatChannel**.

3. **Client-side setup**: On the client side, you need to establish a WebSocket connection using JavaScript. Here is how you might set it up using Phoenix's provided JavaScript client library:

```javascript
1. let socket = new Phoenix.Socket("/socket", {params: {userToken:
   "Token"}})
2.
3. socket.connect()
4.
5. let channel = socket.channel("room:lobby", {})
6.
7. channel.join()
8.   .receive("ok", resp => { console.log("Joined successfully",
   resp) })
9.   .receive("error", resp => { console.log("Unable to join", resp)
   })
10.
11. channel.on("new_msg", payload => {
12.   console.log("New message:", payload.body)
13. })
14.
15. // To send a message
16. document.getElementById("send-button").addEventListener("click",
    function() {
17.   let messageInput = document.getElementById("message-input")
18.   channel.push("new_msg", {body: messageInput.value})
19.   messageInput.value = ""
20. })
```

In this JavaScript code:

- A new socket is created and connected.

- A channel is joined on the topic **room:lobby**.

- Event listeners are set up to handle the **"ok"** and **"error"** responses from joining the channel, and to listen for **"new_msg"** events that include new messages being broadcast.

- An event listener on a button (send-button) sends a new message to the channel when clicked.

This simple chat application demonstrates the basic setup and functionality of Phoenix Channels, allowing real-time, bidirectional communication between the client and the server. Channels are incredibly powerful for any feature that requires real-time user interaction, such as games, notifications, live updates, and more. The scalability and robustness of Phoenix Channels make them an ideal choice for these kinds of applications.

# Data management and security

Data management and security are crucial aspects of building reliable and secure web applications. In Phoenix, these areas are primarily handled through Ecto for data operations and Phoenix contexts for organizing business logic and data interactions. Additionally, authentication and authorization are critical components for securing applications.

## Ecto

Ecto is an integral part of the Phoenix framework that provides a **domain-specific language** (**DSL**) for communicating with databases. It allows developers to define schemas, changesets, and queries that are both expressive and efficient.

The key features of Ecto are:

- **Schema definitions**: Ecto schemas are mappings to database tables that define the structure of your data, including fields and types.

- **Changesets**: Changesets are used for data validation and transformations before writing to or updating the database.

- **Querying**: Ecto provides a powerful query API that abstracts SQL queries into Elixir expressions, making database interactions safe and efficient.

## Schema definitions in Ecto

Schema definitions are a central concept in Ecto, acting as a mapping between Elixir structs and database tables. They define the structure of data, including the fields and their types, and how these fields correspond to the columns in your database.

The importance of schema definitions in application development:

- **Data structure and validation**: Schemas help ensure that the data flowing in and out of your database matches expected formats and types. This is crucial for maintaining data integrity and preventing invalid data from corrupting your application or database.

- **Type safety**: By defining field types in your schemas, you are leveraging Elixir's ability to enforce type safety. This reduces bugs and issues related to data handling by catching type mismatches early in the development process.

- **Readability and maintainability**: Schemas make your code more readable and easier to maintain. They provide a clear blueprint of what your data looks like and how it is structured, which can be especially useful for new developers or when returning to a project after some time.

- **Abstraction and decoupling**: Schemas abstract the specifics of database interactions, allowing most of your application's code to remain decoupled from the database technology you use. This makes it easier to change your database backend without affecting the rest of your application.

# Practical example

Here is an example of how you might define a simple schema for a user in an Ecto-powered Phoenix application:

```
01. defmodule MyApp.Accounts.User do
02.   use Ecto.Schema
03.   import Ecto.Changeset
04.
05.   # Mapping the Elixir struct to the database table 'users'
06.   schema "users" do
07.     field :name, :string
08.     field :email, :string
09.     field :is_active, :boolean, default: true
10.     timestamps()
11.   end
12.
13.   # Changeset function for validating and structuring changes to user
      records
14.   def changeset(user, attrs) do
15.     user
16.     |> cast(attrs, [:name, :email, :is_active])
17.     |> validate_required([:name, :email])
18.     |> unique_constraint(:email)
19.   end
20. end
```

In the above schema:

- Fields are defined with their types (:**string**, :**boolean**). This helps Ecto understand how to handle the data when it is read from or written to the database.

- The changeset function validates data before it is written to the database. It uses functions like cast to filter params, **validate_required** to ensure necessary fields are present, and **unique_constraint** to enforce the uniqueness of the email field.

By defining this schema, you ensure that any interactions with the user's table are structured and safe, adhering to the rules and validations you have set. This schema acts as a single source of truth for what a User is within your application, centralizing and simplifying data management tasks.

# Virtual fields

Virtual fields in Ecto are attributes defined in your schemas that do not correspond to any column in your database. They are used to hold data temporarily, which can be useful for validation, transformations, or any operation that should not be persisted directly in the database. Virtual fields are particularly helpful in scenarios like user registration, where you might want to handle passwords or other sensitive information carefully.

## Example use case of handling passwords

Suppose you have a user schema, and you need to handle user-created passwords that should not be stored directly in the database but instead stored as a hashed version. Here is how you could define and use a virtual field for the password:

```
01. defmodule MyApp.Accounts.User do
02.   use Ecto.Schema
03.   import Ecto.Changeset
04.
05.   schema "users" do
06.     field :email, :string
07.     field :password_hash, :string
08.     field :password, :string, virtual: true  # Virtual field
09.     timestamps()
10.   end
11.
12.   def changeset(user, attrs) do
13.     user
```

```
14.       |> cast(attrs, [:email, :password])
15.       |> validate_required([:email, :password])
16.       |> put_pass_hash()
17.    end
18.
19.    defp put_pass_hash(changeset) do
20.       case changeset do
21.          %Ecto.Changeset{valid?: true, changes: %{password: pass}} ->
22.             hash = Bcrypt.hash_pwd_salt(pass)
23.             put_change(changeset, :password_hash, hash)
24.          _ ->
25.             changeset
26.       end
27.    end
28. end
```

The following is a detailed explanation of virtual fields and password management in Ecto:

- **Schema definition**: The password field is defined as a virtual field. This means it will be used in the application logic but not stored in the database.

- **Changeset function**: In the changeset function, the password is accepted and validated like any other field. However, because it is virtual, it will not persist.

- **Password hashing**: The private function **put_pass_hash** is used to convert the plain password into a hash before storing it in the database under the **password_hash** field. The original password, stored temporarily in the virtual field, is not saved.

This approach keeps the plain password out of the database, enhancing security by storing only the hashed version. Virtual fields are useful because they allow you to work with transient data in a structured way and leverage Ecto's powerful changeset features for validation and transformations without affecting your database schema.

# Querying in Ecto

Querying in Ecto is a powerful feature that allows developers to interact with databases concisely, expressively, and safely. Ecto provides a rich query API that abstracts away the complexities of raw SQL, utilizing Elixir's functional capabilities to build queries programmatically.

The key concepts of Ecto querying are:

- **Ecto.Query module**: This is the primary interface for writing queries in Ecto. It provides a DSL for building queries using Elixir syntax.

- **Composability**: Ecto queries are highly composable; you can build small, reusable query functions that can be combined to perform complex queries. This keeps the code **Don't Repeat Yourself** (**DRY**) and clean.

- **Safety**: Ecto queries prevent SQL Injection attacks by safely parameterizing inputs when queries are constructed using its DSL.

- **Adapters**: It supports multiple databases through adapters (like *Postgres, MySQL*), allowing the same query API to be used regardless of the underlying database.

# Practical example of fetching data

Suppose you have a Blog application with a Posts table, and you want to fetch published posts and order them by their publish date. For this, follow the steps given here:

1. **Defining the Post schema**: The following is how you can structure the Post schema:

```
1. defmodule Blog.Post do
2.   use Ecto.Schema
3.
4.   schema "posts" do
5.     field :title, :string
6.     field :body, :text
7.     field :published_at, :naive_datetime
8.     field :status, :string # "draft", "published", etc.
9.   end
10. end
```

2. **Querying published posts**: Here is how you might write a query to fetch only the published posts, ordered by the **published_at** field:

```
1. defmodule Blog.Repo do
2.   use Ecto.Repo, otp_app: :blog
3.
4.   # Function to fetch published posts
5.   def fetch_published_posts do
6.     import Ecto.Query, only: [from: 2]
7.
8.     query = from p in Blog.Post,
9.           where: p.status == "published",
10.          order_by: [desc: p.published_at],
```

```
11.                select: p
12.
13.      Repo.all(query)
14.  end
15. end
```

The key features demonstrated above are:

- **from/2**: Constructs a query. The macro sets up the initial query source (**Blog.Post**) and allows specifying the fields and conditions.

- **where**: Filters the results based on a condition. In this case, it filters posts where the status is **"published"**.

- **order_by**: Orders the results. This example orders the posts by the **published_at** field in descending order.

- **select**: Specifies which fields to retrieve. Here, it retrieves all fields from the posts that match the query.

- **Repo.all**: Executes the query and fetches all results that match the specified conditions.

# Repo.one/1

**Use case**: Retrieve a single record that meets specific criteria:

```
1. query = from p in Post, where: p.id == 1, select: p
2. post = Repo.one(query)
```

**Repo.one/1** returns a single result or nil if no result is found. This is useful for fetching a specific record by ID or another unique attribute.

# Repo.get/2

**Use case**: Fetch a single post by its primary key:

```
1. post = Repo.get(Post, 1)
```

This function is straightforward and is used when you know the primary key of the record.

# Repo.get_by/2

**Use case**: Fetch a single record using conditions other than the primary key:

```
1. post = Repo.get_by(Post, title: "Introduction to Ecto")
```

This is similar to **get/2** but allows fetching based on other fields. It is particularly useful for retrieving records by unique fields like username or email.

# Repo.insert/2

**Use case**: Insert a new record into the database:

```
1. changeset = Post.changeset(%Post{}, %{title: "New Post", body: "Hello,
   World!"})
2. {:ok, post} = Repo.insert(changeset)
```

**Repo.insert/2** is used to create a new record. The function takes a changeset and returns the inserted record.

# Repo.update/2

**Use case**: Update an existing record:

```
1. post = Repo.get(Post, 1)
2. changeset = Post.changeset(post, %{body: "Updated content"})
3. {:ok, updated_post} = Repo.update(changeset)
```

This is used to update records that already exist in the database. The changeset contains the changes to be applied.

# Repo.delete/1

**Use case**: Delete a record:

```
1. post = Repo.get(Post, 1)
2. {:ok, _} = Repo.delete(post)
```

This function removes a record from the database. It is straightforward but powerful and should be used cautiously.

# Repo.insert_all/3

**Use case**: Insert multiple records into the database in a single query:

```
1. posts = [%{title: "Post 1", body: "Body 1"}, %{title: "Post 2", body:
   "Body 2"}]
2. {:ok, _} = Repo.insert_all(Post, posts)
```

This is efficient for batch inserting data, reducing the number of database queries needed.

# Repo.update_all/3

**Use case**: Update multiple records based on a given condition:

```
1. query = from p in Post, where: p.published == false
2. Repo.update_all(query, set: [published: true])
```

This updates all records that meet the conditions specified by the query. It is useful for bulk updates, like activating multiple user accounts at once.

# Repo.delete_all/2

**Use case**: Delete multiple records based on a condition:

```
1. query = from p in Post, where: p.published == false

2. Repo.delete_all(query)
```

Similar to **update_all**, but for deleting multiple records. It is useful for cleaning up data or removing test records in bulk.

# Repo.aggregate/3

**Use case**: Perform an aggregation, such as counting records:

```
1. count = Repo.aggregate(from(p in Post), :count, :id)
```

This is used to perform aggregate functions like **count**, **sum**, **avg**, etc., over a query.

# Repo.transaction/1

**Use case**: Execute multiple database operations in a transaction:

```
1. Repo.transaction(fn ->
2.     Repo.insert(changeset1)
3.     Repo.insert(changeset2)
4. end)
```

This wraps multiple operations in a transaction, ensuring that all operations must succeed or they are all rolled back. This is critical for maintaining data integrity when multiple related changes must be made together.

Querying with Ecto offers a robust, secure, and flexible way to interact with databases in Elixir applications. By leveraging Ecto's powerful query DSL, developers can write complex queries in a more readable and maintainable way than raw SQL. The ability to compose queries and the built-in safety features help maintain the integrity and security of your data, making Ecto a compelling choice for data access in Elixir projects.

# Ecto association

In Ecto, associations define relationships between different schema entities in an Elixir application, mirroring the relationships that might exist between tables in a relational database. Associations help manage and query related data efficiently. The most common types of associations in Ecto are **belongs_to**, **has_many**, **has_one**, and **many_to_many**.

The different types of associations are:

- **belongs_to**: Indicates that one entity belongs to another. It is typically used in the schema that holds the foreign key.

- **has_many**: Specifies that one entity can have many other entities associated with it. For example, a user might have many posts.

- **has_one**: Used when an entity should only have one of another entity and that other entity exclusively belongs to it.

- **many_to_many**: Defines a relationship where many entities are associated with many other entities. Ecto handles this through a join table.

## Practical example of user and posts

Consider a simple blog system where you have users and posts. Each user can write many posts, but each post is written by one user. This is a classic example of a **has_many** and **belongs_to** association. Follow the given steps:

1. **Defining the schemas**: Start by defining the user schema within your accounts module. This schema will include basic fields such as name and email, along with a **has_many** relationship to posts, indicating that each user can have multiple posts. Additionally, the post schema is defined in your content module, including fields for title, body, and a **belongs_to** association that links each post to a specific user. This setup underscores the one-to-many relationship between users and posts.

   Here is how you would structure the **user** and **post** schemas, along with their respective changeset functions, which will handle validations and casting of incoming data for creating or updating records:

```
01. defmodule MyApp.Accounts.User do
02.   use Ecto.Schema
03.   import Ecto.Changeset
04.
05.   schema "users" do
06.     field :name, :string
07.     field :email, :string
```

```
08.        has_many :posts, MyApp.Content.Post
09.
10.        timestamps()
11.    end
12.
13.    def changeset(user, attrs) do
14.        user
15.        |> cast(attrs, [:name, :email])
16.        |> validate_required([:name, :email])
17.    end
18. end
19.
20. defmodule MyApp.Content.Post do
21.    use Ecto.Schema
22.    import Ecto.Changeset
23.
24.    schema "posts" do
25.        field :title, :string
26.        field :body, :text
27.        belongs_to :user, MyApp.Accounts.User
28.
29.        timestamps()
30.    end
31.
32.    def changeset(post, attrs) do
33.        post
34.        |> cast(attrs, [:title, :body, :user_id])
35.        |> validate_required([:title, :body])
36.    end
37. end
```

2.  **Using the associations**: With these associations set up, you can easily fetch associated data using Ecto's query syntax. For example, to get all posts written by a specific user:

```
1. posts = Repo.all(
2.    from p in Post,
```

```
3.    where: p.user_id == ^user_id,
4.    preload: [:user]
5.  )
```

Here, preload is used to load the associated user for each post, which helps in reducing the number of database queries and improves performance in data retrieval tasks.

3. **Adding and manipulating associated data**: When creating a new post for a user, you can leverage the changeset functions:

```
1.  %Post{}
2.  |> Post.changeset(%{title: "New Post", body: "Content of new
    post", user_id: user_id})
3.  |> Repo.insert()
```

## Importance of associations in Ecto

Associations in Ecto are crucial for several reasons:

- **Data integrity**: They help maintain referential integrity between different data entities.

- **Query efficiency**: Associations make fetching and manipulating related data easier and more efficient with fewer lines of code and potentially fewer database queries.

- **Application structure**: They provide a clear and organized way of managing related data, which can simplify the development and maintenance of the application.

Understanding and properly implementing associations in Ecto can greatly enhance your application's capabilities and performance, providing a solid foundation for complex data operations and relationships.

# Implementing user authentication and authorization in Phoenix

Authentication and authorization are fundamental aspects of web application security. Phoenix provides an efficient solution called Phoenix.Token, which facilitates stateless authentication, a method where no user session is stored on the server, making it ideal for stateless API services.

## Phoenix.Token for stateless authentication

Phoenix.Token is a built-in feature in Phoenix designed for creating and validating bearer tokens. These tokens are essential for verifying user identities and session information without the need to maintain a server-side session state. This approach is particularly advantageous for APIs where maintaining state can be cumbersome and inefficient.

Here is a practical guide on how to implement Phoenix.Token for API authentication:

**Example 8.2**: Token generation and verification.

Follow the given steps:

1. **Generate a token**:

   Begin by creating a token that includes a user identifier, which can then be securely transmitted between the client and server.

   ```
   1. user_id = 1
   2. token = Phoenix.Token.sign(MyAppWeb.Endpoint, "user salt", user_
      id)
   ```

2. **Verify a token**: When the token is presented back to the server, verify its validity and check for expiration.

   ```
   1. case Phoenix.Token.verify(MyAppWeb.Endpoint, "user salt", token,
      max_age: 86_400) do
   2.   {:ok, user_id} -> # Token is valid
   3.   {:error, _reason} -> # Token is invalid or expired
   4. End
   ```

This token system is useful for cases where you need a secure, tamper-proof way to authenticate users without maintaining a session state, such as in stateless API services. It ensures that the token cannot be modified without access to the secret key, and it can be configured to expire within a specified timeframe.

# Using mix phx.gen.auth for full authentication

mix phx.gen.auth is a generator that provides a ready-to-use authentication system for Phoenix applications. Use the **mix phx.gen.auth** command to generate the authentication system. This command structures an entire authentication workflow, including user registration, login, email confirmation, and password recovery:

```
1. mix phx.gen.auth Accounts User users
```

**Generate the authentication system**: Run **mix phx.gen.auth Accounts User** users, where:

- **Accounts**: The context module.
- **User**: The user schema that represents an individual user.
- **users**: The database table name.

  Since this generator installed additional dependencies in **mix.exs**, let us fetch those:

  ```
  1. mix deps.get
  ```

Before using the authentication system, you need to create the database and tables:

```
1. mix ecto.setup
```

Start the Phoenix server:

```
1. mix phx.server
```

Now, you can visit **http://localhost:4000** to see the registration and login flows in action.

The following are the steps to register a user:

1. Navigate to **http://localhost:4000/users/register**.
2. Fill out the form and submit it.
3. Show students the data in the database to demonstrate how it handles user data securely, storing hashed passwords, not plain text.

The following are the steps to log in:

1. Go to **http://localhost:4000/users/login**.
2. Enter the credentials of a registered user.

Suppose you want to add additional fields to the user schema, such as a **"nickname"**. The steps are given as follows:

1. **Update the migration**: First, create a new migration to add the nickname column to the users table:

```
1. mix ecto.gen.migration add_nickname_to_users
```

Then, modify the generated migration file:

```
1. defmodule MyApp.Repo.Migrations.AddNicknameToUsers do
2.   use Ecto.Migration
3.
4.   def change do
5.     alter table(:users) do
6.       add :nickname, :string
7.     end
8.   end
9. end
```

Run the migration to update your database:

```
1. mix ecto.migrate
```

2. **Modify the user schema**: Add the new field to your user schema, located typically in `lib/my_app/accounts/user.ex`:

```
1. schema "users" do
2.   field :email, :string
3.   field :nickname, :string  # new field
4.   field :hashed_password, :string
5.   field :is_admin, :boolean, default: false
6.
7.   timestamps()
8. end
```

3. **Update changeset function**: Add validation for the new field and implement password complexity checks:

```
1. def changeset(user, attrs) do
2.   user
3.   |> cast(attrs, [:email, :nickname, :password, :is_admin])
4.   |> validate_required([:email, :nickname, :password])
5.   |> validate_length(:password, min: 12)   # enforcing password length
6.   |> validate_format(:password, ~r/(?=.*\d)(?=.*[a-z])(?=.*[A-Z])(?=.*[\W])/)  # password must include digits, lower and upper case letters, and special characters
7.   |> hash_password()
8. end
```

These tools provide robust solutions for managing authentication and authorization in your Phoenix applications, ensuring security and scalability, whether you need a stateless mechanism with Phoenix.Token for APIs or a full-fledged user authentication system with `mix phx.gen.auth`, Phoenix supports both with efficiency and ease.

# Conclusion

Throughout this chapter, we explored a wide range of functionalities offered by Phoenix, from basic routing and controller setups to complex features like authentication and real-time communication. We learned how Phoenix leverages the Elixir ecosystem to provide a robust framework for building efficient and maintainable web applications. By now, you should feel confident in your ability to develop applications using Phoenix, apply best practices in web development, and harness the full power of real-time features and database management with Ecto. This knowledge sets a solid foundation for practical application development and further exploration of advanced Phoenix features.

As you continue your journey into Elixir, the next chapter will introduce you to the release mechanism of Elixir. You will learn how to bundle your application and runtime into a single package that can be deployed anywhere with Mix. This includes understanding the intricacies of release management, creating releases, and deploying your Elixir applications effectively. This chapter will be instrumental in taking your applications from development to production, encapsulating them in deployable units while discussing best practices for deployment.

# Practical exercises

## Exercise 8.1

**Objective**: How to create and use a custom plug to check if a user is authenticated?

Follow the steps explained here:

1. **Define the plug**: Create a new file in **lib/your_app_web/plugs/verify_user.ex** and define a module:

```
1. defmodule YourAppWeb.Plugs.VerifyUser do
2.   import Plug.Conn
3.
4.   def init(default), do: default
5.
6.   def call(conn, _opts) do
7.     case conn.assigns[:current_user] do
8.       nil ->
9.         conn
10.        |> Phoenix.Controller.redirect(to: "/login")
11.        |> halt()
12.      _user ->
13.        conn
14.     end
15.   end
16. end
```

This plug checks if **:current_user** is assigned in the connection. If not, it redirects the user to the login page.

2. **Add the plug to your router or controller**: Depending on your needs, you can add this plug to a specific controller or a pipeline in your router.

3. **Adding to a controller**: Directly add the plug to a specific controller to ensure that authentication is enforced for all actions handled by that controller:

```
1. defmodule YourAppWeb.PostController do
2.   use YourAppWeb, :controller
3.   plug YourAppWeb.Plugs.VerifyUser
4.
5.   def index(conn, _params) do
6.     # Your code here
7.   end
8. end
```

4. **Adding to the router**: Include the plug in a pipeline in your router configuration. This approach applies the authentication check broadly to all routes processed through the pipeline:

```
1. pipeline :browser do
2.   plug :fetch_session
3.   plug :put_flash
4.   plug :protect_from_forgery
5.   plug :fetch_live_flash
6.   plug YourAppWeb.Plugs.VerifyUser
7. End
```

This setup ensures that the plug is called for each request that goes through the browser pipeline, verifying user authentication before processing any controller actions.

Custom plugs are a powerful feature in Phoenix that allows you to cleanly handle cross-cutting concerns such as user authentication, logging, and more. By structuring your code with custom plugs, you can make your application more modular, reusable, and easy to maintain.

**Exercise 8.2**

**Objective**: How can you implement multilingual support in a Phoenix application to cater to a diverse user base with different language preferences?

To add multilingual support in a Phoenix application, you can use the gettext package, which Phoenix supports out of the box for internationalization (i18n).

Here is a step-by-step approach:

1. **Setup gettext**: Ensure gettext is in your **mix.exs** dependencies. Phoenix usually includes it by default.

   Run **mix deps.get** to fetch the dependency if needed.

2. **Prepare locale files**: Create translation files using **.po** and **.pot** formats within the **priv/gettext** directory. Use the **mix gettext.extract** and **mix gettext.merge** commands to handle these files:

   a. **Extract strings**: Run **mix gettext.extract** to scan your project and extract strings, generating or updating a **.pot** file.

   b. **Merge translations**: Run **mix gettext.merge priv/gettext** to update **.po** files based on the **.pot** file. This prepares the **.po** files for new translations without losing existing translations.

   This system ensures that translations are managed efficiently and updates to the text in your application do not require starting the translation process from scratch. Translators work primarily with **.po** files, translating new entries as your application evolves.

3. **Setting up language files**: You will find directories within **priv/gettext** corresponding to each locale, such as en, fr, and es for English, French, and Spanish, respectively.

   Each directory will contain **.po** files where you need to provide the translated strings. For instance, for Spanish:

   ```
   1. msgid "Hello, World!"
   2. msgstr "¡Hola, Mundo!"
   ```

4. **Using translations in your application**: Use the gettext function in your Elixir code and templates to refer to translatable strings:

   ```
   1. # In a Phoenix template:
   2. <h1><%= gettext("Hello, World!") %></h1>
   ```

   Phoenix will automatically fetch the correct translation based on the current user's locale.

5. **Handling locale switching**: Implement functionality to allow users to switch locales (e.g., through a dropdown menu).

   Store the chosen locale in the session or a cookie and configure Phoenix to use this locale for each request.

6. **Configuring locale dynamically**: Use a plug to read the locale setting from the session or cookie and set it for each request:

```
1. defmodule MyAppWeb.LocalePlug do
2.   import Plug.Conn
3.
4.   def init(default), do: default
5.
6.   def call(conn, _opts) do
7.     locale = get_session(conn, :locale) || "en"
8.     Gettext.put_locale(MyAppWeb.Gettext, locale)
9.     conn
10.  end
11. End
```

This setup ensures that each user can view your application in their preferred language, enhancing accessibility and user experience. Remember to maintain your translation files as your application evolves to include new translatable strings.

# Points to remember

- **Framework basics**: Understand the foundational concepts of Phoenix, integration with the Elixir ecosystem, and MVC architecture.

- **Setup and installation**: Master the initial steps of setting up a Phoenix project, including installation and configuration of the development environment.

- **Routing and controllers**: Gain proficiency in defining routes and creating controllers to effectively handle web requests and responses.

- **Views and templates**: Learn how to dynamically use Phoenix's templating engine to render HTML content.

- **Real-time communication**: Implement real-time features using Phoenix Channels, understanding the role of WebSockets.

- **Ecto for data management**: Utilize Ecto for database interactions, schema management, and performing CRUD operations.

- **Authentication system**: Implement and customize user authentication and authorization using mix phx.gen.auth and understand stateless authentication using Phoenix.Token.

- **Security practices**: Always prioritize security, especially in authentication flows and data handling.

# Join our Discord space

Join our Discord workspace for latest updates, offers, tech happenings around the world, new releases, and sessions with the authors:

https://discord.bpbonline.com

# CHAPTER 9

# Creating Deployable Releases

## Introduction

In this chapter, we will explore the concept of deployable releases in Elixir using the Phoenix framework. We will create a new Phoenix application to serve as a practical example as we explore various aspects of release management. This chapter aims to equip you with the knowledge and skills needed to effectively manage and deploy Phoenix applications.

## Structure

This chapter will cover the following topics:

- Understanding release management in Elixir
- Creating releases with Mix and deploying them to production

## Objectives

The objective of this chapter is to equip readers with a thorough understanding of creating deployable releases in Elixir, with a focus on the Phoenix framework. We aim to provide a solid foundation in release management principles, including versioning, dependency management, and configuration. They will learn how to use Mix, Elixir's build tool, to compile and package Phoenix applications into self-contained releases that include all necessary dependencies and the Erlang runtime.

Additionally, this chapter will cover the practical aspects of deploying releases to production environments, such as setting up environment variables, running migrations, and starting the application. Emphasis will be placed on adhering to best practices for release management and deployment to ensure smooth and efficient deployment of Phoenix applications. By the end of this chapter, readers will have the skills and knowledge to confidently manage and deploy Elixir applications, ensuring they are reliable, scalable, and production-ready. Practical exercises will also be provided to reinforce the concepts covered and offer hands-on experience in creating and deploying releases.

# Understanding release management in Elixir

Release management in Elixir is a crucial process for deploying applications efficiently and consistently across various environments. It involves packaging your application along with all its dependencies, including the Erlang runtime, into a self-contained bundle known as a **release**. This release can be deployed without the need for a local Elixir or Erlang installation on the target system.

The essence of Elixir releases lies in their inclusion of the Erlang runtime (the BEAM virtual machine) within the release package itself. This bundled runtime allows your compiled Elixir application to run independently of the host system's installed languages or frameworks. As a result, you can deploy your application to any environment that supports the operating system for which the release was built, ensuring portability and reducing the potential for environment-specific issues.

## Key components of release management

Effective release management ensures that your Elixir application is built, packaged, and deployed in a consistent and reliable manner. It involves several critical components, each contributing to the stability and maintainability of your application throughout its lifecycle. The following are the key elements of release management, along with practical examples to help you understand their significance:

- **Versioning**: Proper versioning is critical in release management. **Semantic Versioning (SemVer)** is commonly used, where versions are formatted as MAJOR.MINOR. PATCH. Changes in the MAJOR version indicate incompatible API changes, MINOR versions add functionality in a backward-compatible manner, and PATCH versions are for backward-compatible bug fixes.

  In your **mix.exs** file, specify the version of your application:

```
1. defmodule MyApp.MixProject do
2.    use Mix.Project
3.
```

```
 4.   def project do
 5.     [
 6.        app: :my_app,
 7.        version: "1.0.0", # Major.Minor.Patch
 8.        elixir: "~> 1.12",
 9.        # Other project details...
10.     ]
11.   end
12.
13.   # Other configurations...
14. End
```

When you make changes:

o   Increase the MAJOR number for breaking changes.

o   Increase the MINOR number of new features that do not break existing functionality.

o   Increase the PATCH number for bug fixes.

- **Dependencies**: Managing dependencies is essential to ensure that your application has all the necessary packages and that they are compatible with each other. Dependency management tools like *Hex* and *Mix* help in managing Elixir and Erlang dependencies, respectively.

- **Configuration**: This involves setting up and maintaining the configuration settings required for different environments (development, test, production, etc.). Elixir applications typically use **config** files (like **config/config.exs**) to manage settings, and releases allow you to provide runtime configuration using tools like **config/releases.exs**.

- **Builds**: The build process compiles your application code and its dependencies into bytecode. In Elixir, this is typically done using the Mix build tool. The build process should be reproducible, ensuring consistent results across different environments.

You can use Mix to compile your application:

```
 1. mix compile
```

This compiles your Elixir code into BEAM bytecode that the Erlang VM can execute.

- **Packaging**: This involves creating a self-contained bundle of your application, which includes the compiled bytecode, the Erlang runtime, and any necessary configuration files and assets. This package, known as a release, can be easily deployed to any target environment.

- **Deployment**: The process of transferring the release package to a target environment (e.g., a server) and starting the application. This can be automated using tools like *Capistrano*, *Docker*, or *Kubernetes*.

- **Monitoring and maintenance**: Once deployed, it is crucial to monitor your application for performance, errors, and other issues. Tools like the *Erlang Observer*, *Telemetry*, and third-party services like *AppSignal* can be used for monitoring. Regular maintenance, including updates and patches, is also necessary to keep the application running smoothly.

# Benefits of using releases

Releases in Elixir provide a streamlined and efficient way to deploy applications by packaging everything needed into a self-contained bundle. This approach simplifies deployment, enhances security, and ensures that applications run consistently across different environments. The following are the key benefits of using releases in Elixir:

- **Portability**: Releases are self-contained and include the Erlang runtime, making them easily deployable across different environments without the need for a local Elixir or Erlang installation.

- **Consistency**: Since releases are built from a specific version of your application and its dependencies, they provide a consistent environment, reducing the *it works on my machine* problem.

- **Performance**: Releases can be optimized for performance, as they allow you to compile your code for a specific target environment.

- **Security**: By bundling only the necessary components and dependencies, releases can help reduce the attack surface of your application.

- **Simplicity**: Deploying a release is often simpler than deploying source code, as it eliminates the need for a build step on the target environment.

Therefore, understanding release management in Elixir involves mastering the lifecycle of your application from development to deployment. By using releases, you can ensure that your application is portable, consistent, performant, secure, and easy to deploy.

# Creating releases with Mix and deploying them to production

Creating a release for a production environment in an Elixir project involves several steps to ensure that your application is compiled, packaged, and ready for deployment. The following is a detailed guide on how to create a release for a production environment using Mix:

1.  **Preparing your application**: Before creating a release, make sure your application is ready for production:

    a.  **Update dependencies**: Ensure that all dependencies are up-to-date in your **mix.exs** file:

        ```
        1. mix deps.get --only prod
        ```

    b.  **Configure your application**: Set up your **config/prod.exs** and **config/releases.exs** for production. In **config/releases.exs**, use environment variables for sensitive information and runtime configuration:

        ```
        1. import Config
        2.
        3. config :my_app, MyApp.Repo,
        4.    url: System.get_env("DATABASE_URL"),
        5.    pool_size: String.to_integer(System.get_env("POOL_SIZE") ||
           "10")
        6.
        7. config :my_app, MyAppWeb.Endpoint,
        8.    secret_key_base: System.get_env("SECRET_KEY_BASE")
        ```

    c.  **Compile static assets**: For Phoenix applications, compile your static assets:

        ```
        1. MIX_ENV=prod mix assets.deploy
        ```

    d.  **Generate release configuration**: Run the following command in your Phoenix project directory:

        **mix phx.gen.release**

        ```
        01. mix phx.gen.release
        02. ==> my_app
        03. * creating rel/overlays/bin/server
        04. * creating rel/overlays/bin/server.bat
        05. * creating rel/overlays/bin/migrate
        06. * creating rel/overlays/bin/migrate.bat
        07. * creating lib/my_app/release.ex
        08.
        09. Your application is ready to be deployed in a release!
        10.
        11.    # To start your system
        ```

```
12.     _build/prod/rel/my_app/bin/my_app start
13.
14.     # To start your system with the Phoenix server running
15.     _build/prod/rel/my_app/bin/server
16.
17.     # To run migrations
18.     _build/prod/rel/my_app/bin/migrate
19.
20. Once the release is running:
21.
22.     # To connect to it remotely
23.     _build/prod/rel/my_app/bin/my_app remote
24.
25.     # To stop it gracefully (you may also send SIGINT/SIGTERM)
26.     _build/prod/rel/my_app/bin/my_app stop
27.
28. To list all commands:
29.
30.     _build/prod/rel/my_app/bin/my_app
```

**Note: If you are a Docker user, you can pass the --docker flag to mix phx.gen.release to generate a Dockerfile ready for deployment.**

The **phx.gen.release** task generated a few files for us to assist in releases. First, it created server and migrate overlay scripts for conveniently running the Phoenix server inside a release for invoking migrations from a release. The files in the **rel/overlays** directory are copied into every release environment. Next, it generated a **release.ex** file, which is used to invoke Ecto migrations without a dependency on mix itself.

```
1. mix phx.gen.release --docker
```

Then, build the Docker image:

```
1. docker build -t my_app:latest .
```

2. **Creating the release**: To create a release, run the following command in your project root:

```
1. MIX_ENV=prod mix release
```

This command will compile your application and build the release, which will be stored in **_build/prod/rel/my_app**.

3. **Deploying the release**: Once you have created your release (and optionally your Docker image), you can deploy it to your production environment:

   a. **Transfer the release**: Copy the release artifact from **_build/prod/rel/my_app** to your production server.

   b. **Set environment variables**: Ensure that all the required environment variables (**DATABASE_URL**, **SECRET_KEY_BASE**, etc.) are set in your production environment.

   c. **Start the application**: Run the release on your production server:

```
1. _build/prod/rel/my_app/bin/my_app start
```

   If you are using Docker, you can start the Docker container instead:

```
1. docker run --env-file .env -p 4000:4000 my_app:latest
```

4. **Running migrations**: In Phoenix, database schemas are typically managed through Ecto migrations. When deploying a release, it is important to have a strategy for running these migrations in your production environment. Phoenix's release mechanism provides a way to include Ecto migrations and custom commands as part of your release:

   a. **Including Ecto migrations in releases**: When you run **mix phx.gen.release**, it generates a **lib/my_app/release.ex** file with a **migrate/0** function. This function is responsible for running your Ecto migrations when the release starts. Here is an example of what this file might look like:

```
01. defmodule MyApp.Release do
02.   @app :my_app
03.
04.   def migrate do
05.     load_app()
06.
07.     for repo <- repos() do
08.       {:ok, _, _} = Ecto.Migrator.with_repo(repo, &Ecto.Migrator.run(&1, :up, all: true))
09.     end
10.   end
11.
12.   def rollback(repo, version) do
```

```
13.      load_app()
14.      {:ok, _, _} = Ecto.Migrator.with_repo(repo, &Ecto.Migrator.
   run(&1, :down, to: version))
15.   end
16.
17.   defp repos do
18.      Application.fetch_env!(@app, :ecto_repos)
19.   end
20.
21.   defp load_app do
22.      Application.load(@app)
23.   end
24. End
```

To run migrations as part of your release, you can use the eval command when starting your application:

```
1. _build/prod/rel/my_app/bin/my_app eval "MyApp.Release.migrate"
```

b.  **Custom commands in releases**: In addition to running migrations, you might want to execute other custom commands as part of your release. You can define these commands in the **MyApp.Release** module or in separate modules, depending on your preference.

For example, you might add a function to reset the database:

```
1. def reset_database do
2.    load_app()
3.
4.    for repo <- repos() do
5.      Ecto.Adapters.SQL.query!(repo, "DROP SCHEMA public CASCADE")
6.      Ecto.Adapters.SQL.query!(repo, "CREATE SCHEMA public")
7.      {:ok, _} = Ecto.Migrator.run(repo, :up, all: true)
8.    end
9.  End
```

Then, you can execute this command using the **eval** command in your release:

```
1. _build/prod/rel/my_app/bin/my_app eval "MyApp.Release.reset_
   database"
```

    c.  **Tips for managing migrations and commands**: They are as follows:

        i.  **Test your migrations**: Always test your migrations in a staging environment before running them in production.

        ii.  **Backup your database**: Consider creating a backup of your database before running migrations or commands that modify the database schema.

        iii.  **Monitor the output**: When running migrations or custom commands, monitor the output for any errors or unexpected behavior.

    d.  By leveraging the `MyApp.Release` module and the `eval` command in your releases, you can effectively manage Ecto migrations and execute custom commands in your Phoenix application's production environment.

        The `load_app()` function in Ecto migrations and releases in a Phoenix application ensures that the application and its configuration are loaded before running any migrations or custom commands.

5.  **Monitoring and maintenance**: After deployment, monitor your application for any issues and perform regular maintenance. Set up logging, error tracking, and performance monitoring to ensure your application runs smoothly in production.

# Conclusion

In this chapter, we explored the essential aspects of creating and deploying releases in Elixir, focusing on Phoenix applications. We covered the importance of release management, including versioning, dependency management, and configuration. We explained the process of creating releases using Mix, packaging our applications into self-contained units that can be deployed across various environments.

We also discussed the practicalities of deploying releases to production, emphasizing the need for a solid strategy for running Ecto migrations and executing custom commands. By adhering to best practices and keeping key points in mind, we can ensure our deployments are smooth, reliable, and secure.

Creating and deploying releases is a critical skill for any Elixir developer, and mastering this process will enable you to manage your applications effectively throughout their lifecycle. As you continue to develop and deploy Elixir applications, remember the importance of automation, testing, and monitoring to maintain the quality and reliability of your releases in production environments.

In the next chapter, we will explore the component-driven approach to building maintainable UIs in Phoenix. You will learn how Phoenix Components differ from traditional views, how to create reusable and modular UI elements, and how to write effective tests for reliability. A mini task tracker application will illustrate these concepts in a simple request or response flow. This foundation will help you structure real-world Phoenix applications more effectively.

# Practical exercises

1. Use Mix to check for outdated dependencies in your project. Update any dependencies that are not up-to-date and resolve any compatibility issues that arise.

   **Solution**:

   a. **Check for outdated dependencies**:

   i. Navigate to the **root** directory of your Phoenix project.

   ii. Use the `mix hex.outdated` command to list all dependencies that have newer versions available:

   ```
   1. mix hex.outdated
   ```

   This command will provide a table showing the current version of each dependency, the latest available version, and whether it is a direct or transitive dependency.

   b. **Update outdated dependencies**:

   i. For each outdated dependency, decide whether to update it based on the version changes and your application's requirements.

   ii. Update individual dependencies using the `mix deps.update <dependency_name>` command:

   ```
   1. mix deps.update phoenix
   ```

   iii. Alternatively, you can update all outdated dependencies at once with:

   ```
   1. mix deps.update -all
   ```

   c. **Resolve compatibility issues**:

   i. After updating dependencies, compile your project to check for any compatibility issues:

   ```
   1. mix compile
   ```

   ii. If there are any compilation errors or warnings, address them by adjusting your code or configuration as needed.

   It may be necessary to consult the documentation or changelogs of the updated dependencies to understand any breaking changes or new requirements.

   d. **Test your application**:

   i. Run your application's test suite to ensure that the updates have not introduced any regressions:

   ```
   1. mix test
   ```

      ii. Perform manual testing as needed to verify that your application is functioning correctly with the updated dependencies.

   e. **Commit changes**: Once you have verified that your application works with the updated dependencies, commit the changes to your `mix.lock` file and any other modified files to your version control system.

By following these steps, you can keep the dependencies of your Phoenix project up-to-date and compatible, ensuring the ongoing health and security of your application.

# Points to remember

- **Use SemVer**: Adopting SemVer helps maintain clarity and consistency in your release process:

    o Format your versions as MAJOR.MINOR.PATCH.

    o Increment the MAJOR version for incompatible API changes, MINOR for new features that are backward-compatible, and PATCH for backward-compatible bug fixes.

- **Automate the build process**: Automating builds ensures consistency and reduces human error during deployment:

    o Use CI tools like GitHub Actions, GitLab CI/CD, or Jenkins to automate the compilation and packaging of your application.

    o Set up pipelines that trigger the build process on code commits or merges to specific branches.

- **Manage configuration carefully**: Proper configuration management enhances security and flexibility across environments:

    o Use environment variables to pass sensitive information to your application. For example, use `System.get_env("DATABASE_URL")` in your config/releases. exs.

    o Consider using tools like AWS Secrets Manager or HashiCorp Vault for managing secrets in a more secure manner.

- **Test your releases**: Thorough testing ensures your release works as expected before reaching production:

    o Set up a staging environment that mirrors your production environment as closely as possible.

    o Run your full suite of automated tests and perform manual testing on the release in this environment before deploying to production.

- **Include migrations in your release**: Managing database migrations as part of your release avoids schema inconsistencies:
    - o   Include a migration module in your release, as described in the Ecto migrations section, and ensure it's called as part of your deployment process.
    - o   Use the eval command in your release to run migrations: `_build/prod/rel/ my_app/bin/my_app eval "MyApp.Release.migrate"`.

- **Use Distillery or Mix releases**: Choose the appropriate release tool based on your Elixir version:
    - o   For projects using Elixir 1.9 or later, use Mix releases (mix release) to package your application.
    - o   For older projects, consider using Distillery, a third-party release management tool.

- **Rollback strategy**: Preparing for rollbacks ensures you can recover quickly from failed deployments:
    - o   Keep previous release artifacts stored in a safe location so you can quickly switch back to them if needed.
    - o   Consider using tools like Ansible, Capistrano, or custom scripts to automate the rollback process.

- **Monitor your application**: Ongoing monitoring is essential for maintaining application health post-deployment:
    - o   Set up monitoring tools like New Relic, AppSignal, or Prometheus to track your application's performance and error rates.
    - o   Use logging libraries like Logger or third-party services to capture and analyze logs.

- **Document the deployment process**: Clear documentation streamlines deployments and reduces the risk of errors:
    - o   Create detailed documentation outlining each step of the deployment process, including any manual checks or commands that need to be run.
    - o   Keep this documentation up-to-date and easily accessible to all team members involved in deployments.

- **Keep up with Elixir and Phoenix updates**: Staying current with updates ensures you benefit from the latest features and security patches:
    - o   Regularly check for updates to Elixir, Phoenix, and other dependencies in your project.
    - o   Use tools like Dependabot or Renovate to automate dependency updates and create pull requests for review.

# CHAPTER 10

# Build Phoenix Components for Real-world Apps

## Introduction

In this chapter, we will start a journey into the world of Phoenix Components, exploring how they form the foundation for building powerful and maintainable applications in the Phoenix ecosystem. We will begin by understanding what components are and why the Phoenix team introduced this concept to streamline the development process. Rather than scattering logic across multiple templates and views, we now have a pattern that brings reusability, modularity, and clarity to the forefront. Through this transition, our goal is to establish a solid understanding of why component-driven architecture is changing the game, how it aligns with common best practices seen in other modern frameworks, and what it means for your future development efforts.

## Structure

The chapter covers the following topics:

- Foundational concepts
- Intermediate techniques
- Testing components
- Mini task tracker with Phoenix Components

# Objectives

By the end of this chapter, you will not only grasp the fundamental concepts behind creating, rendering, and organizing Phoenix Components, but you will also be able to confidently use them to build small features and more complex interfaces. You will learn how to pass data into components, handle state and dynamic attributes, and elegantly manage conditional rendering to ensure each component behaves as intended. Moving beyond the basics, you will explore more advanced patterns, such as using slots to compose flexible, reusable layouts and writing tests to safeguard your components against regressions. Ultimately, these skills will empower you to build clean, reliable, and future-proof code that stands strong as your application grows.

# Foundational concepts

Before exploring complex interactions and layouts, it is essential to establish a strong understanding of what Phoenix Components are, how they differ from traditional rendering techniques, and the basic steps needed to create and incorporate them into your application. In this section, we will focus on the fundamentals: defining simple components, rendering them in templates, and passing data to them. This foundation will help you appreciate the more advanced techniques introduced later.

## Phoenix Components

A Phoenix Component is essentially a function that returns a precompiled HTML template. Think of it as a self-contained UI building block, responsible for a specific piece of the interface, like a button, card, or navigation element. By using components, you can write once and reuse these elements throughout your application, which encourages consistency, reduces duplication, and makes your code easier to maintain.

In older versions of Phoenix, you might rely on views and templates scattered across different files. Components centralize logic and markup, and because they are just functions, they are straightforward to test, refactor, and integrate. Unlike using full-blown LiveView (which offers interactive, real-time features), we will keep these components simple and static for now, focusing purely on how to define and render them in a traditional request/response flow.

## Setting stage for Phoenix.Component module

In order to create components, Phoenix provides a dedicated API through the Phoenix. Component module. By using this module and the ~H sigil, you can write your HTML templates inline within your component definitions. This approach keeps your HTML and Elixir logic together, making it easier to see how data flows through your UI. For example, a simple heading component, as shown in the following:

```
01. defmodule MyAppWeb.Components.Title do
02.    use Phoenix.Component
03.
04.    # A simple component that displays a page title
05.    def title(assigns) do
06.      ~H"""
07.      <h1 class="text-2xl font-bold"><%= @text %></h1>
08.      """
09.    end
10. End
```

In the above code snippet, we have defined a component named title that expects an assign (a piece of data passed into the component) called **@text**. Notice how **@text** appears within the ~H template; because this variable is provided by the caller, you can dynamically change the text displayed without altering the component's internal logic.

# Rendering components in templates

Once a component module is in place, you can call it from any **.heex** template. To make the first example crystal clear, we will start with the fully qualified form, spelling out the entire module path, then show the shorter version most developers use in day-to-day work.

Use the fully-qualified call:

```
01. <!-- Fully-qualified invocation -->
02. <MyAppWeb.Components.Title.title text="Welcome to the Task Dashboard" />
```

We can break down the code into the following:

- **MyAppWeb.Components.Title** is the module that houses the component.
- **title** is the function component.
- **text=Welcome** to the Task Dashboard is the assign passed in.

When the page loads, Phoenix turns this call into an **<h1>** element containing **Welcome to the Task Dashboard**.

## Aliased or shorthand call

Typing the full module path quickly becomes tedious, so in a real template, you normally **alias** the module once and then use Phoenix's shorthand syntax:

```
01. # At the top of the template or view module
02. alias MyAppWeb.Components.Title
```

```
03.
04. <!-- Shorthand invocation -->
05. <.title text="Welcome to the Task Dashboard" />
```

The aliased version renders the same HTML, but only the call site is more concise. Use whichever style best fits your context.

When the page loads, the `<h1>` element defined in the component will appear, populated with the text `Welcome to the Task Dashboard`. This separation allows you to keep logic for how a title should look and behave entirely within the `Title` component and simply specify which text should appear when you render it.

# Data passing and assigns

Data passing is at the heart of Phoenix Components. Every piece of data a component needs is provided through assigns, key-value pairs that get passed into the component function. In practice, you will often provide these assignments directly in your templates, ensuring that each component receives the exact data it needs. For example, passing data to a component, as shown in the following:

```
01. <.title text="My Tasks for Today" />
```

Here, the text `My Tasks for Today` is assigned. Inside the component, it is accessed as `@text`. If you need multiple assigns, you can list them all, as shown in the following:

```
01. <.task_card title="Buy Groceries" completed={false} />
```

On the component side, you will be able to reference `@title` and `@completed` to dynamically render or style content.

# Difference between views and components in Phoenix 1.7+

Earlier to Phoenix 1.7, developers typically relied on *views* along with separate template files to render their HTML pages. A view was a module containing helper functions, while the actual HTML lived in .eex template files. You might have something like `MyAppWeb.PageView` combined with `templates/page/index.html.eex`, where the layout and logic were spread out, often making it less obvious how everything was tied together.

## Changes introduced in Phoenix 1.7+

Phoenix introduced function components, allowing you to define UI logic and markup right inside your `MyAppWeb.Components modules`. Instead of scattering code across multiple files (a view module and separate template files), a function component encapsulates everything you need, data handling, and the resulting HTML, into a single place.

A concrete example is given in the following:

- Old way with views (Pre-1.7) is:

  o **PageView module**: It might contain helper functions like **format_title(title)**.

  o **Template file (index.html.eex)**: The following is how you might structure your code in older Phoenix versions, relying on separate view modules and template files before the shift to a more component-centric approach:

```
01.  # page_view.ex
02.  defmodule MyAppWeb.PageView do
03.    use MyAppWeb, :view
04.
05.    def format_title(title), do: String.upcase(title)
06.  end
07.
08.  <!-- templates/page/index.html.eex -->
09.  <h1><%= format_title(@page_title) %></h1>
10.  <p>Welcome to the homepage!</p>
```

In this scenario, you jump between the view (for logic) and the template file (for HTML), which may live in separate directories.

- New way with components (Phoenix 1.7+) is:

  o **Title component**: In Phoenix 1.7 and beyond, you can consolidate markup and logic into a single component module, as shown in the following:

```
01.  # components/title.ex
02.  defmodule MyAppWeb.Components.Title do
03.    use Phoenix.Component
04.
05.    def title(assigns) do
06.      ~H"""
07.      <h1 class="text-2xl font-bold"><%= String.upcase(@text) %></h1>
08.      """
09.    end
10.  end
```

```
11.
12.    <!-- index.html.heex -->
13.    <.title text="Welcome to the homepage!" />
```

Here, the logic (**String.upcase(@text)**) and the **HTML** (**<h1>...</h1>**) live side-by-side, making it easy to see how your data transforms into HTML. You no longer need a separate view for helper functions and a separate template file for HTML; the component encapsulates both. In essence, this comparison highlights how components streamline both development and maintenance by unifying your markup and logic in one place, contrasting the more scattered approach used in older Phoenix versions:

o **Views**: Often rely on multiple files (view modules + templates), making code more scattered.

o **Components**: Combine logic and markup in one place, improving discoverability and maintainability.

## Improving components in reusability and readability

Components shine when you need to reuse UI elements across multiple parts of your application. Without components, you might copy and paste the same markup and logic into multiple templates and later update them all if something changes. For example, a reusable button.

Let us see a scenario without a component. Imagine you have a styled button you use on your homepage, about page, and contact page. If you do not use components, you might create something similar in three different templates:

```
01. <!-- homepage.html.eex -->
02. <button class="px-4 py-2 bg-blue-500 text-white rounded">Click Me</
    button>
03.
04. <!-- about.html.eex -->
05. <button class="px-4 py-2 bg-blue-500 text-white rounded">Click Me</
    button>
06.
07. <!-- contact.html.eex -->
08. <button class="px-4 py-2 bg-blue-500 text-white rounded">Click Me</button>
```

If you decide to change the button's background color, you must open each template and update the class. This is both tedious and prone to error.

Let us see the same scenario with a component. Define the button once as a component, as shown in the following:

```
01. # components/button.ex
02. defmodule MyAppWeb.Components.Button do
03.   use Phoenix.Component
04.
05.   def button(assigns) do
06.     ~H"""
07.     <button class="px-4 py-2 bg-blue-500 text-white rounded">
08.       <%= @text %>
09.     </button>
10.     """
11.   end
12. End
```

Now, to use it anywhere, you type the command mentioned in the following:

```
01. <.button text="Click Me" />
```

If you need to change the button's style later (for instance, changing the background color to red), you edit it in one place, the **button.ex** component file. Every page using **<.button>** instantly updates, saving you time and ensuring consistency.

## Readability through encapsulation

Components also improve readability by grouping related logic and HTML. Instead of jumping between files to understand how something works, you open a single component module and see the entire picture at once.

For example, if someone new joins your team and wants to understand how tasks are displayed, they open **TaskCard** component's file, as shown in the following:

```
01. defmodule MyAppWeb.Components.TaskCard do
02.   use Phoenix.Component
03.
04.   def task_card(assigns) do
05.     ~H"""
06.     <div class={"#{if @completed, do: "bg-gray-200", else: "bg-white"}
     p-4 rounded shadow"}>
07.       <h2 class="font-bold text-lg"><%= @title %></h2>
08.       <p><%= @description %></p>
09.       <!-- Static button without LiveView events, for demonstration -->
```

```
10.        <button class="mt-2 px-4 py-2 bg-blue-500 text-white rounded">
11.          Toggle Completion
12.        </button>
13.      </div>
14.      """
15.  end
16. End
```

Here, the logic (if **@completed**) and the HTML (**<div class="...">...</div>**) sit side-by-side. There is no guesswork about where the styling or logic comes from. Everything you need to know about how a single task is displayed is right here in one file. This self-contained design makes it easier to read, reason about, and change in the future.

**In a Nutshell**: The following is a quick overview of the primary benefits that components bring to your application design:

- **Reusability**: Define an element once, use it everywhere, and update it in one place.

- **Readability**: Keep logic and markup together, so it is easier to understand what is happening at a glance.

By using components, you write less code, maintain fewer files, and end up with a more coherent and manageable codebase. As your application grows, these advantages become even more pronounced, making components a foundational building block for scalable Phoenix applications.

# Incremental complexity

As your application grows, it is natural to add new features and more intricate designs, but that does not mean the learning curve has to be steep. By starting with core principles and gradually building upon them, you can ensure that each step remains manageable. Let us focus on the most essential building blocks:

- **Defining a component**: Creating a function that returns a template using **~H**.

- **Rendering a component**: Invoking **<.component_name>** in templates.

- **Passing data**: Supplying assigns that the component can use to produce dynamic, data-driven output.

With these basics in hand, you already possess the core skill set to start organizing your UI with components. As we progress, you will see how these same fundamentals scale up when we tackle more advanced scenarios, such as dealing with multiple layers of components, conditional rendering, and slot-based layouts.

Some practical tips for beginners are mentioned in the following:

- **Keep it simple first**: Start with extremely simple components, like a styled heading or a static button, to get comfortable with the syntax and concepts.

- **Consistent naming**: Name your components and their functions clearly to reflect their purpose, like `Title`, `TaskCard`, or `AddTaskForm`.

- **Test as you go**: Even though we will talk about testing later, it is helpful to think early about how easily testable your components are. Components defined as pure functions returning templates are simpler to test and reason about.

Having established these foundational concepts, what components are, how to define and render them, and how to pass in data, we are ready to move into the next stage. In the following sections, we will build on this knowledge, introducing intermediate techniques that will let you create more flexible and dynamic components. By the end of this journey, you will be well-equipped to confidently construct a wide range of UI patterns, all grounded in the solid understanding you have gained here.

# Intermediate techniques

With the foundational understanding of defining components, passing data through assigns, and integrating them into templates, you have gained the core building blocks to start thinking more creatively about how to structure your UI. In this section, we are going to push beyond the basics and explore the following three key intermediate-level concepts:

- **Dynamic attributes**: Learning to tailor the attributes of your HTML elements based on passed-in assigns, allowing you to create components that adapt to different contexts and data states.

- **Conditional rendering**: Using logic within your templates to show or hide elements based on dynamic conditions, ensuring your components gracefully handle various scenarios without duplicating code.

- **Slots**: Leveraging slots to create *containers* and *layout* components that can wrap other components or HTML elements, making your system more composable and flexible as your application grows.

By mastering these techniques, you will expand your toolkit to build more versatile and maintainable interfaces. Each concept is firmly rooted in practical examples, so you can immediately see how these patterns improve your day-to-day development workflow.

# Dynamic attributes for adaptable components

As your application's user interface grows more sophisticated, your components will need to do more than just display static content. They will need to adapt to various contexts, handle different data inputs, and present themselves differently based on state or configuration.

Dynamic attributes enable this flexibility, allowing you to modify HTML element attributes at runtime depending on the data assigned to your component.

This adaptability is crucial for building a truly reusable component library. Instead of hardcoding multiple variants of the same UI element, you can create a single component that adjusts its appearance and behavior based on how it is invoked.

## Usage dynamic attributes

Consider a simple button. Early in your project, you might define a single style and size, but as requirements evolve, you will need multiple variants: primary, secondary, disabled, large, small, and so on. Without dynamic attributes, you might end up creating many separate components or scattering conditional code throughout your templates. Dynamic attributes let you centralize all these variations in one place, making it easy to introduce new variants or states later.

Some key benefits are mentioned in the following:

- **Maintainability**: Update one component definition rather than multiple hardcoded templates.

- **Consistency**: Ensure uniform behavior and styling across your entire application.

- **Scalability**: Easily introduce new states or variants without rewriting large portions of your code.

# Flexible button component

Let us revisit the button component introduced earlier, but now in more detail. Our goal is to have a single button component that can display differently based on a type assigned (`:primary`, `:secondary`, `:danger`) and an optional disabled state.

# Component definition of flexible button

Following is an example of a flexible button component that adapts its appearance and behavior based on assigned values, such as button type (`:primary`, `:secondary`, `:danger`) and a disabled state, demonstrating how to use dynamic attributes in Phoenix Components:

```
01. defmodule MyAppWeb.Components.Button do
02.   use Phoenix.Component
03.
04.   def button(assigns) do
05.     type = assigns[:type] || :primary
06.     disabled = assigns[:disabled] || false
07.
```

```
08.      # Define a base set of CSS classes that all buttons share.
09.      base_classes = "px-4 py-2 rounded font-medium"
10.
11.      # Adjust styling based on the button type.
12.      color_classes =
13.        case type do
14.          :primary -> "bg-blue-500 text-white hover:bg-blue-600"
15.          :secondary -> "bg-gray-200 text-black hover:bg-gray-300"
16.          :danger -> "bg-red-500 text-white hover:bg-red-600"
17.          _ -> "bg-gray-500 text-white hover:bg-gray-600"
18.        end
19.
20.      # If the button is disabled, we add different classes and disable
    hover effects.
21.      disabled_classes = if disabled, do: "opacity-50 cursor-not-allowed
    hover:bg-blue-500", else: ""
22.
23.      # Combine all the classes into one final class string.
24.      final_classes = Enum.join([base_classes, color_classes, disabled_
    classes], " ")
25.
26.      ~H"""
27.      <button class={final_classes} disabled={@disabled}>
28.        <%= @text %>
29.      </button>
30.      """
31.    end
32. End
```

The explanation of the code is mentioned in the following:

- We accept **@type** and **@disabled** assigns from the caller. If not provided, **@type** defaults to **:primary** and **@disabled** defaults to false.

- Using a case statement, we select a color scheme based on **@type**.

- If **@disabled** is true, we adjust the styling and add the disabled attribute to prevent user interaction.

- We dynamically build the class and disabled attributes of the **\<button\>** element from the assigns, rather than hardcoding them.

A usage example is shown in the following:

```
01. <.button text="Submit" type={:primary} />
02. <.button text="Cancel" type={:secondary} />
03. <.button text="Delete Account" type={:danger} disabled={true} />
```

Each of these calls uses the same button component but produces a different appearance and behavior.

## Dynamic accessibility attributes

Dynamic attributes are not limited to styling. They can also adjust accessibility attributes (**aria-** attributes), **data-** attributes, or even URLs based on user input. Let us consider a navigation link component that adapts its attributes based on the current page and accessibility needs.

# Component definition of dynamic attribute

Following is a navigation link component illustrating how dynamic attributes can handle accessibility and visual cues. By comparing **@current_page** to the link's **@href**, we selectively add **aria-current=page** and highlight the active link, demonstrating how Phoenix Components can adapt HTML attributes based on user input:

```
01. defmodule MyAppWeb.Components.NavLink do
02.   use Phoenix.Component
03.
04.   def nav_link(assigns) do
05.     current_page = assigns[:current_page] || ""
06.     href = assigns[:href] || "#"
07.
08.     # Check if this link points to the current page:
09.     is_current = current_page == href
10.
11.     # Base classes for all nav links:
12.     base_classes = "inline-block px-3 py-2 rounded hover:bg-gray-100"
13.
14.     # Highlight the current page's link.
15.     active_classes = if is_current, do: "bg-blue-100 font-bold", else:
        ""
```

```
16.
17.      # Accessibility: indicate the current page for screen readers if
     active.
18.      aria_current = if is_current, do: "page", else: nil
19.
20.      final_classes = Enum.join([base_classes, active_classes], " ")
21.
22.      ~H"""
23.      <a href={href} class={final_classes} aria-current={aria_current}>
24.        <%= @text %>
25.      </a>
26.      """
27.    end
28. end
```

The code is explained in the following:

- We take an assign **@current_page** that represents the user's current location.
- We compare **@current_page** to the link's **@href** to determine if the link is currently active.
- Based on that, we dynamically add **aria-current=page** and emphasize the link visually.
- If it is not the current page, we omit the **aria-current** attribute and the highlighting classes, leaving the link as a regular navigation option.

A usage example is shown in the following:

```
01. <.nav_link text="Home" href="/" current_page={@conn.request_path} />
02. <.nav_link text="Blog" href="/blog" current_page={@conn.request_path} />
03. <.nav_link text="Contact" href="/contact" current_page={@conn.request_
    path} />
```

If the user is currently on **/blog**, the **Blog** link will have **aria-current=page** and different styling to indicate it is the active link, while **Home** and **Contact** remain normal.

The tips and best practices for dynamic attributes are mentioned in the following:

- **Default values**: Always provide sensible defaults for your dynamic attributes, so the component renders gracefully even if the caller does not supply all assigns.
- **Keep logic simple**: While you can go wild with conditionals, try to keep the logic straightforward. If a component becomes overloaded with conditions, consider

refactoring into smaller, more focused components or using pattern matching in the function head to handle different scenarios.

- **Reusability first**: Start by implementing general, reusable patterns. You might not need every variant from day one, but by laying a flexible foundation, you can easily add new variants as your application grows.

- **Consistency in naming**: If you use assigns like **@type**, **@disabled**, **@current_page**, keep the naming clear and descriptive. Good naming conventions make it easier to understand what the component's dynamic attributes do without reading all the code.

Dynamic attributes empower you to build components that are not only reusable but also context-aware. By controlling CSS classes, attributes, and even content based on input data, you can keep your component library lean, expressive, and easy to maintain. Instead of duplicating code for every slight variation, you write once and let dynamic attributes handle the rest.

With these techniques in your toolbox, you are well on your way to crafting a flexible UI architecture that elegantly adapts to your application's changing requirements.

# Conditional rendering to hide and show elements

As your application matures, you will encounter scenarios where certain parts of the interface should only appear under specific conditions. Instead of creating multiple versions of a component for each scenario, you can rely on conditional rendering, using standard Elixir logic directly within your component templates to show or hide elements based on dynamic state. This approach keeps your UI code lean, expressive, and easy to maintain.

# Importance of conditional rendering

Without conditional rendering, you might find yourself duplicating templates or creating a tangle of slightly different components for each condition. By using simple **if**/**else** statements or case logic within a single component, you can tailor its output to various situations. This helps with the following things:

- **Reduce repetition**: One component handles multiple states, avoiding the need for separate variants.

- **Improve maintainability**: When conditions change, you adjust logic in one place rather than hunting through multiple files.

- **Enhance clarity**: The logic that determines what is displayed is right alongside the markup, making the component's behavior easy to understand.

## Task card that displays a completed label

Let us revisit a simplified version of our **TaskCard** component. Suppose you want to visually indicate when a task is done by adding a **Completed** label. Instead of having one template for completed tasks and another for pending tasks, you will use a conditional to render the label only when **@completed** is true.

# Component definition of conditional rendering

Following is a simplified **TaskCard** component showcasing conditional rendering: it adjusts the background color and selectively displays a **Completed** label based on the value of **@completed**, all within a single component definition:

```
01. defmodule MyAppWeb.Components.TaskCard do
02.    use Phoenix.Component
03.
04.    def task_card(assigns) do
05.        ~H"""
06.        <div class={"#{if @completed, do: "bg-gray-200", else: "bg-white"}
    p-4 rounded shadow"}>
07.            <h2 class="font-bold text-lg"><%= @title %></h2>
08.            <p><%= @description %></p>
09.
10.            <%= if @completed do %>
11.                <span class="inline-block bg-green-200 text-green-800 text-xs
    font-semibold px-2 py-1 rounded-full mt-2">
12.                    Completed
13.                </span>
14.            <% end %>
15.        </div>
16.        """
17.    end
18. end
```

The explanation of the code is given in the following:

- The background color of the card changes based on **@completed**.

- An if condition checks **@completed**. If true, the **Completed** label is rendered; if false, that portion of the template is skipped entirely.

- With a single component, you handle both states. Updating the condition or styling is straightforward, as it all lives in one place.

A usage example is shown in the following:

```
01. <.task_card title="Buy Groceries" description="Eggs, Milk, Bread"
    completed={false} />
02. <.task_card title="Clean the Garage" description="Organize tools and
    boxes" completed={true} />
```

In the second card, the **Completed** label appears automatically, while the first card displays no such label.

**Example 11.1:** Displaying alerts only when needed:

Conditional rendering can also manage more transient UI elements, like warnings or success messages. Imagine a banner component that optionally displays a dismissible alert box only if there is a relevant message to show.

# Component definition of AlertBanner

Following is an **AlertBanner** component that uses conditional rendering to display a dismissible alert only when **@alert_message** is present, avoiding empty space or redundant markup if no alert is needed:

```
01. defmodule MyAppWeb.Components.AlertBanner do
02.   use Phoenix.Component
03.
04.   def alert_banner(assigns) do
05.     ~H"""
06.     <div class="mb-4">
07.       <%= if @alert_message do %>
08.         <div class="bg-yellow-100 border border-yellow-300 text-
    yellow-800 px-4 py-3 rounded relative">
09.           <strong class="font-bold">Notice:</strong>
10.           <span class="block sm:inline"><%= @alert_message %></span>
11.         </div>
12.       <% end %>
13.     </div>
14.     """
15.   end
16. end
```

The explanation of the code is mentioned in the following:

- If **@alert_message** is present, the alert box is rendered.

- If **@alert_message** is nil (or not passed in), the alert box section is skipped, resulting in a clean layout with no empty space.

- The logic is fully contained within this component, making it easy to adjust how alerts are displayed or what triggers them.

A usage example is shown in the following:

```
01. <.alert_banner alert_message="Your account password expires in 3 days!"
    />
02. <.alert_banner /> <!-- No alert_message assign, so no alert is shown -->
```

**Note:** In Phoenix function components, the assigns map is passed into the component function, and inside the ~H template, you reference assigns using the @ syntax. This @ syntax is a convenience provided by the template compiler. When you write @alert_message inside the ~H template, it is essentially shorthand for assigns[:alert_message].

The tips and best practices for conditional rendering are mentioned in the following:

- **Keep conditions simple**: Keep your conditional logic straightforward and readable. If you find yourself nesting too many if or case statements, consider breaking parts of the UI into smaller, specialized components.

- **Use guards and pattern matching in assigns (if needed)**: Sometimes you can simplify conditional logic by using Elixir's pattern matching and guards at the function head. For instance, you might define multiple function clauses for a component that handles different assigns. For a single condition, though, a simple if in the template is often the most direct approach.

- **Combine with dynamic attributes**: Conditional rendering pairs well with dynamic attributes. For example, you might hide certain elements or modify their classes only when certain conditions are met.

- **Avoid over-complication**: While conditional rendering is powerful, do not try to solve every problem in one component. If a component becomes too complex due to extensive conditions, consider refactoring or introducing a new, smaller component that handles a specific scenario.

Conditional rendering gives you fine-grained control over what appears in your UI without increasing complexity. By using basic Elixir logic directly in your templates, you can tailor a single component to multiple states, making your code more efficient, maintainable, and easier to reason about. Combined with dynamic attributes and other intermediate techniques, conditional rendering helps you craft a component library that remains flexible and adaptable as your application evolves.

# Slots for composing and reusing container layouts

As your application's complexity grows, you will often need more than just components that render static content. You will want to create container components, the ones that wrap other components or content, providing structure and layout. Slots allow you to do exactly this, turning your components into flexible, composable building blocks.

Slots let you define *placeholders* within a component's template, which the caller can fill with their own content. This approach is especially powerful for creating reusable layouts, cards, modals, or other UI elements that have a common outer structure but need customizable inner content. By leveraging slots, you can reduce code repetition, ensure consistent styling, and give developers the freedom to compose layouts in a modular, maintainable fashion.

## Understanding the working of slots

When you define a slot in a component, you are essentially saying: *Here is a region inside this component where callers can inject their own markup or components.* The caller then provides that markup or set of components between the component's opening and closing tags, or via named slot tags, depending on how you structure the component.

The key benefits are mentioned in the following:

- **Reusability**: Define a common layout once. Consumers of that component can customize just the parts they need to change.

- **Composition**: Build complex layouts from smaller, single-purpose components without scattering your layout logic all over the place.

- **Flexibility**: Easily update or enhance the container's layout without affecting how callers provide their content.

**Example 11.2:** A simple card with a main content slot:

Let us start with a basic **card** component that serves as a container for content. We will define a slot for the card's main body content so the caller can insert any HTML or component they wish.

The following is a basic **Card** component that leverages Phoenix's built-in **@inner_block** slot, enabling callers to inject their own markup or components into the card's main content area, ensuring a consistent layout while allowing customizable content:

```
01. defmodule MyAppWeb.Components.Card do
02.   use Phoenix.Component
03.
04.   # By default, a component has an `@inner_block` slot representing the
        main content area.
05.   def card(assigns) do
```

```
06.     ~H"""
07.     <div class="border rounded p-4 bg-white shadow-sm">
08.        <%= render_slot(@inner_block) %>
09.     </div>
10.     """
11.   end
12. end
```

The explanation of the code is mentioned in the following:

- **@inner_block** is the default slot available in function components. Whatever you place between **<.card>** and **</.card>** in the caller's template is what **@inner_block** represents.

- **render_slot(@inner_block)** outputs that user-supplied content inside the card's layout.

A usage example is mentioned in the following:

```
01. <.card>
02.   <h2 class="text-lg font-bold">Profile Overview</h2>
03.   <p>User: Jane Doe</p>
04.   <p>Member since: 2021</p>
05. </.card>
```

In this case, the card layout remains consistent, while the caller customizes the content inside it. If tomorrow you decide all cards should have a slightly different background color or padding, you update the card once, and all places that use **<.card>** automatically benefit from this change.

**Example 11.3:** Named slots for more complex layouts:

While **@inner_block** works well for a single content area, more complex components may have multiple distinct regions. This is where named slots shine. You can define multiple slots and allow callers to fill each one with specific content. Think of a modal component that has a header, a body, and a footer, three distinct areas, each with its own slot.

# Component definition modal with named slots

The following is a **Modal** component featuring named slots (**:header**, **:footer**) in addition to the default **@inner_block**, enabling distinct sections: **header**, **body**, and **footer**, to be optionally provided by the caller, allowing for a more flexible and organized layout:

```
01. defmodule MyAppWeb.Components.Modal do
02.   use Phoenix.Component
```

```
03.
04.    slot :header
05.    slot :footer
06.
07.    def modal(assigns) do
08.      ~H"""
09.      <div class="fixed inset-0 flex items-center justify-center bg-gray-900 bg-opacity-50 p-4">
10.        <div class="bg-white rounded shadow-lg w-full max-w-md">
11.          <!-- Header slot (if provided) -->
12.          <%= if @header != [] do %>
13.            <div class="border-b px-4 py-2 font-bold text-lg">
14.              <%= render_slot(@header) %>
15.            </div>
16.          <% end %>
17.
18.          <!-- Inner block (main content) -->
19.          <div class="p-4">
20.            <%= render_slot(@inner_block) %>
21.          </div>
22.
23.          <!-- Footer slot (if provided) -->
24.          <%= if @footer != [] do %>
25.            <div class="border-t px-4 py-2 text-right">
26.              <%= render_slot(@footer) %>
27.            </div>
28.          <% end %>
29.        </div>
30.      </div>
31.      """
32.    end
33. End
```

The explanation of the code is mentioned in the following:

- We define two named slots: **header** and **footer**. Each named slot is declared using the slot macro.

- Inside the template, we conditionally render these slots only if they have been provided by the caller. This gives flexibility; callers can supply a header, a footer, both, or neither.

- The **@inner_block** is still available for the main modal content, ensuring callers can fill the body freely.

A usage example is mentioned in the following:

```
01. <.modal>
02.    <:header>
03.       Confirm Deletion
04.    </:header>
05.
06.    Are you sure you want to delete this item? This action cannot be undone.
07.
08.    <:footer>
09.       <button class="bg-red-500 text-white px-4 py-2 rounded">Delete</button>
10.       <button class="bg-gray-300 text-black px-4 py-2 rounded ml-2">Cancel</button>
11.    </:footer>
12. </.modal>
```

In the above snippet, the following things can be noticed:

- The **header** slot content (**Confirm Deletion**) appears in the modal's header area.

- The **:footer** slot includes two buttons for user actions.

- Everything not wrapped in a named slot goes into the **@inner_block**, representing the modal's main content area.

> Note: **Named slots make components incredibly flexible. You can add or remove named slots as your layout needs to evolve. If you want a sidebar or another special section, just define a new named slot.**

The tips and best practices for using slots are mentioned in the following:

- **Start simple**: Begin with a single slot (**@inner_block**) if your component has only one content area. Introduce named slots gradually as the complexity of your layout grows.

- **Use named slots judiciously**: While named slots are powerful, adding too many can overcomplicate your component. Keep your designs modular and consider whether multiple small components might be clearer than one extremely configurable component.

- **Leverage conditional rendering**: Combine conditional rendering with slots to make sections optional. For instance, only show the footer if the caller provides one. This keeps your layouts versatile and reduces the need for separate components.

- **Document your slots**: Clear documentation or examples help other developers understand how to use your slots. This is because callers must know what each slot represents, and good docs are key for maintainability.

Note: **If you find yourself creating a complex hierarchy of slots and nested components, consider your design's overall architecture. Sometimes, extracting shared logic into smaller, focused components can make your layout more maintainable in the long run.**

Slots are a powerful feature that elevates your components from simple renderers of static content to flexible containers that structure your UI. By defining placeholders where consumers can inject custom content, you can build reusable layouts, cards, and models that adapt to a variety of needs.

Combined with dynamic attributes and conditional rendering, slots round out your toolkit for creating a scalable and maintainable component architecture. As you continue to refine your components, you will find yourself building increasingly sophisticated UIs with minimal duplication and a high degree of flexibility.

# Testing components

As your Phoenix application scales, components become the building blocks of your UI. However, introducing many components, each with unique states and behaviors, naturally raises the question: *How do I ensure they all work as intended?* This is where component testing comes into play. Testing components directly provides fast, reliable feedback and helps prevent regressions, instilling confidence in your codebase as it evolves.

In this section, we will explore a *professional* approach to testing Phoenix Components in a purely request/response application (such as no LiveView). We will cover everything from setting up the test environment to writing detailed component tests with real-world examples. The goal is to demonstrate best practices that keep your tests organized, maintainable, and easy to understand.

The following are some key reasons why component testing is an essential practice, helping you maintain and evolve your Phoenix applications with greater confidence and clarity:

- **Regression prevention**: As you refine or refactor components, tests will confirm that changes do not break existing functionality.

- **Confidence in iteration**: When adding new features or states, you can trust that your baseline functionality remains intact.

- **Executable documentation**: Each test demonstrates how a component is intended to be used, acting as a reference for other developers (and your future self).

- **Faster feedback loop**: Component tests run quickly, avoiding the overhead of a full browser-based integration test or a running server.

# Setting up the testing environment

Phoenix 1.7 provides convenient testing helpers for components. By default, you will have a test directory containing support files such as **conn_case.ex** or **data_case.ex**. To test components effectively, you can either use the existing **ConnCase** or create a dedicated **ComponentCase** module.

**Example 11.4:** A Simple ComponentCase:

Following is a **ComponentCase** setup demonstrating how Phoenix 1.7's testing helpers can be streamlined into a shared testing environment, allowing you to easily render and test components without a running server:

```
01. # test/support/component_case.ex
02. defmodule MyAppWeb.ComponentCase do
03.   use ExUnit.CaseTemplate
04.
05.   using do
06.     quote do
07.       import Phoenix.Component
08.       import Phoenix.Component.HTML
09.       import Phoenix.ConnTest, only: [build_conn: 0]
10.
11.       # You can also import custom helpers here if needed.
12.     end
13.   end
14. end
```

The explanation of the code is given in the following:

- **ExUnit.CaseTemplate**: This allows you to define a shared testing setup for multiple test modules.

- **import Phoenix.Component**: This provides functions like **render_component/2** or **render_to_string/2**.

- **import Phoenix.ConnTest**: This lets you generate a test **conn** object. It is useful for components that rely on **@conn** (e.g., for form routes).

In order to use this **ComponentCase**, simply use **MyAppWeb.ComponentCase** in your test files.

# Introducing a test helper file

In order to keep your tests **Do not Repeat Yourself** (**DRY**), define small helper functions that return common assigns. This is especially helpful if your component requires multiple fields (**@id**, **@title**, **@completed**, etc.). Place these helpers in a file like **test/support/component_test_helpers.ex**, as shown in the following:

```
01. defmodule MyAppWeb.ComponentTestHelpers do
02.   def default_task_card_assigns(overrides \\ []) do
03.     Enum.into(overrides, %{
04.       conn: Phoenix.ConnTest.build_conn(),
05.       id: 1,
06.       title: "Default Title",
07.       description: "Default Description",
08.       completed: false
09.     })
10.   end
11.
12.   def default_task_list_assigns(overrides \\ []) do
13.     Enum.into(overrides, %{
14.       conn: Phoenix.ConnTest.build_conn(),
15.       tasks: []
16.     })
17.   end
18.
19.   # Add more helpers for other components as needed...
20. end
```

You can then import these helpers into your component test modules to reduce boilerplate. This module (**component_test_helpers.ex**) defines the following two such helper functions:

- **default_task_card_assigns/1**
- **default_task_list_assigns/1**

These functions return maps containing default values for the keys expected by certain components (like **TaskCard** or **TaskList**). If you need to change a value (for example, make completed: true instead of false), you pass a keyword list or map of overrides, and the function merges them into the base set.

# Phoenix.ConnTest.build_conn()

This function comes from **Phoenix.ConnTest**. In a Phoenix application, each HTTP request is represented by a connection struct (**conn**). During tests, you typically do not have a real HTTP request, so you use **build_conn()** to create a fake or mock connection object that simulates certain aspects of a real HTTP connection. It includes headers, parameters, and other metadata in a test-friendly environment.

The purpose of the conn is many Phoenix Components require **@conn** to generate URLs (for example, **Routes.task_path(@conn, :index)**) or to render forms (**form_for @conn, ...**). Without a valid **conn**, those calls would fail or produce incomplete output in tests.

Let us take this helper function in the following example: **default_task_list_assigns/1**

```
01. def default_task_list_assigns(overrides \\ []) do
02.    Enum.into(overrides, %{
03.      conn: Phoenix.ConnTest.build_conn(),
04.      tasks: []
05.    })
06. end
```

The following is the breakdown of the default map generated by the function, showing how **conn** and tasks are set:

- **Default map**: The function initializes **conn** with **Phoenix.ConnTest.build_conn()**, ensuring the component can properly generate routes or handle forms, and defaults **tasks** to an empty list unless you choose to override it with your own data:

  o  **conn**: Again, we use **Phoenix.ConnTest.build_conn()** to create a mock connection.

  o  **tasks []**: By default, we assume there are no tasks unless you override them with a list of tasks.

- **Overriding the defaults:** If you want to test a scenario where multiple tasks are present, you can attempt the following code:

```
01. tasks = [
02.    %{id: 1, title: "Task 1", description: "Desc 1", completed:
       false},
```

```
03.    %{id: 2, title: "Task 2", description: "Desc 2", completed:
       true}
04. ]
05. assigns = default_task_list_assigns(tasks: tasks)
```

- **Final map**: Finally, the following is a rough idea of what the final assigned map looks like after merging:

```
01. %{
02.    conn: %Plug.Conn{...},   # test connection
03.    tasks: [
04.      %{id: 1, title: "Task 1", description: "Desc 1", completed:
         false},
05.      %{id: 2, title: "Task 2", description: "Desc 2", completed:
         true}
06.    ]
07. }
08.
```

## Result of these functions

The following is a summary of how these helper functions streamline your testing workflow, allowing you to pass a ready-to-use map of assigns to your component tests:

o **Simplifies test setup**: You do not have to rewrite boilerplate data (like **conn**, **id**, **title**, etc.) for every test.

o **Keeps tests DRY**: When you have many components or repeated scenarios, a single helper function can be adjusted centrally rather than editing many test files.

o **Provides default values**: If your component expects certain keys but you only want to override a few, you can do so without worrying about the rest.

o **Ensures a valid conn**: The conn generated by **build_conn()** will be sufficient for testing form submissions, route helpers, or other actions that rely on a connection struct.

# Rendering components in tests

When testing a component, you will typically use one of the following approaches:

- **render_to_string/2**: Renders the component to a raw HTML string, which you can assert upon.

- **render_component/2**: Similar to **render_to_string/2** but returns a special data structure you can analyze or manipulate further. For most simple use cases, **render_to_string/2** suffices.

The following are two common function calls you might use to render components in your tests, each accepting a component function (or reference) and a map of assigns:

```
01. render_to_string(MyAppWeb.Components.TaskCard.task_card, assigns)
02. render_component(&MyAppWeb.Components.TaskCard.task_card/1, assigns)
```

Both accept the component function (or a reference to it) and a map of assigns.

# Example tests for sample components

The following are example test modules that showcase how to verify key behaviors for several components—**TaskCard**, **TaskList**, **AddTaskForm**, and **Navigation**, in a Phoenix application. Each snippet demonstrates the use of helper functions, rendering strategies, and targeted assertions that confirm the component's expected output:

- **Testing the TaskCard component**: The following is a test module illustrating how to render and verify a task's details, including conditional background color and toggle button text:

  o **Goal**: Ensure the component renders a task's details correctly, including conditional background color and toggle button text. Refer to the following code for a better understanding:

```
01. # test/my_app_web/components/task_card_test.exs
02. defmodule MyAppWeb.Components.TaskCardTest do
03.   use MyAppWeb.ComponentCase, async: true
04.
05.   alias MyAppWeb.Components.TaskCard
06.   import MyAppWeb.ComponentTestHelpers
07.
08.   test "renders a task card for a pending task" do
09.     assigns = default_task_card_assigns(
10.       title: "Buy Groceries",
11.       description: "Eggs, Milk, Bread"
12.     )
13.
14.     html = render_to_string(TaskCard.task_card, assigns)
```

```
15.        assert html =~ "Buy Groceries"
16.        assert html =~ "Eggs, Milk, Bread"
17.        refute html =~ "bg-green-100"
18.        assert html =~ "Mark as Completed"
19.    end
20.
21.    test "renders a task card for a completed task" do
22.        assigns = default_task_card_assigns(
23.          id: 2,
24.          title: "Clean the Garage",
25.          description: "Organize tools",
26.          completed: true
27.        )
28.
29.        html = render_to_string(TaskCard.task_card, assigns)
30.        assert html =~ "Clean the Garage"
31.        assert html =~ "Organize tools"
32.        assert html =~ "bg-green-100"
33.        assert html =~ "Mark as Pending"
34.    end
35. End
```

The explanation is mentioned in the following:

- We use **default_task_card_assigns/1** to get a basic set of assigns and override only what we need for each scenario.

- We check for CSS class changes (**bg-green-100**) and button labels that differ depending on whether the task is completed.

- The test is short, clear, and focuses on the component's output.

- **Testing the TaskList component**: The following module demonstrates how to check for multiple tasks in the rendered output and confirm a fallback message appears if no tasks are present:

  o **Goal**: Confirm the list renders multiple tasks or shows a fallback message when no tasks exist:

```
01. # test/my_app_web/components/task_list_test.exs
02. defmodule MyAppWeb.Components.TaskListTest do
```

```
03.    use MyAppWeb.ComponentCase, async: true
04.
05.    alias MyAppWeb.Components.TaskList
06.    import MyAppWeb.ComponentTestHelpers
07.
08.    test "renders a list of tasks" do
09.      tasks = [
10.        %{id: 1, title: "Task 1", description: "First",
completed: false},
11.        %{id: 2, title: "Task 2", description: "Second",
completed: true}
12.      ]
13.
14.      assigns = default_task_list_assigns(tasks: tasks)
15.      html = render_to_string(TaskList.task_list, assigns)
16.
17.      assert html =~ "Task 1"
18.      assert html =~ "Task 2"
19.      assert html =~ "First"
20.      assert html =~ "Second"
21.    end
22.
23.    test "shows a message when no tasks are present" do
24.      html = render_to_string(TaskList.task_list, default_
task_list_assigns())
25.      assert html =~ "No tasks found."
26.    end
27. end
```

The explanation is mentioned in the following:

- One test verifies that two tasks appear in the rendered HTML.

- Another check is the fallback text when the task is an empty list.

- The logic is straightforward yet covers critical UI states.

- **Testing the AddTaskForm component**: Below is a test module confirming that the form correctly includes the expected fields and a submit button for adding new tasks:

o    **Goal**: Verify the presence of form elements and the submit button:

```
01.    # test/my_app_web/components/add_task_form_test.exs
02.    defmodule MyAppWeb.Components.AddTaskFormTest do
03.      use MyAppWeb.ComponentCase, async: true
04.
05.      alias MyAppWeb.Components.AddTaskForm
06.
07.      test "renders the form with title and description fields" do
08.        conn = Phoenix.ConnTest.build_conn()
09.        html = render_to_string(AddTaskForm.add_task_form,
    %{conn: conn})
10.
11.        # Check for form, title field, description field, and button
12.        assert html =~ "<form"
13.        assert html =~ "name=\"task[title]\""
14.        assert html =~ "name=\"task[description]\""
15.        assert html =~ "Add Task"
16.      end
17.    end
```

The explanation is mentioned in the following:

- Since the only required assign is **conn**, we provide it directly.
- We confirm the presence of the correct form fields and button text.
- This ensures that the user-facing form matches our expectations.

- **Testing the navigation component**: Here is a test module that verifies the presence of links for different task filters and checks for proper branding text:

o    **Goal**: Confirm navigation links for different task filters exist, as well as a site title or branding:

```
01.    # test/my_app_web/components/navigation_test.exs
02.    defmodule MyAppWeb.Components.NavigationTest do
03.      use MyAppWeb.ComponentCase, async: true
04.
05.      alias MyAppWeb.Components.Navigation
06.
07.      test "renders navigation with filter links" do
```

```
08.          conn = Phoenix.ConnTest.build_conn()
09.          html = render_to_string(Navigation.navigation, %{conn: conn})
10.
11.          assert html =~ "My Task Tracker"
12.          assert html =~ Routes.task_path(conn, :index, filter: "all")
13.          assert html =~ Routes.task_path(conn, :index, filter:
        "completed")
14.          assert html =~ Routes.task_path(conn, :index, filter: "pending")
15.     end
16.  end
```

The explanation is mentioned in the following:

- We check that the navigation component includes links to the **all**, **completed**, and **pending** filters.

- We also verify branding text (**My Task Tracker**).

Some additional professional tips are mentioned in the following:

- **Describe blocks for grouping scenarios**: Elixir allows you to group related tests with describe when the task is completed **do … end**, making the suite more readable.

- **Edge cases and error handling**: Test how components behave under unusual conditions (for example, missing assigns, extremely long text, or special characters).

- **Refactoring and consistency:** As your test suite grows, watch for repeated patterns. Factor them into helper functions to keep tests clean and DRY.

- **Integration testing**: Component tests are one layer. You can further test the full user flow via integration or controller tests, ensuring all pieces (controller, templates, components) work together correctly.

# Using Floki to parse and inspect HTML

If you need to assert more than just raw text, in other words, if you want to check specific HTML elements, attributes, or structures, consider using *Floki*, an HTML parsing library. For example:

```
01. {:ok, document} = Floki.parse_document(html)
02. assert Floki.find(document, "button[type='submit']") != []
```

Floki is most beneficial when:

- **Your tests require detailed HTML structure checks**: For example, if you need to verify specific nested elements, attributes, or the presence/absence of particular tags beyond simple substring matching.

- **Complex or nested rendering**: If your component produces deeply nested HTML (e.g., multiple levels of `<div>s` and `<ul>s`) and you want to verify correctness at multiple levels, Floki can make those assertions more readable.

- **Conditional elements or class manipulations**: When your UI changes many classes or data attributes based on props, Floki can help you assert that certain classes or elements are present or absent in a more structured way than raw string matching.

In the mini Task Tracker examples, **substring matching** was sufficient because of the following reasons:

- We only needed to confirm the presence of certain keywords or classes (for example, `bg-green-100`, `No tasks found`, `Mark as Completed`, etc.).

- The HTML output was relatively simple (a few `<div>s`, **buttons**, and **text checks**).

- Tests were primarily confirming conditional text and CSS classes, rather than verifying intricate nested structures.

Thus, **Floki was not strictly necessary** to demonstrate how to test a typical component's output. In real-world scenarios where HTML structures are more complex, you might find it easier to parse the rendered HTML via Floki, especially if:

- You need to confirm that certain elements exist in a specific hierarchy (for example, a `<button>` inside a `<div>` with a particular **id**).

- You want to check for an attribute like **data-test-id** or **aria-label**.

# Example to use Floki

If you were to incorporate Floki for a slightly more detailed check, it might look like the following:

```
01. defmodule MyAppWeb.Components.TaskCardTest do
02.   use MyAppWeb.ComponentCase, async: true
03.   import MyAppWeb.ComponentTestHelpers
04.   alias MyAppWeb.Components.TaskCard
05.
06.   test "renders a task card and verifies a toggle button with Floki" do
07.     assigns = default_task_card_assigns(
08.       title: "Buy Groceries",
09.       description: "Eggs, Milk, Bread",
10.       completed: false
11.     )
```

```
12.
13.      html = render_to_string(TaskCard.task_card, assigns)
14.      {:ok, document} = Floki.parse_document(html)
15.
16.      # Check for the presence of a form
17.      assert Floki.find(document, "form[method='post']") != []
18.
19.      # Check for a button with the text 'Mark as Completed'
20.      buttons = Floki.find(document, "button")
21.      assert Enum.any?(buttons, fn button_html ->
22.        Floki.text(button_html) == "Mark as Completed"
23.      end)
24.    end
25. end
```

The explanation of the code is mentioned in the following:

- Parse the rendered HTML with **Floki.parse_document/1**.

- Search for specific elements using **Floki.find(document, <selector>)**.

- Extract text content with **Floki.text(...)**.

This approach is often more robust than plain substring checks if you need to pinpoint elements or attributes precisely. You can decide which approach best fits each scenario. In many cases, you might start with substring matching and introduce Floki if or when the complexity of your HTML testing needs increases.

# Mini task tracker with Phoenix Components

In order to conclude our chapter on Phoenix Components, let us walk through a simple Task Tracker application that demonstrates how multiple components can work together to create a cohesive user interface. We will focus on the front-end, request or response flow, showing how to wire up components for navigation, forms, and dynamic listing, without exploring the database schema or context logic, which we will cover in detail in the next chapter when we build a more complete application.

The following is a quick look at how the user's journey unfolds in our mini Task Tracker, highlighting how each component seamlessly contributes to the overall experience, from visiting the tasks page and adding new items to filtering, displaying, and toggling tasks:

- **User arrives**: The user visits the **/tasks** page. Our layout component provides the overarching page structure, while a navigation component sits in the header, offering links to filter tasks by *All*, *Completed*, or *Pending*.

- **Adding a task**: Beneath the navigation, the user sees an *Add Task* form component, allowing them to submit a new task with a title and description.

- **Listing and managing tasks**: The main content area displays a list of tasks using a task list component. Each item in this list is rendered by a task card component, featuring a toggle button to mark it as completed or revert it to pending.

- **Completing a task**: When the user toggles a task, a standard POST request triggers a server-side action that flips the task's state. The page refreshes, and the task card's background color and button label update accordingly.

Through these four steps, our mini Task Tracker illustrates how components can structure the UI in a modular, maintainable way. Let us see how each piece fits together:

1. **Layout component (layout.ex)**: Following is how we define a layout component using named slots (**:nav**, **:main**) to organize header and main content areas without duplicating code across multiple templates:

```
01. defmodule MyAppWeb.Components.Layout do
02.   use Phoenix.Component
03.
04.   slot :nav
05.   slot :main
06.
07.   def layout(assigns) do
08.     ~H"""
09.     <div class="min-h-screen flex flex-col">
10.       <header class="bg-gray-800 text-white p-4">
11.         <%= if @nav != [] do %>
12.           <%= render_slot(@nav) %>
13.         <% else %>
14.           <h1 class="text-xl font-bold">My Task Tracker</h1>
15.         <% end %>
16.       </header>
17.
18.       <main class="flex-1 p-6 bg-gray-100">
19.         <%= if @main != [] do %>
```

```
20.            <%= render_slot(@main) %>
21.          <% else %>
22.            <p>Welcome to the Task Tracker</p>
23.          <% end %>
24.      </main>
25.
26.      <footer class="bg-gray-200 text-center p-2">
27.        <p>&copy; 2024 MyApp. All rights reserved.</p>
28.      </footer>
29.    </div>
30.    """
31.  end
32. end
```

When a user loads the **/tasks** page, we wrap the entire content in **<.layout>**. This layout defines our page's header, main section, and footer. It uses named slots (**:nav**, **:main**) to let us insert a custom navigation bar and main content area. Without this slot-based design, we would have to repeat header/footer code across multiple templates, making changes cumbersome.

2. **Navigation component (navigation.ex)**: The following is the navigation component, which appears in the layout's **:nav** slot to provide links for filtering tasks:

```
01. defmodule MyAppWeb.Components.Navigation do
02.   use Phoenix.Component
03.
04.   def navigation(assigns) do
05.     ~H"""
06.     <nav class="flex items-center justify-between">
07.       <div class="font-bold text-lg">
08.         <a href="<%= Routes.task_path(@conn, :index) %>">My Task
    Tracker</a>
09.       </div>
10.       <div class="space-x-4">
11.         <a href="<%= Routes.task_path(@conn, :index, filter:
    "all") %>" class="underline">All</a>
12.         <a href="<%= Routes.task_path(@conn, :index, filter:
    "completed") %>" class="underline">Completed</a>
```

```
13.            <a href="<%= Routes.task_path(@conn, :index, filter:
    "pending") %>" class="underline">Pending</a>
14.         </div>
15.       </nav>
16.       """
17.   end
18. end
```

This navigation sits in the header slot. The user sees a brand-like title (**My Task Tracker**) and three links to filter tasks. Clicking **Completed** or **Pending** triggers a new request that refreshes the page, displaying only tasks that match that filter. Notice how the **@conn** is used to generate the correct routes; this is a pure request or response pattern (no **LiveView**).

3. **Add task form component (add_task_form.ex)**: Next is the form component for creating a new task, which sits in the following navigation:

```
01. defmodule MyAppWeb.Components.AddTaskForm do
02.   use Phoenix.Component
03.
04.   def add_task_form(assigns) do
05.     ~H"""
06.     <div class="bg-white p--4 rounded shadow mb-6">
07.       <h2 class="font-bold text-lg mb-2">Add a New Task</h2>
08.       <%= form_for @conn, Routes.task_path(@conn, :create),
    [method: :post], fn f -> %>
09.         <div class="mb-2">
10.           <%= label f, :title, "Title:", class: "block mb-1" %>
11.           <%= text_input f, :title, class: "border rounded p-1
    w-full" %>
12.         </div>
13.
14.         <div class="mb-2">
15.           <%= label f, :description, "Description:", class:
    "block mb-1" %>
16.           <%= textarea f, :description, class: "border rounded
    p-1 w-full" %>
17.         </div>
18.
```

```
19.            <button type="submit" class="bg-green-500 text-white px-4
    py-2 rounded">Add Task</button>
20.         <% end %>
21.      </div>
22.      """
23.   end
24. end
```

The user sees this **Add Task** form right beneath the navigation. Submitting the form posts to an endpoint (like **/tasks/add**) and creating a new task behind the scenes. The page then reloads, and the new task appears in the list. This form component encapsulates form rendering, styling, and action handling, making it reusable or easy to move if the layout changes later.

4. **Task card component (task_card.ex)**: The following is a component for displaying individual tasks, including logic to toggle completion status:

```
01. defmodule MyAppWeb.Components.TaskCard do
02.   use Phoenix.Component
03.
04.   def task_card(assigns) do
05.     background = if @completed, do: "bg-green-100", else: "bg-white"
06.
07.     ~H"""
08.     <div class={"border rounded p-4 shadow #{background}"}>
09.        <h2 class="font-bold text-lg"><%= @title %></h2>
10.        <p><%= @description %></p>
11.
12.        <!-- Toggle button to mark as completed or revert to pending -->
13.        <%= form_for @conn, Routes.task_path(@conn, :toggle, @id),
    [method: :post], fn _f -> %>
14.           <button type="submit" class="mt-2 px-4 py-2 bg-blue-500
    text-white rounded">
15.              <%= if @completed, do: "Mark as Pending", else: "Mark
    as Completed" %>
16.           </button>
17.        <% end %>
```

```
18.    </div>
19.        """
20.  end
21. end
```

Each task is displayed as a task card. If **@completed** is true, the card's background becomes light green to indicate its state. The user can click the button to send a **POST** request that toggles the task's completion. The reloaded page immediately reflects the updated state.

5. **Task list component (task_list.ex)**: Following is the task list component, which iterates over tasks and renders a **TaskCard** for each:

```
01. defmodule MyAppWeb.Components.TaskList do
02.   use Phoenix.Component
03.
04.   def task_list(assigns) do
05.     ~H"""
06.     <div class="space-y-4">
07.       <%= if Enum.empty?(@tasks) do %>
08.         <p class="text-gray-600">No tasks found.</p>
09.       <% else %>
10.         <%= for task <- @tasks do %>
11.           <.task_card
12.             conn={@conn}
13.             id={task.id}
14.             title={task.title}
15.             description={task.description}
16.             completed={task.completed}
17.           />
18.         <% end %>
19.       <% end %>
20.     </div>
21.     """
22.   end
23. end
```

The task list is responsible for iterating over a collection of tasks and rendering a task card for each. If no tasks match the selected filter, it displays a helpful **"No tasks found"** message instead. This design keeps the task card logic separate from the list logic, making each component more focused and testable.

6. **Putting it all together in a template (index.html.heex)**: Finally, here is how we assemble everything in the Phoenix template:

```
01. <.layout>
02.    <:nav>
03.      <.navigation conn={@conn} />
04.    </:nav>
05.
06.    <:main>
07.      <!-- Add a New Task -->
08.      <.add_task_form conn={@conn} />
09.
10.      <!-- Display All Tasks (Possibly Filtered) -->
11.      <.task_list conn={@conn} tasks={@tasks} />
12.    </:main>
13. </.layout>
```

Here is where everything merges into a final page. We use the layout component to provide a header and a footer structure. We fill the **:nav** slot with our navigation component, and the :main slot with the form to add a task and the task list. Phoenix automatically injects **@tasks** from the controller, and each component picks up exactly the data it needs.

We have mentioned a quick user experience recap in the following:

- **Arriving at /tasks**: The layout loads, showing a header with navigation links. The main area includes a form for adding tasks and a list of existing tasks.

- **Adding a task**: The user types a title and description, submits the form, and reloads the page with the new task at the top (or in the correct place in the list).

- **Filtering tasks**: The user clicks **Completed** to see only completed tasks. Another request fetches and displays only tasks **completed: true**.

- **Toggling task state**: On each task card, a button toggles its completion status. A quick refresh reveals an updated background color and a changed label (**Mark as Pending** or **Mark as Completed**).

## Mini Task Tracker component architecture

Following is how our mini Task Tracker application relies on a simple request or response flow, avoiding the complexity of LiveView while still providing a clean, modular UI, with each component fulfilling a distinct role in the overall architecture:

- Layout sets the page structure, offering named slots.

- Navigation focuses on filtering logic, letting users view relevant tasks.

- AddTaskForm encapsulates form creation, styling, and submission.

- TaskList organizes task data, delegating individual display to TaskCard.

- TaskCard handles toggling states and conditional rendering.

Through this project, we see how each component plays a distinct role and how, together, they form a cohesive interface for managing tasks. When combined with good testing practices, you will have a system that is both easy to maintain and confidently extensible, a perfect foundation before we move on to building a more fully featured application in the next chapter.

# Conclusion

By adopting a component-driven mindset, you have laid the groundwork for building Phoenix applications with code that is easy to maintain, test, and extend. You have seen how everything from basic function components to slots, dynamic attributes, and conditional rendering can work together to create a modular, flexible architecture. Our mini Task Tracker provided a real-world glimpse into these ideas, demonstrating how each component can address a specific concern while still fitting into a cohesive, reusable UI.

In the next chapter, we will build on these concepts by integrating more robust application logic, exploring schema and context code in-depth, and tackling more advanced design patterns. With your new expertise in Phoenix Components, you are well-equipped to scale up from these foundational pieces to a full-fledged, production-ready system.

# Practical exercises

1. **Setting up the project:**
    a. Create a new Phoenix project named expense_tracker.
    b. Add user authentication with mix phx.gen.auth.
    c. Run migrations and verify login and registration functionality.

2. **Adding expenses:**
    a. Generate a context and schema for expenses with fields like description, amount, and date.

    b.   Write tests for creating an expense and implement the functionality.

    c.   Verify expenses are saved and displayed on the dashboard.

3. **Filtering and viewing expenses:**

    a.   Extend the expense listing to filter by date or category.

    b.   Add a test to confirm filtering returns only the expected records.

    c.   Implement the filter in your controller and component.

4. **Budgets and alerts:**

    a.   Create a budget table linked to users.

    b.   Write a test to check that an alert is triggered when expenses exceed the budget.

    c.   Implement the alert mechanism in the dashboard.

5. **Generating reports:**

    a.   Implement a function to calculate monthly totals.

    b.   Add a chart component that displays expense distribution.

    c.   Write a test to verify the correctness of the report data.

# Points to remember

- **Components vs. views in Phoenix 1.7+**: Components focus on modular, reusable UI elements, while the older view and template approach scatters logic across multiple files.

- **Reusability and readability**: By encapsulating logic and markup in a single function component, you reduce duplication and make your codebase easier to navigate.

- **Dynamic attributes and conditional rendering**: Dynamically change classes, attributes, or entire content blocks based on assigned data, making your components adaptable to different scenarios.

- **Slots for layout and composition**: Use named slots to create containers or layout components. This keeps your layout flexible and maintainable, especially in more complex UIs.

- **Testing components**: Rely on Phoenix's component test helpers to render components in isolation. Substring checks or an HTML parser (Floki) let you verify output under various states without a running server.

- **When components get too big**: If you find yourself juggling too many slots and nested components, break them down into smaller, more focused pieces. This keeps your code modular and maintainable in the long run.

- **Mini task tracker application**: A simple, request/response-driven app can illustrate all these principles, layout, navigation, form handling, dynamic rendering, and reusable components, without the complexity of LiveView.

# Join our Discord space

Join our Discord workspace for latest updates, offers, tech happenings around the world, new releases, and sessions with the authors:

https://discord.bpbonline.com

# CHAPTER 11

# Project on Building Real-world Application

## Introduction

In this chapter, we will embark on a practical journey to build a real-world application, a Task Management **Create, Read, Update, and Delete (CRUD)** app. This project will serve as a culmination of the concepts we have explored throughout the book, providing hands-on experience in designing, developing, and deploying a fully functional web application with the Phoenix framework in Elixir. By focusing on a common yet essential tool that many individuals use, this project will help solidify your understanding of Elixir and Phoenix in a tangible way.

The skills gained here are domain-driven context design, reusable component patterns, edge-case testing, and production hardening, forming a blueprint for any CRUD-centric web service, enabling rapid delivery of robust, maintainable applications in real-world teams.

## Structure

The chapter discusses the following topics:

- Project setup
- Listing records
- Showing single record

- Creating records

- Editing records

- Deleting records

- Refactor with Phoenix Components

- Refinement and debugging

- Deployment

# Objectives

This chapter guides the reader through building a complete CRUD web application with Phoenix 1.7, strictly following current best practices. The process starts with a fresh Phoenix project and proceeds step-by-step through listing, creating, editing, and deleting tasks, with each feature first captured in an automated test and only then implemented in code. LiveView is intentionally omitted to keep the focus on traditional server-rendered HTML and to reinforce the core concepts of the Phoenix framework.

Throughout the exercise, developers learn how to structure a new Phoenix project; define Ecto schemas and contexts; craft controllers, HEEx templates, and reusable Phoenix Components; and write and run a comprehensive test suite. The chapter also covers form handling, validation, user-feedback mechanisms, and robust error management, all aimed at producing clean, maintainable code.

By the end, readers will not only have a fully working task-management application packaged for deployment but also the practical skills and confidence to create their own CRUD-based projects using a disciplined TDD workflow and component-driven design.

# Project setup

The first step in building our Task Management CRUD app is setting up a new Phoenix project. We will configure the necessary dependencies and prepare the environment for development.

Follow the steps to generate the project, inspect its structure, and verify that everything compiles correctly:

1. **Create a new Phoenix project**: To create a new Phoenix project, navigate to your workspace directory and run the following command:

```
mix phx.new tasks_app --no-live --binary-id
```

Here is what the flags mean:

- **--no-live**: We will not use Phoenix LiveView in this chapter, focusing on traditional server-rendered HTML.

- **--binary-id**: Tells Phoenix to use UUIDs for primary keys instead of integers, which is a modern and recommended practice for new apps.

The generated project will include everything needed to get started, including a folder structure for controllers, views, templates, and Ecto integration for database access.

2. **Navigating the project structure**: Once the command completes, switch to your new project directory:

```
1. cd tasks_app
```

Let us briefly review the most important folders and files Phoenix generated:

- **lib/tasks_app/**: Contains your application's core Elixir modules (business logic, contexts, schemas).

- **lib/tasks_app_web/**: Houses all web-specific code (controllers, components, templates, HTML helpers, router).

- **test/**: Contains automated tests for your application, organized by context and functionality.

- **config/**: Holds your application configuration files for different environments (development, test, production).

- **assets/**: Where static files (JavaScript, CSS, images) and build tools (like esbuild) are managed.

- **priv/repo/migrations/**: Stores your database migration scripts.

Understanding this structure will help you feel comfortable as you build out your application in the following sections.

3. **Set up necessary configurations and dependencies**: With the skeleton generated, our next task is to configure the database, fetch dependencies, and prepare assets so the application can run locally without errors:

a. **Database setup**: Since we are using Ecto, we need to configure the database. By default, Phoenix uses PostgreSQL. Update the **config/dev.exs** and **config/test.exs** files with your database credentials:

```
1. config :tasks_app, TasksApp.Repo,
2.   username: "your_db_username",
3.   password: "your_db_password",
4.   database: "tasks_app_dev",
5.   hostname: "localhost",
6.   show_sensitive_data_on_connection_error: true,
7.   pool_size: 10
```

b. **Install dependencies**: Install all dependencies using the following command:

```
1. mix deps.get
```

c. **Create and migrate the database**: Create the database:

```
1. mix ecto.create
```

Run the initial migration:

```
1. mix ecto.migrate
```

d. **Integrate Tailwind CSS for styling**: Since we are using Phoenix version 1.7, Tailwind CSS comes integrated by default, so we do not need to manually configure Tailwind. However, you can run the following command to ensure that all necessary CSS assets are bundled correctly:

```
1. mix assets.deploy
```

e. **Run the server**: After setting up everything, run the Phoenix server to test the application:

```
mix phx.server
```

Navigate to: **http://localhost:4000/**

You should see the default Phoenix welcome page, confirming that everything is set up correctly.

4. **Running the test suite:** As a best practice, run the default test suite to make sure your environment is healthy:

```
1. mix test
```

All tests should pass.

# Listing records

One of the first features in any CRUD app is the ability to display a list of records, in this case, a list of tasks. This section will guide you through building a feature that fetches all tasks from your database and displays them on a web page. We will follow the **test-driven development** (**TDD**) approach: write a test first, then implement just enough code to make it pass:

1. **Writing the test first**: Let us start with a test that describes the desired behavior. When a user visits **/tasks**, the page should display the title **Listing Tasks**. Open (or create, if needed) the file **test/tasks_app_web/controllers/task_controller_test.exs** and add the following test:

```
01. test "GET /tasks", %{conn: conn} do
02.   conn = get(conn, ~p"/tasks")
```

```
03.   assert html_response(conn, 200) =~ "Listing Tasks"
04. end
```

Run your tests with:

```
01. mix test
```

You will see this test fail because the route and logic do not exist yet. This is the *red* phase of TDD.

2. **Implementing the feature**: Follow the numbered steps below to turn the failing test green by wiring up the data layer, routes, controller, and template:

   a. **Generate task schema and context**: Let us generate the files for managing tasks:

   ```
   01. mix phx.gen.context Tasks Task tasks title:string
          description:string
   ```

   Running this command scaffolds the entire **Tasks** domain: context module, schema, and migration, so we have a clean starting point before wiring it into the database:

   b. This command creates the **Tasks** context and **Task** schema, plus a migration for the tasks table.

   c. We do not use the **phx.gen.html** generator to practice hand-crafting our controllers and components.

   Run the migration to update the database:

   ```
   01. mix ecto.migrate
   ```

3. **Add the index route**: Open **lib/tasks_app_web/router.ex** and add:

   ```
   01. resources "/tasks", TaskController, only: [:index]
   ```

4. **Create the controller**: Create **lib/tasks_app_web/controllers/task_controller.ex** with:

   ```
   01. defmodule TasksAppWeb.TaskController do
   02.   use TasksAppWeb, :controller
   03.   alias TasksApp.Tasks
   04.
   05.   def index(conn, _params) do
   06.     tasks = Tasks.list_tasks()
   07.     render(conn, :index, tasks: tasks)
   08.   end
   09. end
   ```

5.  **Create the index template**: First, create the directory if it does not exist:

```
01. mkdir -p lib/tasks_app_web/controllers/task_html
```

Now add the template file **lib/tasks_app_web/controllers/task_html/index. html.heex**:

```
01. <.header>
02.   Listing Tasks
03. </.header>
04.
05. <div>
06.   <%= for task <- @tasks do %>
07.     <div class="mb-4 border rounded p-3">
08.       <div class="font-semibold"><%= task.title %></div>
09.       <div class="text-sm text-gray-500"><%= task.description
       %></div>
10.     </div>
11.   <% end %>
12. </div>
```

6.  **Define the HTML module**: Create or edit **lib/tasks_app_web/controllers/task_ html.ex**:

```
01. defmodule TasksAppWeb.TaskHTML do
02.   use TasksAppWeb, :html
03.
04.   embed_templates "task_html/*"
05. end
```

7.  **Re-run your test:**

```
01. mix test
```

Now your **GET /tasks** test should pass.

You have implemented the minimal code needed to display a list of tasks.

8.  **Refactoring with a custom component**: Let us make your code more reusable and modern by extracting each task's display into a Phoenix component.

Create **lib/tasks_app_web/components/task_components.ex**:

```
01. defmodule TasksAppWeb.TaskComponents do
02.   use Phoenix.Component
```

```
03.
04.    attr :task, :map, required: true
05.
06.    def task_row(assigns) do
07.      ~H"""
08.      <div class="mb-4 border rounded p-3 flex justify-between
    items-center">
09.        <div>
10.          <div class="font-semibold"><%= @task.title %></div>
11.          <div class="text-sm text-gray-500"><%= @task.description
    %></div>
12.        </div>
13.        <!-- Future: add actions here -->
14.      </div>
15.      """
16.    end
17. end
```

Now update **index.html.heex** to use this component:

```
01. <.header>
02.   Listing Tasks
03. </.header>
04.
05. <div>
06.   <%= for task <- @tasks do %>
07.     <TasksAppWeb.TaskComponents.task_row task={task} />
08.   <% end %>
09. </div>
```

With your project setup complete and your index listing working, you are ready to move on to *Showing single record*.

# Showing single record

After learning how to list all records, the next step in a CRUD app is to display the details of a single item. In this section, you will build the ability to view the details of an individual task by clicking on it in the list. This feature is commonly called the **show** operation in CRUD.

Just like before, we will use TDD: start with a failing test, then implement just enough code to make it pass. Follow these steps:

1. **Writing the test first**: Open **test/tasks_app_web/controllers/task_controller_test.exs** and add the following test if it is not already present:

```
01. test "GET /tasks/:id shows chosen task", %{conn: conn} do
02.   {:ok, task} = Tasks.create_task(%{title: "Test task",
         description: "Testing show action"})
03.   conn = get(conn, ~p"/tasks/#{task.id}")
04.   assert html_response(conn, 200) =~ task.title
05. end
```

Run your tests with:

```
01. mix test
```

You will see this test fail, since the show route and action are not set up yet. That is expected in TDD.

2. **Implementing the show feature**: Follow the steps below to add the route, controller action, template, and linking so the new **show** test passes.

3. **Add the show route**: Open **lib/tasks_app_web/router.ex** and update your resource routes to include **:show**:

```
01. resources "/tasks", TaskController, only: [:index, :show]
```

4. **Add the show action to your controller**: Open (or create) **lib/tasks_app_web/controllers/task_controller.ex** and add:

```
01. def show(conn, %{"id" => id}) do
02.   task = Tasks.get_task!(id)
03.   render(conn, :show, task: task)
04. end
```

This action fetches the task by ID and renders the show template.

5. **Create the show template**: Create **lib/tasks_app_web/controllers/task_html/show.html.heex** with:

```
01. <.header>Task Details</.header>
02.
03. <section class="mt-4">
04.   <p><strong>Title:</strong> <%= @task.title %></p>
05.   <p><strong>Description:</strong> <%= @task.description || "—"
```

```
     %></p>
06. </section>
07.
08. <div class="mt-6">
09.    <.link navigate={~p"/tasks"} class="mr-4">← Back to list</.
       link>
10.    <.link navigate={~p"/tasks/#{@task.id}/edit"}>Edit</.link>
11. </div>
```

6. **Add show Links to the index page:** To allow users to access the details page, add a **Show link** to each task in your index listing. If you are using a custom **task_row** component, pass the **show** path as a prop.

In your **index.html.heex**:

```
01. <.header>Listing Tasks</.header>
02.
03. <div>
04.    <%= for task <- @tasks do %>
05.      <TasksAppWeb.TaskComponents.task_row
06.        task={task}
07.        show_path={~p"/tasks/#{task.id}"}
08.        edit_path={~p"/tasks/#{task.id}/edit"}
09.        delete_path={~p"/tasks/#{task.id}"}
10.      />
11.    <% end %>
12. </div>
```

Also, in your **task_row** component:

```
01. attr :task, :map, required: true
02. attr :show_path, :string, required: true
03. attr :edit_path, :string, required: true
04. attr :delete_path, :string, required: true
05.
06. def task_row(assigns) do
07.    ~H"""
08.    <div class="flex items-center justify-between border rounded
       px-4 py-3 mb-3 bg-white shadow-sm">
```

```
09.    <div>
10.      <div class="font-semibold"><%= @task.title %></div>
11.      <div class="text-sm text-gray-500"><%= @task.description
     %></div>
12.    </div>
13.    <div class="flex gap-3">
14.      <.link navigate={@edit_path} class="text-blue-600
     hover:underline">Edit</.link>
15.      <.link navigate={@show_path} class="text-gray-700
     hover:underline">Show</.link>
16.      <.form :let={f} for={%{}} action={@delete_path}
     method="delete" class="inline">
17.        <button type="submit"
18.          data-confirm="Are you sure you want to delete this
     task?"
19.          class="text-red-600 hover:underline bg-transparent
     border-0 cursor-pointer">
20.          Delete
21.        </button>
22.      </.form>
23.    </div>
24.  </div>
25.  """
26. end
```

7. **Re-run your test**: Run your tests again:

```
01. mix test
```

Now your **GET /tasks/:id** shows the chosen task test should pass. You can also visit the **Show** page in your browser by clicking the **Show link** next to a task on the listing page.

With listing and showing single records working, you are now ready to move on to the next CRUD operation: creating records (C in CRUD).

# Creating records

Creating new records is a central part of any CRUD application. In this section, you will learn how to build a form for adding new tasks, process form submissions, handle errors, and provide feedback to users, all using the TDD approach. Follow these steps:

1. **Writing the test first:** Let us start by specifying what we expect from the *new task* feature.

   Open your **test/tasks_app_web/controllers/task_controller_test.exs** file and add these tests:

   ```
   01. test "GET /tasks/new renders form", %{conn: conn} do
   02.    conn = get(conn, ~p"/tasks/new")
   03.    assert html_response(conn, 200) =~ "New Task"
   04. end
   05.
   06. test "POST /tasks creates task", %{conn: conn} do
   07.    conn = post(conn, ~p"/tasks", task: %{title: "Write a book",
          description: "Write a Phoenix book chapter"})
   08.    assert redirected_to(conn) =~ "/tasks/"
   09. End
   ```

   What these two tests verify:
   o   The first test ensures the form for a new task appears at **/tasks/new**.
   o   The second test checks that submitting valid data creates a task and redirects to its detail page.

   Run your tests:

   ```
   01. mix test
   ```

   These tests should fail, since you have not created the new task page or action yet.

2. **Implementing the feature**: Follow the steps below to turn the failing tests green by wiring up routing, controller logic, and a form template.

3. **Add the routes**: Open **lib/tasks_app_web/router.ex** and make sure your resources line includes **:new** and **:create**:

   ```
   01. resources "/tasks", TaskController, only: [:index, :show, :new,
          :create]
   ```

4. **Add the controller actions**: Open **lib/tasks_app_web/controllers/task_controller.ex** and add the following:

   ```
   01. def new(conn, _params) do
   02.    changeset = Tasks.change_task(%Tasks.Task{})
   03.    render(conn, :new, changeset: changeset)
   04. end
   05.
   ```

```
06. def create(conn, %{"task" => task_params}) do
07.   case Tasks.create_task(task_params) do
08.     {:ok, task} ->
09.       conn
10.       |> put_flash(:info, "Task created!")
11.       |> redirect(to: ~p"/tasks/#{task.id}")
12.
13.     {:error, changeset} ->
14.       render(conn, :new, changeset: changeset)
15.   end
16. end
```

You may need to add the **change_task/1** function in your context if it does not already exist (usually generated with **phx.gen.context**):

```
01. def change_task(%Task{} = task, attrs \\ %{}) do
02.   Task.changeset(task, attrs)
03. end
```

5. **Create the new task form template**: Create the file **lib/tasks_app_web/controllers/ task_html/new.html.heex**:

```
01. <.header>New Task</.header>
02.
03. <.simple_form :let={f} for={@changeset} as={:task} action={~p"/
    tasks"} method="post">
04.   <.input field={f[:title]} type="text" label="Title" required />
05.   <.input field={f[:description]} type="textarea"
    label="Description" />
06.
07.   <:actions>
08.     <.button>Create Task</.button>
09.   </:actions>
10. </.simple_form>
11.
12. <div class="mt-4">
13.   <.link navigate={~p"/tasks"}>← Back to list</.link>
14. </div>
```

A few implementation notes about the form itself:

- The **:let={f}** syntax lets you reference form fields with **f[:title]** and **f[:description]**.

- The form uses Phoenix's latest components for clean, accessible markup.

6. **Add a New Task button to the listing page**: To make it easy for users to add tasks, add a **New Task** link to your index page, preferably at the top right:

```
01. <div class="flex justify-between items-center mb-8">
02.    <.header class="mb-0">Listing Tasks</.header>
03.    <.link
04.      navigate={~p"/tasks/new"}
05.      class="bg-blue-600 hover:bg-blue-700 text-white font-semibold
    py-2 px-4 rounded"
06.    >
07.      + New Task
08.    </.link>
09. </div>
```

Run your tests

```
01. mix test
```

Now both your **GET /tasks/new** and **POST /tasks** tests should pass.

7. **Try it out**: Run your Phoenix server:

```
01. mix phx.server
```

Visit **http://localhost:4000/tasks/new**, fill out the form, and submit.

You should see your new task created and redirected to its details page.

Next, you will learn how to edit and update existing records to complete your CRUD journey.

# Editing records

Editing existing records is a crucial part of a CRUD application. In this section, you will add the ability to update tasks. You will learn how to display an edit form pre-filled with existing data, handle user submissions, and update the database, all with TDD.

The following steps test the behavior we expect when users load the edit form and submit changes:

1. **Writing the test first:** Begin by writing tests for editing a task. Open **test/tasks_app_ web/controllers/task_controller_test.exs** and add:

```
01. test "GET /tasks/:id/edit renders edit form", %{conn: conn} do
02.   {:ok, task} = Tasks.create_task(%{title: "Original",
      description: "Edit me"})
03.   conn = get(conn, ~p"/tasks/#{task.id}/edit")
04.   assert html_response(conn, 200) =~ "Edit Task"
05. end
06.
07. test "PUT /tasks/:id updates task and redirects", %{conn: conn}
    do
08.   {:ok, task} = Tasks.create_task(%{title: "Original",
      description: "Edit me"})
09.   conn = put(conn, ~p"/tasks/#{task.id}", task: %{title:
      "Updated", description: "Changed"})
10.   assert redirected_to(conn) == ~p"/tasks/#{task.id}"
11.
12.   # Optionally, follow up and check the updated content
13.   conn = get(conn, ~p"/tasks/#{task.id}")
14.   assert html_response(conn, 200) =~ "Updated"
15. end
```

Run the tests and confirm they fail (since you have not built the edit/update feature yet:

```
01. mix test
```

2.  **Implementing the feature**: Follow the steps below to turn the failing tests green by wiring up routing, controller logic, templates, and links:

    a.  **Add routes for edit and update**: In **lib/tasks_app_web/router.ex**, update your resources to include **:edit** and **:update**:

    ```
    01.   resources "/tasks", TaskController, only: [:index, :show,
          :new, :create, :edit, :update]
    ```

    b.  **Add controller actions**: In **lib/tasks_app_web/controllers/task_controller.ex**, add:

    ```
    01. def edit(conn, %{"id" => id}) do
    02.   task = Tasks.get_task!(id)
    03.   changeset = Tasks.change_task(task)
    04.   render(conn, :edit, task: task, changeset: changeset)
    05. end
    ```

```
06.
07.  def update(conn, %{"id" => id, "task" => task_params}) do
08.    task = Tasks.get_task!(id)
09.    case Tasks.update_task(task, task_params) do
10.      {:ok, task} ->
11.        conn
12.        |> put_flash(:info, "Task updated successfully.")
13.        |> redirect(to: ~p"/tasks/#{task.id}")
14.      {:error, changeset} ->
15.        render(conn, :edit, task: task, changeset: changeset)
16.    end
17.  end
```

3. **Create the edit form template**: Create **lib/tasks_app_web/controllers/task_html/edit.html.heex**:

```
01. <.header>Edit Task</.header>
02.
03. <.simple_form :let={f} for={@changeset} as={:task} action={~p"/
    tasks/#{@task.id}"} method="put">
04.   <.input field={f[:title]} type="text" label="Title" required />
05.   <.input field={f[:description]} type="textarea"
    label="Description" />
06.
07.   <:actions>
08.     <.button>Update Task</.button>
09.   </:actions>
10. </.simple_form>
11.
12. <div class="mt-4">
13.   <.link navigate={~p"/tasks/#{@task.id}"}>← Back to task
    details</.link>
14. </div>
```

4. **Add an edit link to the task list**: Make it easy for users to access the edit form by adding an **Edit** link to each task row in your list, using your custom component. For example, in **index.html.heex**:

```
01. <%= for task <- @tasks do %>
02.   <TasksAppWeb.TaskComponents.task_row
03.     task={task}
04.     edit_path={~p"/tasks/#{task.id}/edit"}
05.     show_path={~p"/tasks/#{task.id}"}
06.     delete_path={~p"/tasks/#{task.id}"}
07.   />
08. <% end %>
```

In your **task_row component** (if you want, you can add a nice label for clarity):

```
01. attr :task, :map, required: true
02. attr :edit_path, :string, required: true
03. attr :show_path, :string, required: true
04. attr :delete_path, :string, required: true
05.
06. def task_row(assigns) do
07.   ~H"""
08.   <div class="flex items-center justify-between border rounded
      px-4 py-3 mb-3 bg-white shadow-sm">
09.     <div>
10.       <div class="font-semibold"><%= @task.title %></div>
11.       <div class="text-sm text-gray-500"><%= @task.description
          %></div>
12.     </div>
13.     <div class="flex gap-3">
14.       <.link navigate={@edit_path} class="text-blue-600
          hover:underline">Edit</.link>
15.       <.link navigate={@show_path} class="text-gray-700
          hover:underline">Show</.link>
16.       <.form :let={f} for={%{}} action={@delete_path}
          method="delete" class="inline">
17.         <button type="submit"
18.           data-confirm="Are you sure you want to delete this
            task?"
19.           class="text-red-600 hover:underline bg-transparent
            border-0 cursor-pointer">
```

```
20.              Delete
21.            </button>
22.          </.form>
23.        </div>
24.      </div>
25.    """
26. end
```

5. **Run your tests:**

```
01. mix test
```

Your edit or update tests should now pass.

6. **Try it out**: Run your Phoenix server:

```
01. mix phx.server
02.
```

   a. Visit **/tasks** to see your tasks.
   b. Click the edit link next to a task, make changes, and submit.
   c. You should see your changes reflected immediately, and a flash message indicating success.

Your application now allows users to create, read (list and show), and update tasks!

Next, let us add the final CRUD operation: *Deleting records.*

# Deleting records

The final piece of CRUD is giving users the ability to delete records. In this section, you will add the ability to remove tasks from your app, with proper test coverage, UI feedback, and safe handling.

The following steps test the behavior we expect when a user deletes a task:

1. **Writing the test first**: Begin by writing a test to define the expected behavior. Open **test/tasks_app_web/controllers/task_controller_test.exs** and add:

```
01. test "DELETE /tasks/:id deletes the task and redirects", %{conn:
    conn} do
02.   {:ok, task} = Tasks.create_task(%{title: "Task to Delete",
      description: "Will be gone"})
03.   conn = delete(conn, ~p"/tasks/#{task.id}")
04.   assert redirected_to(conn) == ~p"/tasks"
05.   assert_error_sent 404, fn ->
```

```
06.        get(conn, ~p"/tasks/#{task.id}")
07.    end
08. end
```

This test verifies that after deleting a task:

- o   The app redirects to the task listing.
- o   Accessing the deleted task gives a **404** error.

Run your tests:

```
01. mix test
```

This test should fail because the delete functionality is not implemented yet.

2.  **Implementing the delete feature**: Follow the steps to turn the failing tests green by wiring up routing, controller logic, template changes, and UI hooks:

    a.  **Update the routes**: Ensure your resource definition in **lib/tasks_app_web/router.ex** includes **:delete**:

```
01.    resources "/tasks", TaskController, only: [:index, :show,
           :new, :create, :edit, :update, :delete]
```

    Otherwise, simply use:

```
01.    resources "/tasks", TaskController
```

    This is to generate all standard routes.

3.  **Add the delete action to the controller**: Open **lib/tasks_app_web/controllers/task_controller.ex** and add:

```
01. def delete(conn, %{"id" => id}) do
02.    task = Tasks.get_task!(id)
03.    {:ok, _task} = Tasks.delete_task(task)
04.
05.    conn
06.    |> put_flash(:info, "Task deleted successfully.")
07.    |> redirect(to: ~p"/tasks")
08. end
```

    Make sure your context module (**lib/tasks_app/tasks.ex**) includes:

```
01. def delete_task(%Task{} = task), do: Repo.delete(task)
```

4.  **Add a delete button to each task row**: You will want users to be able to delete tasks from the list. The safest way to do this in Phoenix is with a form using the **HTTP DELETE** method, which includes CSRF protection.

In your custom **task_row** component:

```
01. def task_row(assigns) do
02.   ~H"""
03.   <div class="flex items-center justify-between border rounded
      px-4 py--3 mb-3 bg-white shadow-sm">
04.     <div>
05.       <div class="font-semibold"><%= @task.title %></div>
06.       <div class="text-sm text-gray-500"><%= @task.description
      %></div>
07.     </div>
08.     <div class="flex gap-3">
09.       <.link navigate={@edit_path} class="text-blue-600
      hover:underline">Edit</.link>
10.       <.link navigate={@show_path} class="text-gray-700
      hover:underline">Show</.link>
11.       <.form :let={f} for={%{}} action={@delete_path}
      method="delete" class="inline">
12.         <button type="submit"
13.           data-confirm="Are you sure you want to delete this
      task?"
14.           class="text-red-600 hover:underline bg-transparent
      border-0 cursor-pointer">
15.           Delete
16.         </button>
17.       </.form>
18.     </div>
19.   </div>
20.   """
21. end
```

The following are that you should remember:

o  The **:let={f}  for={%{}}** syntax gives you a valid form context without needing a changeset.

o  The **action={@delete_path}** points to the correct delete route.

o  **method="delete"** ensures the form issues an **HTTP DELETE** request.

o  **data-confirm** triggers a browser confirmation dialog before deletion.

In your **index.html.heex**:

```
01. <div class="flex justify-between items-center mb-8">
02.   <.header class="mb-0">Listing Tasks</.header>
03.   <.link
04.     navigate={~p"/tasks/new"}
05.     class="bg-blue-600 hover:bg-blue-700 text-white font-semibold
       py-2 px-4 rounded"
06.   >
07.     + New Task
08.   </.link>
09. </div>
10.
11. <div>
12.   <%= for task <- @tasks do %>
13.     <TasksAppWeb.TaskComponents.task_row
14.       task={task}
15.       edit_path={~p"/tasks/#{task.id}/edit"}
16.       show_path={~p"/tasks/#{task.id}"}
17.       delete_path={~p"/tasks/#{task.id}"}
18.     />
19.   <% end %>
20. </div>
```

5.  **Run your tests:**

```
01. mix test
02.
```

Your delete test (and all others) should now pass.

6.  **Try it out**: Run your Phoenix server:

```
01. mix phx.server
```

7.  **Visit /tasks to see your tasks:** Click the *Delete* button for any task. You should see a confirmation dialog, and after confirming, the task will be removed and you will be redirected to the list page.

You now have a complete, test-driven CRUD app in Phoenix, with clear and maintainable code.

# Refactor with Phoenix Components

As your Phoenix application develops, your codebase will naturally expand. What may start as a simple and clear template can quickly become cluttered as you add new features or adjust existing ones. This is especially true in CRUD applications, where you often display similar information in multiple places, like listing tasks, showing a task's details, and rendering forms for new or edited tasks. Without careful attention, you may find yourself copying and pasting the same HTML, logic, and markup into several templates, making your code harder to read, maintain, and test.

## Importance of refactoring with components

Refactoring with Phoenix Components helps you address these problems by encouraging you to:

- **Avoid duplication**: If you notice the same HTML or logic repeated in multiple templates, extract it into a reusable component. This means you only have to make changes in one place when your design or logic changes.

- **Keep the code Do not Repeat Yourself (DRY)**: A DRY codebase is easier to maintain and extend. Repetition leads to bugs; if you forget to update every copy, your app becomes inconsistent.

- **Improve readability**: Components let you replace long chunks of HTML with clear, meaningful tags like `<TasksAppWeb.TaskComponents.task_row ... />`, making your templates shorter and easier to understand at a glance.

- **Encourage reuse and consistency**: When all your *task rows* or *action buttons* are rendered by a single component, your UI stays consistent across the app. Updates to a component are instantly reflected everywhere it is used.

- **Support testing and refactoring**: Components help you break complex templates into smaller, focused parts, which are easier to test, update, or even move between projects.

The following pattern shows how to wrap varied page content in a single, reusable panel by leveraging component slots:

- **Flexible layouts with slots**:
  - **Reason**: Sometimes, you have repeating wrapper markup (like a **card** or **panel**), but the content inside it changes. Instead of duplicating the wrapper, use a slot so your component can accept any inner content you want. This is powerful for layouts and page sections.

  - **Ways**: Create a generic **panel** component with a slot:

```
01.    # In the same TaskComponents module
02.
```

```
03.   def panel(assigns) do
04.     ~H"""
05.     <div class="p-4 rounded border mb-6 bg-gray-50 shadow">
06.       <%= render_slot(@inner_block) %>
07.     </div>
08.     """
09.   end
```

The special **@inner_block** variable is a slot in Phoenix.

When you use the component, you can put any content inside **<TasksAppWeb. TaskComponents.panel>** ... **</...>**.

Usage in a template:

```
01. <TasksAppWeb.TaskComponents.panel>
02.   <.header>Listing Tasks</.header>
03.   <%= for task <- @tasks do %>
04.     <TasksAppWeb.TaskComponents.task_row
05.       task={task}
06.       edit_path={~p"/tasks/#{task.id}/edit"}
07.       show_path={~p"/tasks/#{task.id}"}
08.       delete_path={~p"/tasks/#{task.id}"}
09.     />
10.   <% end %>
11. </TasksAppWeb.TaskComponents.panel>
```

Now your list page is wrapped in a consistent, styled panel, and you can use the same panel for other content anywhere in your app.

- **Centralizing forms**: If your new and edit forms are nearly identical, extract a **TaskForm** component.

This is because the new and edit screens share almost identical form markup, so we can eliminate duplication by pulling the form into its own.

- **TaskForm component:** Create the component. Here is the definition of that reusable form component:

```
01. attr :changeset, :map, required: true
02. attr :action, :string, required: true
03. attr :button_label, :string, default: "Save Task"
```

```
04.
05. def task_form(assigns) do
06.    ~H"""
07.    <.simple_form :let={f} for={@changeset} as={:task} action={@
    action} method="post">
08.       <.input field={f[:title]} type="text" label="Title" required
    />
09.       <.input field={f[:description]} type="textarea"
    label="Description" />
10.       <:actions>
11.          <.button><%= @button_label %></.button>
12.       </:actions>
13.    </.simple_form>
14.    """
15. end
```

Now, use it for both new and editing:

o **In new.html.heex**:

```
01.    <.header>New Task</.header>
02.    <TasksAppWeb.TaskComponents.task_form
03.       changeset={@changeset}
04.       action={~p"/tasks"}
05.       button_label="Create Task"
06.    />
07.    <.link navigate={~p"/tasks"}>← Back to list</.link>
```

o **In edit.html.heex**:

```
01.    <.header>Edit Task</.header>
02.    <TasksAppWeb.TaskComponents.task_form
03.       changeset={@changeset}
04.       action={~p"/tasks/#{@task.id}"}
05.       button_label="Update Task"
06.    />
07.    <.link navigate={~p"/tasks/#{@task.id}"}>← Back to task
    details</.link>
```

# Refinement and debugging

The refinement and debugging stage is crucial for ensuring that our Task Management CRUD app runs smoothly and meets the requirements we have set throughout the development process. During this stage, we focus on polishing the code, fixing any bugs, and optimizing performance. We also ensure that all tests pass, guaranteeing that our features work as expected and are reliable for end users.

Let us proceed step by step, covering key areas such as test validation, debugging strategies, and code optimization:

1. **Running and reviewing tests**: The first step in refinement and debugging is to run all the tests we have written so far to identify any failures or inconsistencies. Run the following command to execute all tests in the project:

   ```
   01. mix test
   ```

   This command runs all the test cases across the application, including tests for task creation, editing, deletion, listing, and any edge cases you may have added.

   If any tests fail, carefully read the error messages and stack traces provided by the Elixir test framework. These messages often contain valuable information about the cause of the failure, such as incorrect values, missing parameters, or logic errors.

2. **Debugging the application**: Once you identify failing tests or bugs in the application, you need a systematic approach to debugging them. The following are some common debugging techniques and tools that can help:

   a. **Logging:** Adding logging to your code can help you track the flow of execution and identify problematic areas. You can add logging using the **Logger** module in Elixir:

   ```
   01.    require Logger
   02.
   03.    def create(conn, %{"task" => task_params}) do
   04.      Logger.info("Creating a task with params: #{inspect(task_params)}")
   05.      # Rest of the code...
   06.    end
   ```

   By adding logs, you can trace the data and understand where things might be going wrong.

   b. **Interactive debugging**: You can use **Interactive Elixir (IEx)** to interact with your application and test specific functions or expressions. Start your Phoenix server with IEx like this:

   ```
   01.    iex -S mix phx.server
   ```

This allows you to execute code snippets and inspect the state of your application in real time, making it easier to diagnose issues.

c.  **Testing edge cases:** During debugging, always include scenarios that the initial test suite may have missed. Verify that the application rejects attempts to create a task with an empty title by returning a validation error, and confirm that requesting a non-existent task produces a **404** response. Add dedicated test cases to prove that these conditions are handled gracefully.

3.  **Refining the code**: Refinement is about making the code cleaner, more efficient, and easier to maintain. Here are some areas to focus on during the refinement process:

    a.  **Code cleanup**: Remove any redundant code, unused variables, or commented-out sections. This keeps the codebase clean and makes it easier for other developers to understand.

    b.  **Refactoring**: Refactor the code to improve its structure without changing its behavior. For instance, if you notice repeated code blocks, consider extracting them into helper functions or components to avoid duplication and improve readability.

    For example, extracting a repeated validation block into a separate function:

```
01.   def validate_title_present(changeset) do
02.       validate_required(changeset, [:title])
03.   end
04.
05.   # Usage in the Task changeset function
06.   def changeset(task, attrs) do
07.       task
08.       |> cast(attrs, [:title, :description])
09.       |> validate_title_present()
10.   end
```

Refactoring like this helps make the code DRY and easier to test.

4.  **Performance optimization**: Look for opportunities to improve the performance of your application. For example, if certain queries are slow, consider adding indexes to the database or optimizing the query logic. Use the **EXPLAIN** command in SQL to analyze the performance of your queries.

5.  **User experience improvements**: During refinement, prioritize the user experience. Provide clear, informative error messages and maintain an intuitive, easy-to-navigate UI. Even small usability tweaks can significantly enhance the application's overall quality.

6. **Ensuring all tests pass**: After making refinements and debugging, run the tests again to ensure that everything still works as expected. Execute the following code:

```
01. mix test
```

All tests should pass without any errors or failures. If any test fails, revisit the related part of the code, make the necessary corrections, and rerun the tests.

7. **Manual testing and user feedback**: In addition to automated testing, it is essential to manually test the application. Go through the main user flows, such as creating a new task, editing and deleting tasks, and viewing task details. Make sure everything works smoothly and there are no usability issues.

If possible, get feedback from potential users or stakeholders. They may identify issues or suggest improvements that you might not have considered.

The refinement and debugging process is vital for ensuring the quality and reliability of the Task Management CRUD app. By running tests, debugging issues, refining the code, and conducting manual testing, we can provide users with a stable and efficient experience. This stage not only helps in fixing issues but also makes the code more maintainable and scalable in the long run.

# Deployment

In this section, we will focus on preparing the Task Management CRUD app for deployment in a production-like environment. While we will not actually deploy the app to a cloud provider, we will set up the necessary configurations to make the application deployment-ready. This process includes configuring the database, environment variables, and ensuring the application is optimized for production use.

Let us proceed step by step, covering essential tasks such as production configuration, environment variable setup, and testing the application in a production-like environment:

1. **Production configuration**: First, we need to adjust the configuration files to prepare the application for deployment. Production settings differ from development settings, especially for database connections and sensitive credentials.

2. **Database configuration**: Open **config/prod.exs** and update the database settings as follows:

```
01. import Config
02.
03. config :tasks_app, TasksApp.Repo,
04.   username: System.get_env("DATABASE_USER"),
05.   password: System.get_env("DATABASE_PASS"),
06.   hostname: System.get_env("DATABASE_HOST"),
```

```
07.   database: System.get_env("DATABASE_NAME"),
08.   pool_size: 10,
09.   ssl: true
```

Explanation for the above code is as follows:

- The production configuration uses environment variables for database credentials.
- This is a secure way to manage sensitive information and ensures credentials are not hardcoded in your codebase.

3. **Endpoint configuration**: Still in **config/prod.exs**, update the endpoint settings:

```
01. config :tasks_app, TasksAppWeb.Endpoint,
02.   http: [port: String.to_integer(System.get_env("PORT") ||
      "4000")],
03.   url: [host: System.get_env("HOSTNAME"), port: 80],
04.   cache_static_manifest: "priv/static/cache_manifest.json",
05.   server: true,
06.   root: ".",
07.   version: Application.spec(:tasks_app, :vsn)
```

Explanation of the above code is as follows:

a. This configuration sets the HTTP port, the public URL, and cache settings for static files.

b. **server: true** ensures the Phoenix server starts automatically in production mode.

4. **Secret key base**: In production, it is critical to set a secure secret key for session encryption.

Generate a secret key using the following code:

```
01. mix phx.gen.secret
```

Copy the generated secret key and set it as an environment variable named **SECRET_ KEY_BASE**.

Update the endpoint configuration in **config/prod.exs**:

```
01. config :tasks_app, TasksAppWeb.Endpoint,
02.   secret_key_base: System.get_env("SECRET_KEY_BASE")
```

5. **Setting up environment variables**: Environment variables configure sensitive information such as database credentials and session secrets, without including them directly in your codebase.

Set up the following environment variables for your production environment:

- **DATABASE_USER**: The database username.
- **DATABASE_PASS**: The database password.
- **DATABASE_HOST**: The hostname or IP address of your database server.
- **DATABASE_NAME**: The name of the production database.
- **PORT**: The port on which the application will run (default is 4000).
- **HOSTNAME**: The hostname or domain for your application.
- **SECRET_KEY_BASE**: The secret key generated earlier for session encryption.

To manage environment variables, you can create a .env file and use tools like direnv or dotenv to load them into your environment.

Here is an example .env file:

```
01. DATABASE_USER=your_db_user
02. DATABASE_PASS=your_db_pass
03. DATABASE_HOST=your_db_host
04. DATABASE_NAME=your_db_name
05. PORT=4000
06. HOSTNAME=your_hostname.com
07. SECRET_KEY_BASE=your_secret_key_base
```

6. **Building a release:** In production, we typically use a release to deploy the application. Phoenix provides tools for creating releases that bundle everything needed to run the app.

7. **Create a release:** Run the following command to build a release:

```
01. MIX_ENV=prod mix release
```

This command creates a release for the Task Management CRUD app in the **_build/ prod/rel/tasks_app** directory.

8. **Run the release**: After building the release, you can run it with:

```
01. _build/prod/rel/tasks_app/bin/tasks_app start
```

This command starts the application in production mode, using the production configuration settings.

9. **Testing the application in a production-like environment**: To ensure the application is ready for deployment, test it in an environment that closely resembles production. You can use a staging server or set up a local production environment.

10. **Docker setup:** You can use Docker to create a production-like environment locally.

Create a Dockerfile in your project root:

```
01. # Use the official Elixir image as a base
02. FROM elixir:1.15
03.
04. # Set environment variables
05. ENV MIX_ENV=prod
06.
07. # Install dependencies
08. RUN apt-get update && \
09.     apt-get install -y postgresql-client
10.
11. # Set working directory
12. WORKDIR /app
13. COPY . .
14.
15. # Install Hex and Rebar
16. RUN mix local.hex --force && \
17.     mix local.rebar --force
18.
19. # Install dependencies
20. RUN mix deps.get --only prod
21.
22. # Compile the application
23. RUN mix compile
24.
25. # Build static assets
26. RUN cd assets && npm install && npm run build && cd ..
27. RUN mix phx.digest
28.
29. # Create a release
30. RUN mix release
31.
32. # Start the application
33. CMD ["_build/prod/rel/tasks_app/bin/tasks_app", "start"]
```

11. **Running the Docker container**: Build and run the Docker container to simulate a production environment:

```
01. docker build -t tasks_app .
02. docker run -p 4000:4000 --env-file .env tasks_app
```

This command runs the application in a Docker container, exposing it on port **4000**.

Setting up the Task Management CRUD app for deployment involves configuring production settings, managing environment variables, and building a release to run the application in a production-like environment.

By following these steps, you can ensure that your application is ready for deployment and can handle real-world use cases. Even though we have not deployed to a cloud provider, this setup gives you a solid foundation for deploying the application when needed.

# Phoenix 1.8 compatibility notes

If you generated your project with Phoenix 1.8, everything in this chapter still applies. The overall flow is router | controller | HEEx templates and components | Ecto are unchanged. The differences are mostly in scaffold defaults and one small controller declaration.

The following are the same:

- Verified routes (~p), router scopes/pipelines, and controller action flow.
- HEEx templates and function components (Phoenix.Component, ~H, attr, slot).
- Ecto contexts, schemas, changesets, queries, and Repo usage.
- Tests and deployment with a mixed release.

The following are different in Phoenix 1.8:

- **Controllers must declare formats:**
  - ○ **What changed**: In Phoenix 1.8, each controller explicitly declares the content types (formats) it serves. This makes compile-time pipelines clearer and prevents accidental ambiguity (e.g., a controller meant for HTML accidentally handling JSON).

    The following is how to write it (1.8):

```
01.    defmodule MyAppWeb.TaskController do
02.      use MyAppWeb, :controller, formats: [:html]    # or
         [:json], or [:html, :json]
03.      # actions...
04.    end
```

The following is how it was written earlier:

```
01.  defmodule MyAppWeb.TaskController do
02.    use MyAppWeb, :controller
03.    # actions...
04.  end
```

- o **Selection criteria:**
  - **UI controllers | formats**: [:html]
  - **JSON APIs | formats**: [:json]
  - **Mixed controllers (only if you intentionally serve both) | formats**: [:html, :json]

- o **Common mistakes:**
  - Forgetting to add formats: and getting confusing render errors.
  - Declaring [:json] but returning HTML, or vice versa. Align your formats with your templates and responses.

- **Single root layout (root.html.heex):**

  - o **What changed**: New 1.8 projects consolidate the base layout into a single root layout:

    ```
    01.  lib/my_app_web/layouts/root.html.heex
    ```

    It wraps your entire HTML tree and is referenced from the router's **:browser** pipeline. You still insert **@inner_content** and can compose smaller layout components.

  - o **Router integration:**

    ```
    01.  pipeline :browser do
    02.    plug :accepts, ["html"]
    03.    plug :fetch_session
    04.    plug :fetch_live_flash
    05.    plug :put_root_layout, {MyAppWeb.Layouts, :root}
    06.    plug :protect_from_forgery
    07.    plug :put_secure_browser_headers
    08.  end
    ```

  - o **Why is it better**: A single, predictable layout simplifies mental overhead and works cleanly with components and verified routes.

- o **Migrating notes:**
  - ▪ If your text/screenshots said **app.html.heex**, readers on 1.8 should look for **layouts/root.html.heex**.
  - ▪ Your usage of **<.flash_group />**, navigation components, and **@inner_content** is unchanged.

- **HTML modules and embedded templates:**
  - o **What changed:** You continue to use *HTML modules with **embed_templates**, but fresh projects often locate templates under a path that mirrors the module name closely, for example:

```
01.  # lib/my_app_web/controllers/task_html.ex
02.  defmodule MyAppWeb.TaskHTML do
03.    use MyAppWeb, :html
04.    import MyAppWeb.TaskComponents
05.    embed_templates "task/*"
06.  end
```

    The templates live under:

```
01.  lib/my_app_web/controllers/task/index.html.heex
02.  lib/my_app_web/controllers/task/show.html.heex
03.  ...
```

  - o **Why it is better:** It keeps controller-related templates near their HTML module and aligns with component-first design.

  - o **Common mistakes:**
    - ▪ Using a stale path like **"task_html/*"** or placing templates under **templates/** from much older versions.
    - ▪ Forgetting to import your component module; if you call **<.task_row />** in a template, the HTML module should import it.

- **Security headers:**
  - o **What changed:** The **:browser** pipeline still calls **put_secure_browser_headers/2**, but 1.8 drops some legacy headers from the defaults (e.g., **x-frame-options**, **x-download-options**) to reflect modern browser guidance.

    If you still need them, add explicitly:

```
01.  plug :put_secure_browser_headers
02.  plug :put_resp_header, "x-frame-options", "SAMEORIGIN"
03.  plug :put_resp_header, "x-download-options", "noopen"
```

- o **Why it is better:** The defaults follow current standards, and teams can opt-in only to the headers they actually need.

- o **Pitfall:** If you depended on older defaults for clickjacking or download behavior, you must add them yourself now.

- **Assets workflow (Tailwind/esbuild) and theming defaults**

  - o **What changed:** Phoenix 1.8 projects ship with asset tooling wired and may include a lightweight theme plugin for Tailwind out of the box, so your UI has sensible defaults immediately.

    The local development is:

    ```
    01.  mix assets.setup
    02.  mix assets.build
    ```

    The production:

    ```
    01.  mix assets.deploy
    ```

  - o **Why it is better:** Faster onboarding; less manual boilerplate for CSS/JS. Theming is optional and does not affect your Elixir/Phoenix code.

  - o **Pitfall:** Using mix assets.deploy during development can minify/bundle in ways that obscure debugging. Prefer assets.build in **dev**.

- **Configuration hygiene (Application.compile_env/3):**

  - o **What changed:** Where you read values at compile time inside modules (e.g., Endpoint/Repo), use **Application.compile_env/3**:

    ```
    01.  config :my_app, MyAppWeb.Endpoint,
    02.    url: [host: Application.compile_env(:my_app, :host,
         "localhost")]
    ```

  - o **Why it is better:** Explicitly conveys compile-time reads and avoids surprising mismatches between runtime env and compiled code.

  - o **Pitfall:** Do not replace every **Application.get_env/3** blindly; use **compile_env** only where you truly need compile-time resolution.

The following are quick migration checklists (from Phoenix 1.7 to 1.8)

- Add formats, such as [:html] (or [:json]) to each controller.

- Use **lib/my_app_web/layouts/root.html.heex** for the main layout (router has **put_root_layout {MyAppWeb.Layouts, :root}**).

- Ensure your HTML modules import any components you call and use **embed_templates "your_path/*"**.

- If you relied on legacy headers, add them explicitly with **put_resp_header/3**.

- Use **mix assets.setup && mix assets.build** in development; reserve **mix assets. deploy** for production.

- Prefer **Application.compile_env/3** for compile-time config reads inside code.

**Note: Phoenix 1.8's changes are evolutionary, not disruptive. If you follow this chapter's 1.7 and apply the small 1.8 notes above (controller formats, root layout name, template paths, optional headers), your code, tests, and deployment will behave exactly as taught, while matching the latest generator defaults.**

# Conclusion

In this chapter, you built a complete Task Management CRUD app with Elixir Phoenix from project bootstrap to a deployment-ready Docker image. You scaffolded the project, then implemented create, read, update, and delete features with a strict TDD loop, guaranteeing reliability at every step. Phoenix Components kept the views DRY and reusable, while refactoring and expanding tests preserved clarity as the codebase grew. Finally, you learned the essentials of production setup: configuring environments, securing secrets, and packaging the release for the cloud. The result is a maintainable, fully tested application that demonstrates modern Phoenix best practices end-to-end.

# Practical exercises

1. **Building a reusable title component:**
   a. Create a function component Title that renders an <h1> with a passed-in text.
   b. Render it in a template using both the fully-qualified path and the shorthand form.
   c. Extend it to accept a second assign (subtitle) and display it below the title.

2. **Conditional rendering in a component:**
   a. Build a StatusTag component that takes an assign (status) with values like *active* or *inactive*.
   b. Render different colors (e.g., green for active, red for inactive) based on the status.
   c. Write an exercise to test how it behaves with unexpected values.

3. **Looping through data in a component:**
   a. Create a UserList component that accepts a list of user maps (%{name: "Alice"}).
   b. Render them as an unordered list (<ul>).
   c. Modify the exercise so students can add a condition: only render users with an "active" field set to true.

4. **Slot-based components:**
   a. Build a Card component that accepts content via slots.
   b. Use it in a template to render multiple cards with different text.
   c. Extend the exercise to add a :header slot and require students to render both a header and body.

5. **Composing components together:**
   a. Create a Dashboard template that uses the Title, StatusTag, and UserList components together.
   b. Change one of the components (e.g., StatusTag) and observe how it affects the dashboard layout.

6. **Refactoring templates into components:**
   a. Take an existing .heex template with repeated HTML (like buttons or form fields).
   b. Refactor the repeated part into a new function component.
   c. Students should update the template to use the new component everywhere.

7. **Challenge project; component library**
   a. Build a mini *UI library* with at least three reusable components (Button, Alert, Card).
   b. Render them in a sample page (demo.html.heex).
   c. Add one more component of your own choice and integrate it into the demo page.

# Points to remember

- Start every feature with a failing test. The TDD cycle: Red | Green | Refactor | ensures correctness and drives clean design.

- Use mix phx.gen.context for domain logic, not phx.gen.html. Hand-crafting controllers and components forces a deeper understanding of Phoenix's structure.

- Keep templates DRY with Phoenix Components. Extract repeated markup (task rows, forms, panels) into reusable components and slots for consistency and easy maintenance.

- Leverage Ecto changesets for validation. Centralized rules prevent invalid data from slipping into the database or the UI.

- Write edge-case tests. Validate empty fields, missing IDs, and other boundary conditions to safeguard user experience.

- Refactor continuously. Small, incremental clean-ups after each passing test keep the codebase readable and flexible.

- Provide clear flash messages and error feedback. Good UX is as important as correct business logic.

- Secure routes with HTTP verbs. Use method="delete" forms for destructive actions to benefit from Phoenix's CSRF protection.

- Automate assets and database tasks. Commands like mix assets.deploy, mix ecto. create, and mix ecto.migrate should be part of your routine.

- Prepare for production early. Manage environment variables, use UUID primary keys, and generate Docker releases so deployment is a push-button affair.

# Join our Discord space

Join our Discord workspace for latest updates, offers, tech happenings around the world, new releases, and sessions with the authors:

https://discord.bpbonline.com

# CHAPTER 12
# Future Directions

## Introduction

As we approach the end of our exploration into the dynamic and functional world of Elixir, it is crucial to take a moment to reflect on the journey we have taken. Starting with the basics of functional programming and the unique features of Elixir, we have traversed through topics as diverse as syntax and tooling, concurrent programming, building with Phoenix and Ecto, and even exploring the advanced field of metaprogramming. Each chapter has not only expanded your toolkit as a developer but also sharpened your problem-solving skills in a functional paradigm.

In this final chapter, we aim to consolidate the knowledge you have gained, ensuring that the principles and practices of Elixir are not just learned but ingrained in your approach to software development. We will revisit the core concepts to reinforce your understanding and confidence in using Elixir effectively. Additionally, we will discuss best practices for code organization and development methodologies that enhance maintainability and scalability, essential qualities in today's fast-evolving tech landscape.

Moreover, we will look ahead to the future directions of Elixir. As the language matures and its community grows, staying informed about its trajectory will help you leverage its full potential and remain at the cutting edge of software development. Whether you are planning to build scalable web applications, contribute to open source, or innovate with new technologies, Elixir offers a robust foundation for building resilient and efficient systems.

# Structure

In this chapter, we will cover the following topics:

- Revisiting learned concepts
- Best practices in Elixir
- Code organization in Elixir
- Resources for further learning
- Future directions of Elixir

# Objectives

In this final chapter, our goal is to provide a cohesive review of all the key concepts you have encountered throughout this book, solidifying your ability to leverage Elixir's functional programming strengths and robust concurrency model. We aim to reinforce best practices for coding and structuring your projects, ensuring the maintainability and scalability that modern applications demand. Finally, by exploring the future directions and resources available for Elixir, we seek to inspire your continued growth, encourage you to contribute to the thriving Elixir community, and equip you to stay at the forefront of evolving technology trends.

By the end of this chapter, you should not only feel competent in your ability to apply Elixir to real-world problems but also inspired to continue exploring, learning, and growing as a developer within the vibrant Elixir ecosystem. Let us embrace these final insights and advice to ensure you are well-equipped for whatever challenges and opportunities lie ahead in your programming endeavors.

# Revisiting learned concepts

Elixir is a functional programming language designed for building scalable and maintainable applications, benefiting from the proven stability of the Erlang VM (BEAM). One of its standout features is the ease with which developers can create highly concurrent programs, thanks to Elixir's lightweight processes and messaging system. Moreover, Elixir offers an elegant syntax that streamlines common tasks, whether it is testing, documentation, or dependency management, ensuring that developers can focus on writing clear, expressive code rather than wrestling with boilerplate.

Following is a summarized list of important Elixir concepts revisited in this section, showcasing how each aspect of the language contributes to building robust and efficient applications:

- **Functional programming (FP):** This paradigm treats computation as the evaluation of mathematical functions and avoids changing state and mutable data. In Elixir, this paradigm provides several advantages that enhance the reliability and maintainability of software systems.

- **Principles of FP**: The following are the principles of FP:

  o **Immutability**: In FP, data is immutable, meaning once a data structure is created, it cannot be changed. This eliminates side effects caused by changes in data state, reducing bugs related to shared mutable state.

  o **First-class functions**: Functions in FP are treated as first-class citizens, meaning they can be passed as arguments, returned from other functions, and assigned to variables. This promotes higher-order functions and function composition.

  o **Pure functions**: These functions always return the same output for the same input and do not cause any side effects, making the code predictable and testable.

- **Benefits over imperative programming**: The Following are the benefits:

  o **Predictability**: Pure functions and immutability make the system behavior predictable. Unlike imperative programming, where the state can be changed from anywhere in the application, FP's immutable data structures and pure functions provide a clear understanding of data flow.

  o **Ease of debugging**: With immutability, the state of an application at any point in time is easier to understand because it does not change unexpectedly. This makes debugging simpler as there is no need to consider the global state or side effects.

  o **Concurrency**: FP's immutable data structures naturally lend themselves to concurrent and parallel programming. Since data cannot be changed, there is no need for locks or synchronization primitives, reducing the potential for concurrency-related bugs.

- **Elixir's syntax and tooling**: Elixir combines the robustness of the Erlang ecosystem with a syntax that is more accessible to newcomers and developers coming from other languages.

  o **Syntax**: Elixir's syntax is designed to be both approachable and powerful, allowing developers to write clean, concise, and maintainable code.

    ▪ **Readable and expressive**: The syntax is clean and easy to understand, making the code expressive and reducing the cognitive load for developers. This simplicity helps developers focus more on solving business problems rather than battling with complex syntax.

    ▪ **Tooling**: Elixir provides a robust set of tools that streamline the development process, making it easier to build, test, and manage applications efficiently.

    ▪ **Mix**: Elixir's build tool that provides tasks for creating, compiling, testing, and managing dependencies in Elixir projects. Mix simplifies many routine tasks in the development process, from project creation to running migrations.

    ▪ **ExUnit**: This built-in test framework is designed to make testing simple and efficient with features like assert macros, set-up blocks, and test tagging, which facilitate unit and integration testing.

For example, creating a new Phoenix project with Mix (`mix phx.new app_name`) automatically sets up the project structure, integrates with Ecto for database use, and prepares testing configurations with ExUnit.

Using ExUnit to write tests for a Phoenix controller ensures that web requests are handled correctly, promoting **test-driven development (TDD)** practices.

- **Concurrency and distribution**: Elixir leverages the Erlang VM (BEAM) to provide a powerful model for concurrent and distributed computing without the typical complexities associated with these paradigms.

  o **Concurrency model**: Elixir's concurrency model, built on the Erlang VM (BEAM), offers a highly efficient and fault-tolerant system for managing multiple processes simultaneously.

    ▪ **Lightweight processes**: Elixir runs each task in separate lightweight processes managed by the BEAM. These processes are not OS processes or threads but are more similar to green threads, which are extremely lightweight and fast to create and destroy.

    ▪ **Message passing**: Processes communicate via message passing, which decouples them and enhances fault tolerance. Each process has a mailbox, and messages are handled asynchronously to ensure that the system remains responsive.

    ▪ **Real-world advantages:** In web applications, this model handles thousands of concurrent connections without significant overhead. The WhatsApp backend, famously built on Erlang (and thus compatible with Elixir), efficiently manages millions of simultaneous connections.

  For **Internet of Things** (**IoT**) devices, where multiple tasks (like reading sensor data and communicating with a server) need to run concurrently, Elixir's processes can be a perfect fit due to their low overhead and isolated nature.

- **Phoenix and Ecto**: Phoenix and Ecto are two crucial parts of the Elixir ecosystem, particularly when it comes to building web applications and interacting with databases.

  o **Phoenix**: Designed for productivity and maintainability, Phoenix is a **Model-View-Controller (MVC)** framework that makes it easy to build reliable web applications. Its real-time capabilities through channels and LiveView offer out-of-the-box support for features that are complex and hard to implement in other frameworks.

  o **Ecto**: This is a database wrapper and query generator in Elixir, allowing developers to write safe and efficient database queries. It is integrated into Phoenix but can also be used independently.

- **Effectiveness in production**: Companies like *Pinterest* and *Discord* have used Elixir and Phoenix to build highly scalable and maintainable applications. *Pinterest* used

Elixir to reduce the response time of certain endpoints by a significant margin, while *Discord* handles millions of concurrent users with real-time messaging, showcasing the real-time capabilities of Phoenix.

These tools and principles collectively make Elixir a top choice for developers.

# Best practices in Elixir

Elixir is a functional, concurrent language built on the Erlang VM, which offers unique advantages for building scalable and maintainable applications. To fully leverage its capabilities, adhering to best practices is essential. Here are some of the core best practices recommended for Elixir developers:

- **Leverage immutability**: One of the foundational aspects of Elixir is its immutable data structures. Immutability leads to safer and more predictable code by eliminating side effects:

  o **Consistent data state**: Since data cannot be changed once created, functions that operate on this data cannot alter its state, preventing bugs that occur from unintended side effects.

  o **Example**: When passing a user structure through various functions to update different attributes, rather than modifying the original user, each function returns a new user instance with the updated attributes.

  The following code snippet demonstrates how an Elixir module can handle updates to a user's location or age without modifying the original data, thus highlighting the benefits of immutability:

```
1. defmodule User do
2.    defstruct [:name, :age, :location]
3.
4.    def update_location(user, new_location) do
5.      %{user | location: new_location}
6.    end
7.
8.    def celebrate_birthday(user) do
9.      %{user | age: user.age + 1}
10.   end
11. End
```

- **Embrace concurrency**: Elixir is renowned for its built-in support for concurrency, utilizing lightweight processes that run on all CPU cores. Employing Elixir's concurrency model effectively can significantly enhance application performance by:

o **Using processes for isolation**: Each task should be run in its own process, where it is possible to isolate failures and maintain system responsiveness.

o **Messaging passing over shared state**: Communicate between processes using message passing rather than shared state to maintain system integrity and simplify debugging.

- **Follow the let it crash philosophy**: Instead of writing defensive code to handle every possible error, Elixir encourages developers to let processes crash and depend on supervisors to restart them:

o **Simplifies code**: By not cluttering code with defensive checks, the code becomes more straightforward and focused on business logic.

o **Resilience**: Use supervisors to define strategies for restarting parts of your application when failures occur, thus ensuring the application recovers gracefully from errors.

In the following snippet, observe how a supervisor is set up to oversee a worker process, automatically restarting it should a crash occur, thereby simplifying error handling and improving resilience:

```
1. defmodule MyApp.Application do
2.    use Application
3.
4.    def start(_type, _args) do
5.      children = [
6.        {MyApp.Worker, []}
7.      ]
8.
9.      opts = [strategy: :one_for_one, name: MyApp.Supervisor]
10.     Supervisor.start_link(children, opts)
11.   end
12. end
```

- **Use pattern matching extensively**: Pattern matching is not just a convenient syntax in Elixir, but a fundamental concept that should be utilized extensively by:

o **Clarifying intent**: Clearer than using conditional statements, as it directly expresses the intent of your code.

o **Reducing boilerplate**: Avoid the need for verbose if or switch statements and make your functions declarative.

Following is a simple example that demonstrates pattern matching in a greeting function, providing different messages based on the language passed in:

```
1. defmodule Greeter do
2.   def greet(%{language: "Spanish"}), do: "Hola"
3.   def greet(%{language: "French"}), do: "Bonjour"
4.   def greet(_), do: "Hello"
5. End
```

- **Document and test thoroughly**: Elixir's built-in tools like *ExDoc* and *ExUnit* make it easy to document and test your code. Always aim to:

  o **Write clear documentation**: Use **@moduledoc** and **@doc** annotations to document modules and functions.

  o **Comprehensive testing**: Use ExUnit to write tests that cover both happy paths and edge cases.

The following example illustrates how to include documentation directly within your module and function definitions, fostering clarity and maintainability:

```
 1. defmodule Math do
 2.   @moduledoc """
 3.   Provides math-related functions.
 4.   """
 5.
 6.   @doc """
 7.   Computes the sum of two numbers.
 8.   """
 9.   def add(a, b), do: a + b
10. End
```

- **Optimize with Erlang libraries**: Since Elixir runs on the Erlang VM, you have access to all Erlang libraries. Use them when they provide a more efficient or suitable solution:

  o **Interoperability**: You can call Erlang functions directly from Elixir, giving you access to a vast array of mature libraries and functionalities.

Here is a quick illustration of how an Erlang library function can be used within your Elixir code for cryptographic hashing:

```
1. :crypto.hash(:sha256, "Use Erlang libraries in Elixir")
```

By following these best practices, Elixir developers can build applications that are not only functional and efficient but also maintainable and scalable. These principles help in exploiting the full potential of Elixir and the Erlang ecosystem, making it easier to handle complex applications with ease.

# Code organization in Elixir

Organizing code efficiently is crucial for building scalable and maintainable applications, especially in a language like Elixir that offers immense flexibility in how you structure your projects. Effective code organization helps in understanding the application flow, making updates, fixing bugs, and onboarding new developers. The following are the key practices and considerations for organizing code in Elixir:

- **Modular design**: Elixir encourages a modular approach, leveraging modules to encapsulate related functions and data. Modules serve as the primary means of organizing code, each acting as a namespace for related functionalities.

  o **Purpose-driven modules**: Create modules that align with specific areas of functionality. For example, a User module might handle everything related to user information and actions, while a Payment module would deal with financial transactions.

  o **API definition**: Use module interfaces to define clear APIs. This means external code interacts with the module through a well-defined set of functions, which improves maintainability and reduces the impact of changes within modules.

  The following is an example of a module in Elixir that demonstrates how to organize user-specific functionalities, such as creation and updating, within a dedicated namespace:

  ```
  1. defmodule MyApp.User do
  2.   def create(attrs), do: # Implementation
  3.   def update(user, attrs), do: # Implementation
  4. End
  ```

- **Leveraging contexts in Phoenix**: In web applications built with Phoenix, contexts are used to group related functionalities, making a clear distinction between the application's business logic and its web interface. Contexts serve as a dedicated boundary that organizes functionalities into a coherent group, usually reflecting a business domain:

  o **Context example**: For a commerce platform, you might have contexts such as Catalog, Sales, and Accounts. Each context handles operations relevant to its domain, potentially interacting with other contexts through well-defined APIs.

  Here is a sample showing two contexts, Catalog and Sales, that separately handle product listing and order placement, illustrating a clear division of responsibilities.

  ```
  1. defmodule MyApp.Catalog do
  2.   def list_products, do: # Implementation
  ```

```
3.   def add_product(attrs), do: # Implementation
4. end
5.
6. defmodule MyApp.Sales do
7.   def place_order(user, product_id), do: # Implementation
8. end
```

- **Project structure**: An effective project structure is critical for navigating and maintaining an Elixir application. Phoenix, for instance, provides a standard directory structure that includes lib (application code), test (test files), assets (JavaScript, CSS), and more:

  o **Lib directory**: Split your lib directory into further directories representing each major component or context of your application. For instance, the **lib/my_app/ accounts** directory could contain all modules related to user accounts.

  o **Maintain a clean root**: Keep the root of your project clean by only including necessary configuration files and directories. This simplifies understanding the project's structure.

- **Dependency management**: Dependencies are managed in Elixir using Mix. Proper management involves keeping your **mix.exs** file organized and updated. This file is not just for defining project dependencies but also includes project configuration and tasks:

  o **Group similar dependencies**: Keep test, development, and production dependencies separate and clearly comment on their purpose and usage.

  o **Keep dependencies updated**: Regularly update your dependencies to leverage improvements and security patches, reducing potential technical debt.

The following snippet from a **mix.exs** file demonstrates how you might structure your dependencies for different environments and specify any test-only libraries:

```
1. defp deps do
2.   [
3.     {:phoenix, "~> 1.5"},
4.     {:ecto, "~> 3.0"},
5.     {:postgrex, "~> 0.15.0"},
6.     {:ex_unit, "~> 1.6", only: :test},   # Test-specific dependency
7.     {:credo, "~> 1.7", only: [:dev, :test], runtime: false}
8.   ]
9. end
```

- **Documentation and comments**: Elixir's documentation tools are first-class citizens in the language. Using **@moduledoc** and **@doc** attributes not only allows you to generate professional documentation but also helps organize your code by explaining the purpose and functionality of modules and functions.

Comments should explain why something is done, not what is done. Avoid over-commenting by writing self-explanatory code and using descriptive functions and variable names.

- **Code formatting and style guides**: Consistency in coding style is important for readability and maintainability. Use the built-in formatter (mix format) to ensure your code adheres to a consistent style. This removes the need for manual style checks during code reviews and maintains uniformity across the codebase.

By implementing these practices in code organization, Elixir projects can achieve a high level of maintainability and scalability, making it easier for teams to develop, test, and deploy their applications efficiently. This organized approach not only enhances the development process but also ensures that the applications are robust and ready for growth.

# Resources for further learning

To continue growing your Elixir skills, consider the following resources:

- **Elixir Forum**: Engage with the community for support and to keep up with new trends.
- **HexDocs**: Always keep an eye on the official documentation for libraries and the language itself.
- **Conferences and meetups**: Participating in community events can provide new insights and networking opportunities.
- **Open-source projects**: Contributing to or examining open-source projects can provide practical experience and a deeper understanding.

# Future directions of Elixir

The future of Elixir looks promising as it continues to gain popularity in areas like telecommunications, financial services, and web development, owing to its fault-tolerance and ability to handle high volumes of traffic. Innovations in Phoenix and Nerves (for embedded systems) will likely keep it at the forefront of development in both the web and IoT sectors. As machine learning and blockchain technologies continue to evolve, the adaptability of Elixir may make it an increasingly attractive option for implementing systems in these domains as well.

# Conclusion

As this book closes, remember that the end of these chapters is just the beginning of your adventures with Elixir. The language's blend of functional programming with Erlang's robust concurrency model offers a unique platform from which to build reliable, scalable, and maintainable applications. Continue exploring, learning, and building with Elixir, and let it open new doors to programming excellence.

# Index

www.ingramcontent.com/pod-product-compliance
Lightning Source LLC
Chambersburg PA
CBHW061801210326
41599CB00034B/6830